Killing History

ALSO BY ROBERT M. PRICE

Deconstructing Jesus

Incredible Shrinking Son of Man: How Reliable Is the Gospel Tradition?

The Empty Tomb: Jesus Beyond the Grave

The Da Vinci Fraud: Why the Truth Is Stranger than Fiction

The Reason-Driven Life: What Am I Here on Earth For?

The Paperback Apocalypse: How the Christian Church Was Left Behind

Top Secret: The Truth behind Today's Pop Mysticism

Inerrant the Wind: The Evangelical Crisis in Biblical Authority

Killing History

Jesus in the NO-SPIN ZONE

Robert M. Price

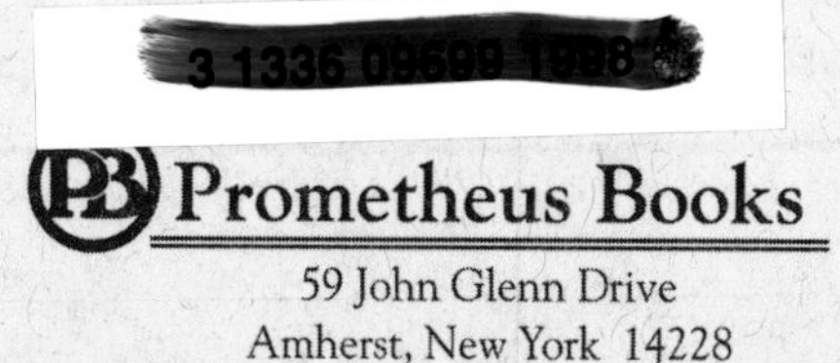

Prometheus Books
59 John Glenn Drive
Amherst, New York 14228

Published 2014 by Prometheus Books

Cover design by Grace M. Conti-Zilsberger

Inquiries should be addressed to
Prometheus Books
59 John Glenn Drive
Amherst, New York 14228
VOICE: 716–691–0133
FAX: 716–691–0137
WWW.PROMETHEUSBOOKS.COM

18 17 16 15 14 5 4 3 2 1

Library of Congress Cataloging-in-Publication Data Pending

ISBN 978-1-61614-966-6
ISBN 978-1-61614-967-3 (ebook)

Printed in the United States of America

CONTENTS

Introduction: Jesus in the No-Spin Zone 7

Chapter One: Historical Background or Historical Ballast? 11
Chapter Two: Bird Man of Nazareth 33
Chapter Three: How Not to Behave in Church 47
Chapter Four: Fishermen, Prostitutes, and Pharisees 63
Chapter Five: The Amazing Jesus 79
Chapter Six: Theology Hidden in Plain Sight 93
Chapter Seven: Liar, Pinhead, or Lord 109
Chapter Eight: Temple Tantrum 123
Chapter Nine: Messiahs and Matchstick Men 137
Chapter Ten: The Imp Act Segment 153
Chapter Eleven: Check, Please 161
Chapter Twelve: Trial and Error 173
Chapter Thirteen: Cross Examined 187

The Missing Chapter: Raising Jesus 205

Appendix One: When Were the Gospels Written? 215

Appendix Two: Do Ancient Historians Mention Jesus? 237

Index of Modern Authors 277

Scripture Index 279

Subject Index 285

Introduction

JESUS IN THE NO-SPIN ZONE

Bill O'Reilly is a phenomenon. He is the host of the top-rated *The O'Reilly Factor* and the coauthor of a number of bestselling historical books, notably *Killing Lincoln* and *Killing Kennedy*. To these he has recently added *Killing Jesus: A History*, written with Martin Dugard. I must confess to being a frequent viewer of *The Factor*. I enjoy Bill O'Reilly's humor, and I usually agree with his social and political opinions (though on some issues he is not quite conservative *enough* to suit me). I want you to be aware of this at the outset, because I want it to be clear I am not one of the man's detractors who look for any opportunity to take him down. This book, a rejoinder to *Killing Jesus*, I felt compelled to write by my professional conscience as a New Testament scholar. It is evident to me that Bill O'Reilly and Martin Dugard are writing way, way out of their fields of expertise and that they simply do not understand either the principles of critical historiography or the difference between a historical and a religious treatment of a topic.

Killing Jesus attempts to apply the same principles of journalistic research that worked well enough in O'Reilly and Dugard's books on the Lincoln and Kennedy assassinations. But it does not work. I hope to show (as much as I regret having to) that the task of reconstructing the events connected with a figure like Jesus Christ, the deity of the Christian faith, and that of writing about modern political figures, is as different as the heavens are from the earth. And *Killing Jesus* depends essentially upon ignoring that difference. I should estimate that reporting the historical truth about Jesus falls somewhere between documenting the facts about Robin Hood and Superman. It is just not the same thing at all. Another thing I aim to demonstrate is that to treat Jesus as one treats Abe Lincoln tends to make nonsense of the gospels, our main source concerning Jesus. If one loves the gospel accounts and wants to appreciate them by the standards by which they were written, one does not come out where O'Reilly and Dugard do. One does not even begin where they begin. If there is any parallel at all between writing about JFK and writing about Jesus, we might have to compare using the gospels for a blow-by-blow account to drawing up *Killing Kennedy* from the mass of conspiracy theories entertained by Dale Gribble. In both cases we are dealing with a genre very different from straight history.

Any biographer of Kennedy or of Lincoln must familiarize himself with the earliest available source material (though the gospels are not nearly so early or reliable as our authors believe) and then do a comprehensive study of previous work in the field. One would, for instance, weigh and compare the very different portraits of Honest Abe drawn by Carl Sandburg and C. A. Tripp, who claimed to have "outed" Lincoln as a homosexual.[1] It is important not to disregard the history of scholarship lest one, impatient to reinvent the wheel, wind up producing a wheel greatly inferior to those already available. There is no sign whatsoever that the authors of *Killing Jesus* have even begun to do their homework here. In the end notes, true, we find a number of book recommendations, but it is revealing that virtually every one of the New Testament and Jesus books mentioned are the work of evangelical/fundamentalist spin doctors dedicated to defending the proposition that the gospels are entirely accurate, miracles and all. We are not in the No-Spin Zone anymore. And it is not that O'Reilly and Dugard actually discuss the arguments of these authors. It seems, rather, that O'Reilly and his collaborator have simply cited these apologists for the faith as a license to treat the gospels as inerrant scripture.

O'Reilly has many times contended that *Killing Jesus* sticks to the facts and stops short of promoting religious doctrine. Please tell me how a purely historical work time and again asserts as simple fact that Jesus fulfilled Old Testament predictions. It is not enough to refrain from calling Jesus "Christ." That does not make the book impartial history. The entire treatment of the Bible bears witness that O'Reilly and Dugard are approaching it as committed religious believers. Both are proud Roman Catholics. So was the late, great New Testament scholar Raymond E. Brown (whose magisterial work *The Death of the Messiah*, thankfully, our authors recommend in the end notes), but Father Brown knew the difference between historical research and proof-texting, between writing a scholarly work and writing a narrative novel with a few pedantic digressions thrown in. Raymond E. Brown, Joseph A. Fitzmyer, John Meier, Hans Küng, Edward Schillebeeckx, Thomas L. Brodie, Herman Hendrickx, Jon Sobrino, all are Roman Catholics—and not one of them would ever be caught with his name on a book like this one.

Killing Jesus has nothing to do with Life of Jesus studies. It is in fact almost a twin to Mel Gibson's oh-so-authentic 2004 film *The Passion of the Christ*. Both are exhibitions of popular piety aimed at reinforcing believers' faith and stilling their doubts by providing a real-seeming illusion about the myths and legends of the gospels. Their function is not dissimilar to that of the numerous End Times movies and novels like *Left Behind*, *Image of the Beast*, and *A Distant Thunder*. Those fictions, whether on screen or page (and *Killing Jesus* is already heading for the screen), help buttress faith in the ever-receding, always deferred Second Coming of Christ by depicting it in narrative form before the eyes of those who would really like to see the Rapture, the Great Tribulation, and so on, occurring on the evening news. They don't. They can't. So End Times fiction is the next best thing, a game of pretend. And that is just the role of *The Passion of the Christ* and *Killing Jesus*. The familiar Sunday school tales are dressed up in pseudo-documentary form to make the Christian reader feel confident that the legends are historical reports, not legends at all. It is all a trick, though Gibson, O'Reilly, and Dugard are presumably tricking themselves as well.

It is not going too far to compare *Killing Jesus* to Dan Brown's pseudo-historical bestseller *The Da Vinci Code*. Like Brown, O'Reilly and Dugard assure the reader that the fast-paced narrative he is about to read is based on historical fact. And just as Brown's "facts" have been gathered from half-cocked "research" like Baigent, Lincoln, and Leigh's cinderblock of misinformation, *Holy Blood, Holy Grail*,[2] O'Reilly and Dugard are too ready to accept the religious apologetics of Craig Evans, Darrell Bock, J. P. Moreland, and William Lane Craig as genuine historical scholarship. The reader of either book is sure to be led astray, though admittedly in very different directions.

O'Reilly and Dugard are like Ben Bernanke, churning out inflated currency that lacks the value of the amount stamped on it. They are like Jay Carney, bald-facedly handing out the inflexible talking points of an institutional party line, in this case that of conservative Christianity. Bill O'Reilly has no trouble at all seeing what is really going on in these political cases, but when it comes to religion he cannot see it. If he even knows about the great legion of critical scholars who classify most of the gospel story as myth and legend, no doubt he considers them pinheads. If political liberalism is, as David Mamet contends, essentially a fact-proof, dogmatic religious faith,[3] it is a shame that Bill O'Reilly can see through those illusions but cannot penetrate those of Christian apologetics. Instead, in *Killing Jesus*, he joins in propagating them.

Whenever evolutionary biologist and militant atheist Richard Dawkins appears on *The Factor* (and it is greatly to Bill's credit that he does), I'm sure many of my readers find themselves cringing at the lame arguments Bill uses in his attempts to set Dawkins straight. Like me, they must wince at the smug self-satisfaction of Bill's boasts after the interview that he has triumphed over Dawkins. He is just plain out of his league. And, I regret to say, in *Killing Jesus* he is even farther in over his head (as tall as he is). And the book you are about to read is an attempt to set things right, to undo the misinformation that constitutes *Killing Jesus*. In other words, the spin stops here.

Chapter One

HISTORICAL BACKGROUND OR HISTORICAL BALLAST?

Bill O'Reilly and Martin Dugard spend a surprising amount of space, perhaps too much, filling in the historical setting of the gospel story. The stories of Julius Caesar, Herod the Great, Herod Antipas, and others are made into novelistic narratives just like the Jesus chapters.[1] One is tempted to say the authors are verging on the docudrama genre. While I have no quibbles about their depictions of these historical figures, I suspect that the material actually turns out to be counterproductive to their purpose, since we are soon going to find out that the gospel appearances of these characters do not match what history tells us about them, suggesting that the historical connection between them and the gospel story of Jesus is less secure than O'Reilly and Dugard would have us believe.

DOES JESUS BELONG IN HISTORY?

First a word about the larger function of these background chapters. It is common, and altogether natural on certain assumptions, to regard the gospel episodes as iceberg tips emerging into view from larger bodies beneath the surface. That is, the gospel stories seem to presuppose much about the culture, the politics, the religions, and so on, of the period in which the episodes are set. The evangelists (gospel writers) may be expected to have taken a good deal for granted, since they could count on their contemporaries to be familiar with the relevant facts. Living so long afterward, modern readers require some help filling in the picture. Bible commentaries are properly filled with such information. But there is a forgotten or unsuspected question being begged here. To some scholars, the Jesus stories bear an unmistakable resemblance to oft-recurring archetypal myths and legends, and we have to ask whether the gospel writers have sought to bring an originally mythical Jesus figure down to earth by clothing him in a plausible historical-cultural setting, much as Herodotus tried to place Hercules as a historical figure in the reign of this or that king. Plutarch similarly figured that Osiris and Isis must have originally been an ancient king and queen of Egypt. Hercules and Osiris were, like Jesus, dying and rising savior deities. And, like them also, Jesus was placed conjecturally and variously in the first century BCE, imagined crucified by Alexander Jannaeus or his widow Helena,[2] or as late as the reign of Claudius.[3] It is perhaps significant that in earlier New Testament epistles we read of Jesus'[4] death being brought about not by any Roman or Jewish government officials but rather by "the Archons [angels] who rule this age" (1 Cor. 2:6–8), "the Principalities and Powers," fallen angels (Col. 2:13–15); while of the Romans we read that they never punish the innocent, only the guilty (Rom. 13:3–4; 1 Pet. 2:13–14). Does it look as if these writers knew the crucifixion story we read in the gospels? The very notion of the Son of God put to death on a cross makes plenty of sense in terms of ancient astronomy and Gnostic mythology, where the celestial cross is the junction of the ecliptic with the zodiac.

The effect as well, perhaps, as the intent of providing a wealth of historical detail as O'Reilly and Dugard do, is to make Jesus seem as real as Julius and Augustus Caesar, Herod the Great, and Herod Antipas. The goal is analogous to having a US president appear in a movie or a comic book. Clinton is made to look like he is announcing a communication from outer space in the Jodie Foster movie *Contact*. Superman has been depicted shaking hands with Clinton and with JFK. Forrest Gump met Kennedy, too, even though Gump never existed. The Incredible Hulk once received a pardon from Lyndon Johnson. Bill O'Reilly himself appears on TV commenting on Stark Industries in *Iron Man 2*.

O'Reilly and Dugard repeatedly simply assume that Jesus must have done what Jews regularly did. On pilgrimage to Jerusalem, pilgrims typically waded into the *mikvah*, a ritual bathing area, for the sake of ceremonial purification, so we read simply that Jesus did it, too. (This is the kind of baseless inference from "what most people did" that led William E. Phipps to suggest, in a once-controversial book, that Jesus was probably married—since most rabbis were.[5]) I think they are a bit too sure about these things, insignificant as most of them are. But it is vivid to tell the tale this way, so they do. It gets worse when our authors make up events from Jesus' life out of whole cloth.

> Passover is a time when Jerusalem is packed with hundreds of thousands of worshippers from all over the world, so it was horrific when Archelaus boldly asserted his authority by ordering his cavalry to charge their horses into the thick crowds filling the Temple courts. Wielding javelins and long, straight steel and bronze swords, Archelaus's Babylonian, Thracian, and Syrian mercenaries massacred three thousand innocent pilgrims. Mary, Joseph, and Jesus saw the bloodbath firsthand and were lucky to escape the Temple with their lives. They were also eyewitnesses to the crucifixion of more than two thousand Jewish rebels outside Jerusalem's city walls when Roman soldiers moved in to quell further revolts. (p. 66)

> He labors six days a week as a carpenter alongside his father, building the roofs and doorposts of Nazareth and laying the foundation stones of sprawling nearby Sepphoris. (p. 81)

Not one word of any of these episodes is mentioned anywhere in the New Testament. These deeds of violence occurred, as we know from Josephus, but the Holy Family is nowhere associated with them. Sepphoris was constructed about this time, but we have no mention of Jesus and his dad donning their hard hats and carrying their lunch pails down the road to join in.[6] Sure, Mary, Joseph, and Jesus *might* have witnessed these Roman atrocities. We can *imagine* them doing so, and that appears to be quite good enough for the authors of *Killing Jesus*.

Reading *Killing Jesus*, one may wonder where the authors got all the vivid detail displayed in their recountings of the very brief and sketchy gospel cameos. Again, strictly from their imaginations. They did just what Anna Katharina Emmerich did in the eighteenth century when she wrote *The Dolorous Passion of our Lord Jesus Christ*, a rather hefty and super-detailed gospel novel (the basis of Mel Gibson's film *The Passion of the Christ*). She claimed to have simply received the whole thing in a series of feverish visions as she lay upon her chronic sickbed, but what seems to have happened is that she attempted to visualize the gospel events in this-worldly detail, and they seemed very real to her as a result. The same technique is brought to bear still today as devout Christians, Catholic and Protestant, meditate their way through the *Spiritual Exercises* of Ignatius Loyola.[7] This is basically what O'Reilly and Dugard have done in *Killing Jesus*. The rule of thumb is to ask oneself, "If this really happened, what would it have been like on the scene?" Think of the old TV show that promised, "All is as it was then, only *you are there*." But you weren't. And neither were O'Reilly and Dugard. And, we might wonder, was Jesus?

HEROD THE GREAT (BEAST)

King Herod was fully the villain O'Reilly and Dugard make him, though they do miss one interesting little detail. They quote Caesar Augustus' quip "I would rather be Herod's pig than his son." It is worth knowing that the remark is a clever pun. The Greek word for "pig" (υικος) is but a single letter different from the word for "son" (υιος), and the joke was that, Herod being nominally Jewish, he would never have a pig slaughtered, but, as a murderous paranoid, he would and did have various of his sons put to death.

Herod's role in the gospels is confined to Matthew's Nativity story (Matt. chap. 2), including the episodes of the Wise Men and of the Slaughter of the Innocents. O'Reilly and Dugard blithely accept this story as accurate history (at least most of it). They trim the apocryphal details that are so familiar from Christmas carols and cards; Matthew

when baby Zeus arrives, his mother Rhea contrives to get him to safety while covering a rock in the swaddling. Kronos swallows it and does not know the difference. Sure enough, Zeus grows up and unseats his father, becoming king of the immortals.

But there are a number of such rescues related of religious and other founders. News of the birth of Octavian (Caesar Augustus) upsets the corrupt senators of the Roman Republic, who know he is the one destined to overthrow their regime, so they conspire to have the infant murdered. They are unsuccessful. When the Iranian prophet Zoroaster is born, he who shall one day convert Prince Vishtaspa to the new faith and cause the Magi caste to lose their position, the chief Magus, Durasan, tries to have the baby hero placed in the path of a stampeding herd, but the cattle swerve around him. The infant is next dropped into a wolves' den, but, like Daniel in the lions' den, he is unharmed. Nimrod learns from his wise men that Abraham, the future scourge of idolatry, has been born, so he tries, unsuccessfully, to have him killed. When Krishna is incarnated, the demons arrange for his wet nurse to smear poison on her breast, but he is rescued. You get the idea. So even if Matthew did not derive the Slaughter of the Innocents specifically from Josephus' story of Moses, we would still have to classify it with these parallels. If all the rest are manifestly mythical, why should Matthew's Nativity of the Son of God be regarded any differently?

Of course, one might point to Herod the Great's bloody record of eradicating anyone he thought might one day plot against him. Josephus catalogs Herod's numerous atrocities. So it sounds reasonable to picture Herod learning of some newborn hailed by a group of potential rebels wanting to use him as a standard to rally the people against Herod, the false king. One can imagine Herod figuring it is not worth the risk to let this seed grow into a real threat—and having all the local children killed, just to be sure. But can we be sure we are dealing with history? Or is it just literary verisimilitude? Herod is the obvious choice if the myth-making imagination is looking to cast the role of the stereotypical nativity villain.

Not only that, but if you're going to appeal to Herod's rap sheet to make the Slaughter of the Innocents look suitably historical, just realize that the argument cuts both ways: the ample, detailed record of Herod's atrocities *does not record this one*. Given all the crimes against humanity Josephus lists, shouldn't this one be on the list? It's not like it was kept quiet, as if such a thing were possible. Matthew 2:3 says that all Jerusalem knew of the reason for the Wise Men's visit and dreaded to hear what Herod might do. If he did what Matthew says he did, they'd have heard about it, and so would Josephus.

STAR TREK

I said that O'Reilly and Dugard include most of the Matthean Herod story, but not all of it. It is not too difficult to see why they tactfully neglected one particular piece of it: the moving star that, like a supernatural GPS system, led the Magi to Mary and Joseph's Bethlehem home (not Luke's stable, which presupposes an entirely different scenario, though O'Reilly and Dugard switch over to Luke when they assure us that Jesus was born in a manger in a stable). Not only does this "star" move through the air close enough to the ground as to hover visibly above a single small dwelling, it is obviously pictured as a tiny object, just like all the ancients imagined the stars to be.

I once had a New Testament professor who, in discussing this story, recalled seeing some low-budget church education film depicting the Nativity. He said he had winced when it reached the point of the star of Bethlehem. He shook his head and summed up by opining, "There are just some things that you shouldn't try to depict." He didn't actually say so, but I was sure he meant that Matthew's moving star, *if represented accurately*, would look like Tinkerbell. And you wouldn't want biblical inerrancy to take a hit like that. D. F. Strauss similarly pointed out how the gospel story of the multiplication of the loaves and fish fell prey to the same cartoonishness.[11] What are we supposed to picture Jesus doing? Stretching each barley roll like a sponge until it divided like a cell in mitosis? You're not really supposed to look too close.

It seems to me as if Matthew is inconsistent about the role of the star. Here's the rub: The Magi explain to King Herod that they know the infant king has been born because they saw his natal star in the East (or "when it rose," same phrase in the Greek). As astrologers, they knew the significance of a stellar event occurring in the constellation Pisces, assigned by them to the Jews. The star had not *moved* anywhere. They simply inferred that, if there was a newborn heir to the Jewish throne, Jerusalem was the place to inquire. Once there, they don't anticipate any flying star; they know to head for Bethlehem because Herod's scribes tell them that's where they ought to look. But then Matthew says the star reappeared and this time moved through the sky to hover over a single house. This is the part O'Reilly and Dugard tactfully omit—because it exposes the story as a piece of pious legend. They refer to a convenient theory that a comet observed by Chinese astronomers in 5 BCE might have been the Wise Men's "star" and conclude that "due to the earth's orbital motion, the comet's light would have been directly in front of the Magi during their journey—hence, they would have truly followed the star" (p. 15). But they are said to have followed the *moving* star only once they reached Jerusalem, and it led them to a particular house in Bethlehem. Tinkerbell.

O'Reilly and Dugard assure us that Jesus was born in a Bethlehem stable and that immediately afterward Mary and Joseph took baby Jesus to the Jerusalem temple to have him circumcised, whereupon they met up with the prophetic pair Simeon and Anna who proclaimed the child's great destiny. The Jerusalem visit comes from Luke. The trouble is that one cannot draw piecemeal from Matthew and Luke, whose Nativity stories diverge at virtually every point, though you will not learn this from the authors of *Killing Jesus*. They interweave as much as they can of the contradictory Nativity stories, for example, noting the irony that, even while Herod's goons were frog-gigging babies in Bethlehem, Mary and Joseph brought their new son to the Jerusalem temple to be circumcised, right under Herod's nose. But would the parents have risked showing up on Herod's doorstep if, as Matthew says, they were anxious to flee the country and take refuge in Egypt? Anyone who does this must not expect miraculous protection from a God who has told them to get packing and go into hiding someplace else. Besides, can you imagine the scene with Simeon and Anna proclaiming to all who would listen that the baby Messiah was in town—when "all Jerusalem" (Matt. 2:3) knew of Herod's murderous designs? Were Simeon and Anna trying to get rid of him, too?

O'Reilly and Dugard simply ignore the larger narrative contexts from which they have cherry-picked the Nativity scenes they use, heedless (or hoping the reader won't notice) that these snippets make no sense thus isolated, then forced into their new context in the Gospel according to O'Reilly. For instance, how did Jesus come to be born in Bethlehem in the first place (one of the very few things Matthew's and Luke's birth stories have in common)? Matthew pictures Mary and Joseph living in Bethlehem. Jesus, presumably, is born *in their home*, where the Magi find him as much as two years later. After the attempt by Herod to snuff the boy, they hasten to put their hovel on the market and hightail it to Egypt. Once they think the coast is clear, some years later, they return, only to find that Herod's no-good son Archelaus has replaced him, so the danger is not past after all. (Why? Mustn't Herod have assumed his plan had worked? Why would his son still be gunning for Jesus?) So they relocate to Nazareth, a new town for them.[12]

Luke has it exactly the other way round. For him, Mary and Joseph live in *Nazareth*. They only make a temporary trip to Bethlehem in order to register for taxation, and that in the strangest tax census anyone has ever heard of: that a man should have to register to file his taxes not where he actually lives, but where his remote ancestors had lived *a thousand years before*. Anyway, the town is overcrowded with people there for the same reason, so that Mary must give birth in the open air, in a stable. (One must ask why Joseph would have dragged his very pregnant wife on such a journey.) Once the baby Jesus arrives, the Holy Family goes *back home* to Nazareth. Thus you cannot have Luke's manger and Matthew's Wise Men and Herodian pogrom in the same story. Mary and Joseph did not stay living in a Bethlehem stable for another two years, waiting for Matthew's Magi to show up.

SCISSORS AND PASTE

Our authors are not writing as critical, that is, modern, historians. R. G. Collingwood explained the difference.[13] Ancient and medieval historians, precritical historians, were what Collingwood dubbed "scissors-and-paste historians." They referred to their documents, inscriptions, and so on, as their "authorities."[14] They felt obliged to take the old documents at face value, to take them at their word, at least until two "authorities" conflicted and one had to choose between them. But once the coin had been flipped, you went back to implicit confidence in the rest of what your "authorities" said. That, obviously, is the approach taken in *Killing Jesus*. Entirely different is the methodology of critical historians. These scholars make their ancient documents sing for their supper. They think of them not as "authorities" to be heeded but rather as "sources" to be scrutinized and evaluated. The maxim of precritical historians is "Innocent until proven guilty,"[15] while that of critical historians is "Guilty until proven innocent." The critical historian recognizes that writers of the past, whether letter writers, chroniclers, essayists, whatever, indulged in deception, spin, propaganda, legend mongering, pseudonymity,[16] and other non-veridical conventions. This doesn't mean such materials are to be rejected as useless. No, the trick is to learn to recognize just what sort of material one is dealing with. If a particular document is propagandistic in nature, well, there is a history of propaganda to be told.[17]

O'Reilly knows this perfectly well when it comes to sniffing out spin when his TV guests start to bloviate. He won't stand for it if what he wants are the facts. But it is not as if the BS his guests hand him tells him nothing about them. It may actually reveal the truth about them more accurately than a straightforward statement of fact would. What we call "spin," New Testament scholar F. C. Baur called *Tendenz* (tendency).[18] An essential tool in the critical historian's kit is tendency criticism, or ideological criticism. But it seems not to occur to O'Reilly to employ it in the case of the New Testament. He is almost completely credulous. I doubt that he and Dugard approached their books on the Lincoln and Kennedy assassinations this way. Those books evaluate secular sources about secular events. *Killing Jesus* is quite different. This is part of what I mean when I say *Killing Jesus* is not, despite its pretentions, a historical treatment but rather a religious one.

The paradigm case of the arbitrary critical procedure in *Killing Jesus* is its authors' treatment of the saying from the cross "Father, forgive them, for they know not what they do," which occurs only in Luke's Gospel (23:34) and not in all manuscripts of that gospel. O'Reilly says he omitted it from his crucifixion scene because, in the circumstances, no one could have heard Jesus say it even if he did. Well, that would appear to rule out *any* of the sayings from the cross, but what about this one? O'Reilly can't bring himself to declare it inauthentic. No, he figures, Jesus must have said these words just a bit earlier, at Golgotha, in the scant minutes before the Romans nailed him up. Somebody might have heard that. Like Collingwood said: scissors and paste.

LURKING FUNDAMENTALISM

The authors say they felt compelled to omit any gospel feature that they could not defend as the product of eyewitness reporting. But where do they come by the notion that the gospels are the work of those who saw and heard Jesus for themselves? From one source, which I must regard as something of a polluted well: the fourth-century church historian Eusebius, quoting from Papias, a second-century bishop from Hierapolis in Asia Minor. He said that Papias had stated that "Matthew was the first to write the words of the Lord, in the Hebrew language, and everyone translated them as well as he could" (Eusebius, *Ecclesiastical History* 3:39).[19]

> Mark, who had been Peter's interpreter, wrote down carefully, but not in order, all that he remembered of the Lord's sayings and doings. For he had not heard the Lord or been one of his followers, but later, as I said, one of Peter's. Peter used to adapt his teaching to the occasion, without making a systematic arrangement of the Lord's sayings, so that Mark was quite justified in writing down some things just as he remembered them.

> For he had one purpose only—to leave out nothing that he had heard, and to make no misstatement about it.[20]

Most have supposed that Papias was referring to the Gospels of Matthew and Mark. D. F. Strauss, however, suggested that this was a gratuitous inference.[21] In fact Papias may as easily have been talking about other documents altogether. Why? Because what Papias says does not appear to describe our familiar Matthew and Mark. For one thing, our Greek Matthew appears to be an original Greek composition, not a translation. For another, most scholars think Matthew is an expansion of Mark, rather than, as Saint Augustine thought, an abridgment of Matthew. Again, Matthew certainly includes many sayings attributed to Jesus, but one would not naturally refer to any of the traditional gospels as simply "the words of the Lord." It looks as if, whatever Papias was referring to, it would more likely have been something on the order of the all-sayings Gospel of Thomas or the Q Source ("Q" standing for *Quelle*, German for "source") that scholars hypothesize existed as one of the two principal sources, along with Mark, employed independently by the second-stage gospel writers Matthew and Luke. Finally, it is worth noting that Origen, Jerome, and others referred to gospels written in Aramaic (sister language to Hebrew), which they took to be the supposed "Hebrew" original of Matthew. But their quotations from them seem rather to represent other documents altogether, such as the *Gospel according to the Hebrews* (though their quotations even of this survive only in Greek translation). Papias may as easily have been referring to one of these. Plus, there were other documents ascribed to Matthew, such as the *Infancy Gospel of Matthew* (to which we shall return). In other words, we can't be as sure as Eusebius was that Papias was talking about our canonical Gospel of Matthew.

Nor does the work Papias ascribes to Mark sound like our Gospel of Mark, for Papias implies it featured teachings of Jesus in no chronological order, whereas our Mark has a clear basic outline (even if it is an artificial order imposed by the author). It sounds to me more like he meant to describe something like the noncanonical *Preachings of Peter* or the *Gospel of Peter*, both of which actually do present themselves as the memoirs of Peter, written down by himself or others, though they are clearly fiction.

O'Reilly and Dugard are willing to take for granted the names Matthew, Mark, Luke, and John that ancient editors used as headings for the gospels. But these designations were applied to the gospels only after each had circulated for a while anonymously. Compare them with, say, the epistles of Paul. Whether or not he really wrote them (and there is a storm of debate over this, too), his name does actually appear as part of the text, both at the opening and occasionally farther on into the body of the letter. There is no such authorship claim in any of the four gospels. Nor did any of them at first require one. It is no surprise that all were originally anonymous, since, as with the compilers of the Mishnah, to use the name of the evangelists might have drawn attention away from Jesus, whom they sought to display for the reader. They likely would not have wanted to leave the impression that they were the real authors of the material (even though, to some extent, they were). Think of how the Book of Mormon was initially published with Joseph Smith listed as author, with subsequent editions omitting his name, lest readers get the impression that he created the whole thing (which of course he *did*). The names were added only once congregations eventually began to receive copies of additional gospels to supplement the single one they had used at first. Hitherto, their practice had been simply to announce "a reading from the Gospel." But once they had a set of two, or three, or four (or more), it became necessary to distinguish which one they meant, and so editors added the qualifier "according to Matthew," "according to Mark," and so on. We don't know where they got these names. It is way too late to tell. Besides, all four names were quite common, "Mark" and "Luke" being nearly as common in the Mediterranean world as "Muhammad" is in the Islamic world today. So even if the four authors did have these names on their chariot licenses, they needn't have automatically been the same as the various New Testament characters with those names. Indeed, one can easily imagine that, once the gospels had been tagged with these names, scribes started looking for New Testament personages bearing the same names so they could peg them as the evangelists. (Nonetheless, I am going to keep referring to the gospels as Matthew, Mark, Luke, and John, without any assumptions as to who may actually have written them.)

Papias didn't say anything, as far as we know, about the Gospels of Luke and John, but Irenaeus (*Against Heresies* 3:1) says (on what basis, we don't know) that Luke, Paul's personal physician (Col. 4:14; 2 Tim. 4:11), had written down the story of Jesus as Paul used to preach it. This is pretty hard to credit, since Paul's letters have almost nothing to say about any historical Jesus. When a saying of Jesus we read in our gospels would have come in quite handy to settle some disputed point, Paul does not mention it, implying he knew of none. On the one occasion (1 Cor. 7:10, cf. 25) where he does appeal to "a command of the Lord," it more probably refers to the kind of "command of the Lord" he believes he had received from the heavenly Lord Jesus (see 1 Cor. 14:37; 1 Thess. 4:15–17, where "the word of the Lord" includes a third-person reference to the Lord Jesus and thus cannot be taken as his own speech). We can't help thinking of how Bill O'Reilly himself felt commanded by the Holy Spirit to write the very book we are talking about. Whether the Holy Ghost also told him to enlist Martin Dugard, Bill has not yet said. Maybe it was like Exodus 4:10–16, where God told Moses not to worry about stage fright; he's sent Aaron along with him as his spokesman.

So Paul does not know of Jesus as an itinerant teacher. Nor does he speak of Jesus as a miracle worker. In 1 Corinthians 1:1:22–23 he virtually denies that Jesus performed any miracles.[22] He never mentions Nazareth. Can this man have been the source of Luke's Jesus material? Even if he had seen Jesus during the latter's earthly sojourn, Luke hadn't, even if he was dependent upon Paul. Nor did anybody think Mark was an eyewitness, reliant as he supposedly was on Peter's decades-old recollections.

JOHNNY ON THE SPOT

O'Reilly and Dugard highly value the eyewitness reliability of the Gospel of John, and indeed it serves as the central source of their version of Jesus' teachings about his identity as the divine Son of God. It is merely church tradition that identifies John, son of Zebedee, as the fourth evangelist. John 21:24 refers to the (unnamed) author of the preceding twenty chapters as a witness and reporter of the things there narrated, but chapter 21 appears to constitute an appendix to the gospel, written by someone else, because 20:30–31 seems intended as the conclusion to the gospel, but chapter 21 starts it up again and paraphrases the original conclusion in 21:25. Thus 21:24 ("This is the disciple who is bearing witness to these things, and who has written these things; and we know that his testimony is true.") is not a claim by the evangelist on his own behalf but rather by someone else, essentially no different from Irenaeus'. Are we to accept that claim? Remember, a critical historian's duty is to not take that for granted. He requires some corroboration. But O'Reilly doesn't.

John 19:34–37 ("But one of the soldiers pierced his side with a spear, and at once there came out blood and water. He who saw it has borne witness—his testimony is true, and he knows that he tells the truth—that you also may believe," etc.) is an overt eyewitness claim, and on this is built the belief in this gospel's eyewitness character. But there is a problem. These verses seem to contradict what comes immediately before them:

> Since it was the day of Preparation, in order to prevent the bodies from remaining on the cross on the Sabbath (for that Sabbath was a high day), the Jews asked Pilate that their [the crucified criminals'] legs might be broken, and that they might be taken away. So the soldiers came and broke the legs of the first, and of the other that had been crucified with him; but when they came to Jesus and saw that he was already dead, they did not break his legs.

Wait a minute here. They already knew he was dead? Then why the spear in the side? The same thing has also been interpolated into some manuscripts of Matthew 27:49: "And another took a spear and pierced his side, and out came water and blood." Without this dubious verse in John 19:34–37, no one would suspect that John was supposed to be an eyewitness record, and it isn't. Just compare John with the other three gospels (together called the Synoptics).[23] As different as they are, they are much more alike than any of them is like John. As scholars have long noted, John not only has the events of Jesus' ministry in a different order but also extends it over three years, unlike the others, which imply a single year. At least as important, the parables, the favorite teaching mode of Jesus in Matthew, Mark, and Luke, are virtually absent from John (though he does include two allegories, the True Vine in 15:1–11 and the Good Shepherd in 10:1–18). Instead, John features numerous artificial-sounding monologues and dialogues constructed on a pattern according to which Jesus' hostile hearers obtusely misunderstand his revelation discourses, giving him the opportunity to clarify them for the readers' sake.

The subject matter in John is very different from that portrayed in Matthew, Mark, and Luke. In them, Jesus is all the time preaching about the kingdom of God, while in John the recurrent theme is "eternal life." The Jesus of Matthew, Mark, and Luke, as Adolf Harnack pointed out, talks about the Father, but in John he talks about the Son.[24] It is not that John never mentions the kingdom or the Father, or that the others never mention eternal life or Jesus as God's Son, but the difference in emphasis is pronounced. No reader not invested in spinning the gospel data will deny that.

Most striking of all, everyone in the Gospel of John speaks the same way, whether that be John the Baptist, Jesus, or the narrator. Sometimes we cannot even tell when a character's speech leaves off and the narrator's comments begin. This idiom and style do not sound like Jesus in the other gospels, but they sound just like the style and idiom of the epistles ascribed (by editors) to John. As Albert Schweitzer urged, if you are going to try to delineate the historical Jesus, you have to make a choice: either John or the Synoptics.[25] But this is precisely what O'Reilly and Dugard refuse to do. Like all precritical gospel scholars and like fundamentalists today, they patch together bits and pieces from John and the others indiscriminately. They are scissors-and-paste "historians."

O'Reilly and Dugard hasten to reassure us that, though once there was serious doubt about the authorship and accuracy of the gospels, recent years have seen a return to traditional views: "Thanks to scholarship and archaeology, there is growing acceptance of their overall historicity and authenticity" (p. 22). This is sheer wishful thinking. O'Reilly and Dugard eventually provide a list of scholars to whom their work is indebted, and most of them are ax-grinding fundamentalist platform debaters and overt spin doctors for biblical inerrancy: William Lane Craig,[26] Craig Evans, Craig Keener, Paul Copan, J. P. Moreland.[27] O'Reilly and Dugard are quite comfortable in this company. But, like these men, they are engaged in nothing but pseudo-scholarly spin.

They admit that some of the details may have become garbled in the process of oral transmission (pp. 103, 126), even though this does not really square with their belief that Matthew and John were penned by those two members of the twelve apostles. In that case, what room would be left for the telephone game of oral tradition? Indeed, the dogmatic insistence on eyewitness authorship is nothing but an ad hoc device to eliminate the whole notion of a fluid, developing oral transmission. Anyhow, it is important to understand how O'Reilly and Dugard use the critical scalpel they have sharpened. They are eager to take just about everything they read in any of the gospels as grist for their mill. They busily stitch every piece of gospel cloth they can into their quilt. It is only when they run across some stubborn tag end that they feel entitled to trim it off. What they do not realize is that, if one can notice difficulties at such minor points, there is no reason not to start cutting elsewhere, anywhere one finds difficulties: contradictions, anachronisms, too-close parallels with extra-biblical sources. But this they will not do.

JESUS THE NERD

Once again I marvel at our authors' blithe willingness to take as a piece of historical repor-*tazh* (as Bill likes to pronounce it) Luke's story of the twelve-year-old Jesus in theological dialogue with the scribes at the Temple. It reminds me of an old Lenny Bruce joke: One day Jesus strolls right into St. Patrick's Cathedral in Manhattan, to the considerable shock of the priest on duty. This poor fellow rushes to the cardinal's office and asks what he should do. The cardinal tells him: "Look busy."

O'Reilly and Dugard are oblivious of the Law of Biographical Analogy. This sort of child prodigy tale is another piece of typical hagiography.[28] Josephus padded his autobiography with an incident just like this. (It is not at all unlikely that this is where Luke got it. It wouldn't be the only place he used Josephus as a source.)

> When I was a child, about 14 years old, I was universally commended for my love of learning, on account of which the high priests and the chief men of the city frequently visited me in a group, to ask my opinion about the accurate understanding of points of the law. (*Life of Flavius Josephus*, 2)

That, my friends, is a tall tale. And so is Luke's. And it is a tall tale of a particular kind. It is the same sort of stuff we find in spades in the pages of the apocryphal Infancy Gospels, like those attributed to Matthew and Thomas, in which Jesus is depicted as a visiting deity in human form. He is alternatively disdainful and pitying of his parents and adults generally. Joseph takes him to a local scribe for schooling, but when the man tries to teach Jesus the letters of the alphabet, the boy already knows them and demands to know if his tutor knows the esoteric significance of the letters. For this effrontery, the teacher smacks Jesus with a ruler, whereupon Jesus strikes him dead with a miracle. Naturally, Joseph scolds him.

Joseph, a carpenter, has been contracted to make a throne for a king, but the bumbling fool cannot seem to get the chair legs the same length. Jesus steps in and, like a fraudulent faith healer today, grabs hold of the legs and stretches them to an equal length.

Jesus is playing outside and some kid tumbles into him. Jesus points at him and says, "You will go no further in your course!" The rambunctious lad keels over dead. This sort of thing happens often enough that Joseph tells Jesus to cool it, lest they get run out of town.

After a rain, Jesus stoops down beside a puddle and fashions some mud into the shape of small birds. A young Pharisee rebukes him for doing this "work" on the Sabbath. Jesus laughs, claps his hands, and the birds come to life and fly away. (This story even made it into the Koran, surah 5:110).

In Luke 2:41–52 we see many of the same elements. Jesus' parents' incredible neglect ("No, I haven't seen him *for three days*. I thought he was with *you*.") is on a par with Joseph's comical ineptitude in the throne story from the Infancy Gospel. His preternatural wisdom, making monkeys of the adults around him, is not mere precocity as O'Reilly and Dugard would have it. That is what Old Testament scholar Niels Peter Lemche[29] calls a "rationalistic paraphrase" of a legendary narrative, smoothing it out in order to make it seem plausible as a piece of history. The adolescent Jesus is clearly pictured in Luke 2:49 as a god masquerading as a mortal. Note that he is not only wiser than the scribes but contemptuous of his oblivious parents who should have known to make a beeline for the Temple if they wanted him. His staying behind when they left for home is no Tom Sawyer mischief; he is acting with superior sovereignty. But he condescends to go with them back home for some milk and cookies.

Even though O'Reilly and Dugard minimize the blatantly legendary character of the story, which is why they make Jesus only a very inquisitive child, they nonetheless double back to cash in on the mythical material by taking the story seriously as Jesus' first public claim to be the Son of God. They are reading Luke 2:49 ("Did you not know I must be in my Father's house?") as if it were John 5:18 ("This was why the Jews sought all the more to kill him, because he not only broke the Sabbath but also called God his Father, making himself equal with God."). O'Reilly and Dugard seem to take the "my Father" reference in the Lukan story the same way Jesus' adversaries do in the Johannine story, against Jesus' intention. He rebuts their inferences in John 10:33–36, but O'Reilly and Dugard apparently agree with the Pharisees. They want Jesus, already as a youth, to claim membership in the Trinity. And any old piece of Jesus folklore is grade-A building material for their project. This is what I mean: *Killing Jesus* is by no stretch of the imagination the purely secular historical account O'Reilly stridently says it is.

Chapter Two

BIRD MAN OF NAZARETH

Bill O'Reilly and Martin Dugard paint a vivid picture in their book of John the Baptist. In doing so, they simultaneously embellish the figure of John and oversimplify it. All four canonical gospels feature John, but they contradict one another in serious respects, as we shall see. The treatment of the Baptizer in *Killing Jesus* is a prime example of the authors' tendency to homogenize the gospel accounts, a method that gives short shrift to any and all of them, cheating the reader, who will come away with no idea of the remarkable distinctiveness of each one. The fundamentalist, the harmonist, the apologist wants to be able to point to a single "truth" about John and his role in the Jesus drama. The fact that there are four different canonical versions is disturbing to him, though not to the genuine historian who is always willing, if necessary, to admit that we cannot arrive at a definitive conclusion. But the apologist for the faith, even if he masquerades as a New Testament historian, is motivated by theology and cannot tolerate such ambiguity. O'Reilly and Dugard, however, are impatient with such "dithering," as they no doubt view it. They have a story to tell, and they want to sound like they know what they're talking about. So they figure the facts must be knowable. The ironic result is that they throw the various accounts of the Baptizer into the textual blender and produce a synthetic product that matches none of the originals. But it looks most like that of John's Gospel. And, as I have argued, this is doubtless the poorest choice of the bunch.[1] What say we take their section on John and the Jordan baptism of Jesus bit by bit?

THE BEAUTIFUL, THE BEAUTIFUL RIVER

What kind of person came out and waited in line to confess his or her sins to John and to receive his absolution? "The believers are mostly poor working people" (p. 95), those whom O'Reilly, on *The Factor*, likes to call "the folks." To today's reader, this sentence would seem to imply that John's ministry attracted only a certain slice of a larger population. This may be misleading, since there weren't many other options. The Roman Empire balanced a tiny elite at the top of the socioeconomic pyramid, the broad base being slaves and desperately poor laborers, shepherds, fishermen, and farmers, even as our authors explain elsewhere in the book. Luke 7:29 adds the hated, quisling tax collectors (or toll collectors) but says "all the people" had been baptized by John, just as Mark says (1:5). O'Reilly and Dugard place "the haughty Pharisees" on the scene, "spying on him from the shore" (p. 95). Here is the old Christian caricature of this pious sect. Pharisees were not aristocrats, much less clergy. There was little overlap between them and the priesthood. They were more analogous to today's Hasidic Jews.

Luke 7:30 says that the Pharisees had boycotted John's baptism, presumably feeling they did not need it. Consistent with this, Luke's account of the baptism (3:1–9), rewritten somewhat from Mark 1:4–8, makes no mention of them being present. It is Matthew, also rewriting Mark, who has introduced the Pharisees, plus the Sadducees, into the baptism story. Luke 3:7 added a passage from the Q Source, giving a detail of the Baptizer's preaching: "He said therefore to the multitude that came out to be baptized by him. 'You brood of vipers! Who warned *you* to flee from the wrath to come?'" Matthew 3:7 added the saying, too, but he made a significant alteration, "But when he saw many of the Pharisees and Sadducees coming for baptism, he said to them, 'You brood of vipers,'" and so on. As you can see from elsewhere in Matthew's Gospel, he really has it in for these groups (see especially chap. 23), so he takes the opportunity to have John give them both barrels. But in doing so, paradoxically, he creates the impression that the Pharisees (and the Sadducees) actually did report for John's baptism, contrary to Luke. Does Matthew mean to imply they were hypocrites, just going through the motions? Why would they? And how would John be in any position to know this? Was he a mind reader? I think the question arises simply from Matthew failing to think his editorial change through. We would have to judge Luke's version more likely, meaning that there were no Pharisees on the scene. But O'Reilly and Dugard happily harmonize Matthew's version with Luke's: "One from column A, one from column B," and thus they conjure "the haughty Pharisees," lounging on the riverbank on their Shroud of Turin beach towels, binoculars at the ready.

But why not add the Gospel of John? In John 1:19–28, we read that certain Temple personnel had been sent by the Pharisees, not to do surreptitious reconnaissance, as O'Reilly and Dugard seem to think, but to interview the Baptizer. The story, as usual in this gospel, is unhistorical, and we can see this for two reasons. First, the Pharisees are said to have sent the priests and Levites (low-level priestly functionaries) on this fact-finding tour, but the evangelist is confused: the Pharisees, a group of pietistic laymen, would not have been in any position to send the Temple priests on some errand. This is the work of someone with no direct knowledge of the Holy Land back before the destruction of the Temple in 70 CE. The evangelist merely imagines "the Jews" (as he usually calls them) as one big gang of villains, with no reason to make distinctions among them.

Second, the interrogation of John, questioning whether he thinks himself to be Elijah, or the predicted Prophet like Moses, or the Messiah, seems to be a Johannine rewrite of Mark's Caesarea Philippi scene (Mark 8:27–30), in which Jesus asks the disciples who the crowds believe him to be, and they answer, "Some say John the Baptist; and others say, Elijah; and others one of the prophets." When Jesus asks the disciples' own opinion, Peter answers, "You are the Christ." John's Gospel has taken this scene and transferred it to John the Baptist. The four options are the same (Elijah, one of the prophets/the Prophet, John the Baptist, the Christ). Both Jesus and John deny being Elijah and a/the p/Prophet, but Jesus, being the Christ, denies being John, while John, being the Baptizer, denies being the Christ. When John's Gospel gets to his version of the Caesarea Philippi scene (though he switches it to Galilee), it is simpler: the contrast between the crowds and the disciples is preserved, but now, instead of Jesus asking, "What do they say? What do you say?" he sees the crowds, mystified at his Bread of Life discourse, abandoning him (John 6:66), and he asks the Twelve, "Will you also go away?" (6:67). Again, it is Peter who replies, and his rewritten response is both simpler and more elaborate: "Lord, to whom shall we go? You have the words of eternal life; and we have believed and have come to know that you are the Holy One of God" (6:68–69).

O'Reilly and Dugard sum up John's preaching this way:

> The end of the known world[2] is coming, John preaches. A new king will come to stand in judgment. Wade into the water and be cleansed of your sins, or this new anointed ruler—this "Christ"—will punish you in the most horrible manner possible. (p. 96)

But this is not in fact what any gospel has John say. He speaks more vaguely of "the Coming One," who will incinerate the unrepentant. This is an ultimatum of apocalyptic doom, that's for sure, but O'Reilly and Dugard are jumping the theological gun here. John says nothing of the Coming One being the Davidic Messiah or any other variety of a king. Albert Schweitzer thought that if these were actually the words of the Baptizer, he was more likely referring to the much-anticipated return of Elijah:

> Behold, I send my messenger to prepare the way before me, and the Lord whom you seek will suddenly come to his temple. . . . Behold, he is coming, says the Lord of hosts (Mal. 3:1); Behold, I will send you Elijah the prophet before the great and terrible Day of the Lord comes. (Mal. 4:5)[3]

Mark's Gospel opens with a quote at Mark 1:2–3 cobbled together from Malachi 3:1 (which I just cited above), with the pronouns changed ("I send my messenger before thy face, who shall prepare *thy* way"), and Isaiah 40:3 ("the voice crying in the wilderness: 'Prepare the way of the Lord, make his paths straight'"), though he names only Isaiah as the source, no big deal. Mark uses the passage to introduce John the Baptizer as the fulfillment of prophecy. John's Gospel puts the Isaiah part of the passage onto John's own lips, making it the Baptizer's reply to the Pharisees' emissaries who want to know what he claims for himself. O'Reilly and Dugard take John's secondary version as fact, unable to discern the subtle redactional alterations of one gospel by another. Nor have they done their homework on Isaiah very well, ascribing Isaiah 40:3 to Isaiah of Jerusalem, who lived eight hundred years before Jesus, when in fact it is the work of the so-called Second Isaiah, a member of the Isaianic sect who wrote just as the Babylonian Exile was about to end, when the Persian emperor Cyrus allowed Jewish subjects to return to Judea. In fact, this is the point of the passage, that God was commanding the preparation of a smooth journey through the desert for his returning people. For their part, O'Reilly and Dugard are quick to read Christian theology into the verses: "Isaiah foretold that a man would come to tell the people about the day the world would end and God would appear on earth." In Isaiah 40:3? Come on.

As if we needed a reminder that O'Reilly and Dugard are writing more of a novel than a historical work, consider this: "Like the Baptist, Jesus of Nazareth has long hair and a beard. He wears sandals and a simple robe. His eyes are clear and his shoulders broad, as if he is a workingman" (p. 103). Oh really, O'Reilly? Where do the gospels say anything like this? I can't help thinking of one morning, decades ago, when I was teaching an Intro to New Testament class and mentioned the belief of some ancient Syrian Christians that Thomas "the Twin" was Jesus' own twin brother. One woman raised her hand and suggested it was because, and here she pointed to an illustration in her Bible, Jesus and Thomas looked so much alike. Hoo boy.

PIGEON ON A STATUE

Again: "Suddenly a dove lands on Jesus's shoulder. When Jesus makes no move to shoo it away, the bird is quite content to remain there" (p. 103). This is another "rationalistic paraphrase." Mark has both more and less than this. "And when he came up out of the water, immediately he saw the heavens opened and the Spirit descending upon him like a dove; and a voice came from heaven, 'Thou art my beloved Son, with thee I am well pleased'" (Mark 1:10–11). Actually the preposition is εις, "into," though most translators, disliking the heretical implications,[4] prefer to pretend the preposition is επι, "upon," which is what Matthew and Luke replace Mark's with. Obviously, O'Reilly and Dugard prefer it, too, since they want the dove to be a flesh-and-blood bird, and it would be pretty grotesque to have the bird penetrate Jesus' body. Did he swallow it? But it is ridiculous for it to come to this. Mark and Matthew say the Spirit descended *as* a dove, not that it *was* a dove. Luke objectifies it, changing Mark's "as a dove" to "in bodily form like a dove" (Luke 3:22), but if he intended an incarnation of the Holy Ghost in a bird's body, it gets even weirder, like the Hindu belief that Vishnu once came to earth as a fish.

O'Reilly and Dugard admit that the gospels diverge over whether the Spirit descended before or after Jesus was immersed. This is one of the rare instances where our authors switch over from fundamentalist literalism to gospel criticism as an expedient when they can think of no other way to get out of a difficulty.

> The Gospels are a combination of oral tradition, written fragments from the life of Christ [=?], and the testimony of eyewitnesses. This would explain the discrepancy. The appearance of the dove may have been coincidental with Jesus' baptism. However, the Gospels were written as many as seventy years after Jesus' death (Mark in the early 50s, Luke between 59 and 63, Matthew in the 70s, and John between 50 and 85). For the dove to remain a part of Jesus's oral tradition for that long indicates that the bird's appearance must have been remembered quite vividly by all who were there. (p. 103)

Good God, but this is nonsense. Earlier our authors assured us that the gospels were eyewitness accounts, but now that would be inconvenient. Can O'Reilly and Dugard even add? If Jesus died in 30 CE, and the gospels were written as late as seventy years after, wouldn't the highest date have to be 100 CE? But the latest date they allow is 85 CE for John. Besides, these dates are preposterously early, dictated by the desire of apologists to minimize the gap between the ostensible time of Jesus and the composition of the gospels. Of course that only matters if you are trying to convince potential converts that all the stuff in the gospels can be trusted as accurate, so they can trust this Jesus, the character in the story they are reading, to be their personal savior and imagine him listening to them during their daily devotional quiet time. It wouldn't work so well if you had only a vague notion of who the historical Jesus might or might not have been. Once in the fold, the convert will be told that none of it matters; the gospels are inspired and without error. Christians can believe them implicitly because they are the infallible Word of God. And that could be equally true if the gospels were written in the 1950s. It is all cynical bait-and-switch, and it is this propaganda tactic that necessitates these early dates for the gospels. It is all mere spin.

Like a whirling dervish, one spins in a circle, and thus it is no surprise that the business about the dove landing on Jesus and the preservation of the scene in oral tradition is viciously circular. Note that O'Reilly and Dugard start out by *assuming* that the incident originated in a remembered fact and was passed down. If it survived, getting repeated for that long after it happened, that proves it must have happened!

THE ALL-SPIN ZONE

Don't let it escape your notice that O'Reilly and Dugard are not truly critical at all. The factors they say would explain slight discrepancies between the gospels are all assumed to be virtual guarantees of gospel accuracy. Let's see: there are oral traditions that are to be judged the more accurate the later we find them, like the late survival of the dove scene. There are written records of Jesus from his own lifetime. Besides being sheer supposition, this guess implies the gospels are giving us at least portions of contemporary testimony in written form. That's even better than accurate oral tradition. Third, we have eyewitness testimony. How does that differ from the other two types? All are accurate. Where is the zone of possible confusion? These "factors," even if they were real and factual, would only make the contradictions more puzzling, not less.

What O'Reilly and Dugard are conspicuously omitting to mention is the very good possibility that, first, the gospels are compilations of fiction and legend and, second, that one evangelist seems to have edited and rewritten his predecessor with considerable freedom, as any glance at one of those three-column parallel comparisons of Matthew, Mark, and Luke will make inescapably clear. And if we must reckon with these "factors," then we cannot pretend to be nearly so sure what really happened in the life of Jesus. The gospels are not unlike the Warren Commission report. Can you really trust them?

In fact, the only way to understand the gaping gospel differences, for example, over the baptism scene, is to "factor" in the possibilities that we are reading fiction, spin, and rewrites. Consider the differences and how much sense they make as polemical rewrites. Mark is the earliest version we have, written probably around 100 CE.[5] Mark has Jesus appear at the Jordan as a face in the crowd. There is not the slightest hint that John the Baptizer knows who he is. Jesus is baptized, then has a vision that only he sees. He sees the heavens open and the Spirit descend. The Baptizer never knows the difference. "Next!"

Early Christians faced competition from the sect of John the Baptist, who believed their own master had been slain by a tyrant, then raised from the dead, and that he was the Messiah. That is why Luke, Acts, and John (Luke 3:15–16; Acts 19:1–7; John 1:8, 20; 3:25–30) bend over backward to have John deny that he is the Messiah. It is aimed at latter-day followers of John whom Christians sought to convert. The John sectarians apparently made much of the fact that Jesus had sought out John's ministry and received his baptism of forgiveness of sins. Does that not indicate that Jesus recognized John's spiritual superiority? This seems to be why Luke, Matthew, John, and even the later Gospel according to the Ebionites handle the baptism with kid gloves, each modifying it, sometimes radically, in their own way.

Luke makes something of a convoluted mess of the baptism, describing John's ministry with material drawn from Mark and Q, as Matthew does, but adds touches of his own, and it is essentially over, with John arrested and hauled off to the slammer, before Luke gets around to telling his readers, in a flashback and in a subordinate clause, that "when all the people were baptized, and when Jesus also had been baptized and was praying, the heaven was opened, and the Holy Spirit descended upon him," and so on (Luke 3:21–22). Why would Luke, perhaps the most elegant stylist of the evangelists, retell the story in so tortuous a manner? It looks like he is trying to minimize, even to obscure, the connection between the Baptizer and Jesus. It's still there if you read it carefully, but it almost opens the door to the idea that somebody else baptized Jesus after John was gone. And notice that, as in Mark, Luke gives not the slightest hint that John knew Jesus before or after his baptism.

Accordingly, when Luke gets to the passage taken from the Q Source, Luke 7:18–20, he has John, languishing in Herod Antipas' dungeon, hearing about a man named Jesus reportedly healing the sick. It dawns on him that this mysterious person might just be the Coming One whose advent he had been proclaiming. "The disciples of John told him of all these things. And John, calling to him two of his disciples, sent them to the Lord, saying, 'Are you he who is to come, or shall we look for another?'" He would not even be asking the question if he had already recognized Jesus as the Messiah. And in Luke, as in Mark, he didn't. Jesus had been merely one more face in the crowd. It is true that Luke's Infancy narrative makes John and Jesus into cousins. And, in an episode too obviously legendary for O'Reilly and Dugard to include, already the fetus John recognizes the embryo Jesus with both still in the womb (Luke 1:44). But this is incompatible with Luke's own episodes of the baptism and the messengers of John being sent to Jesus. It is, in fact, part of Luke's polemical effort to reconcile Christianity with the rival John the Baptist sect and to co-opt their members. It doesn't matter to Luke that one of his stories is inconsistent with another as long as each is consistent with his larger purpose.

Matthew has the same anxieties about the gibe of John's believers that John, having baptized Jesus, must be Jesus' superior. So what does he do with the baptism scene? This: "Then Jesus came from Galilee to the Jordan to John, to be baptized by him. John would have prevented him, saying, 'I need to be baptized by you, and do you come to me?' But Jesus answered him, 'Let it be so now; for thus it is fitting for us to fulfill all righteousness.' Then he consented" (Matt. 3:13–15). In this version, John the Baptizer recognizes Jesus as the Coming One the minute he sees him, just the opposite of the way the story goes in Mark and Luke. Why this rather drastic change? Matthew wants to reassure readers that Jesus is the greater figure, despite the claims of the John sectarians: John discouraged Jesus from receiving his baptism ("What's a nice savior like you doing in a place like this?") and tried to reverse their roles, but Jesus declined his offer, insisting on going through with John's baptism. Can you imagine that, if it had actually happened this way, Mark and Luke would not have included this little exchange between Jesus and John? No way. What Matthew adds to the story he did not get from oral tradition, eyewitness testimony, or written records from Jesus' own lifetime. He made it up. Obviously. But it is not obvious to O'Reilly and Dugard, who tell us it really happened. They are not, despite O'Reilly's oft-repeated claims, writing history. They are engaged in apologetics, spin, on behalf of the doctrine of biblical inerrancy.

O'Reilly and Dugard cherry-pick several of these items and stitch them together. Then they place this Frankenstein's monster into a context derived from John's Gospel, even though it doesn't fit. John has the Baptizer recognize Jesus, all right, contradicting both Mark and Luke, but he also contradicts Matthew, who had the Baptizer know

Jesus as the Coming One even before he beheld the descent of the Spirit after Jesus' immersion. In John's Gospel, the Baptizer knows Jesus for the Coming One only once he witnesses the descent of the Spirit, not before. As we have seen, O'Reilly and Dugard do realize there is an inconsistency here, but they try to hide behind the ambiguity of the sources. The point of such an appeal is not to show that the gospel sources cannot be relied upon for history but merely to wave away a difference in detail. But the contradiction between John and the rest is that John never even says Jesus got baptized! John the Baptist merely points Jesus out in the crowd and announces that whoever commissioned him to start baptizing informed him that he was only doing it to gain a bully pulpit from which to draw public attention to a man upon whom he should eventually behold the Spirit descending. The circumstances of this vision of Jesus being marked out as receiving God's Spirit are not named. Certainly not a baptism, and that is an amazing omission. But in omitting it, John the evangelist hoped to cut the rug from under the feet of the Baptist sect and their gloating over the fact that Jesus was baptized by the superior John.

O'Reilly and Dugard have squeezed every bit of ill-fitting gospel material into one patchwork quilt. But that is not good enough for these modern gospel writers (for that is what they are, not historians). So they start making stuff up again. "So now, speaking softly with John the Baptist, Jesus does declare who he is" (p. 104). But, uh, he doesn't, even in the new and improved O'Reilly and Dugard version. All he does is mouth the words taken from Matthew 3:15: "Let it be so now; for thus it is fitting for us to fulfill all righteousness." But maybe the Holy Spirit just forgot to tell his faithful scribes O'Reilly and Dugard the rest of Jesus' supposed self-declaration, because the Baptizer now knows enough to announce to the crowds, "I have seen and I testify that this is the Son of God" (John 1:34), a little detail conspicuously absent from all three of the other gospels. Or is it? Actually, it is just that the evangelist John has transferred what the voice from heaven says in Matthew, Mark, and Luke into the mouth of John the Baptist. Why? Because, remember, the evangelist John decided to sidestep the embarrassment of Jesus having received John's baptism of repentance by omitting the baptism altogether. For him, the whole baptizing project was just a pretext for the Baptizer to gain the public ear so he could announce Jesus. So if he is going to have Jesus declared Son of God in connection with John the Baptist, he is going to have to make John himself, and not a heavenly voice, say it. Was John the gospel author writing straight history? No more than novelists O'Reilly and Dugard. And here is a bit more of their fictionalization of the gospel narrative:

> The believers drop to their knees and press their faces into the earth. Jesus does not react to this sign or worship. He does nothing to discourage it either. The Nazarene simply wades down into the water and takes his place alongside John, waiting to be baptized. . . . The crowd remains on its knees as Jesus steps onto the shore and keeps on walking. (pp. 104, 105)

This little sequence has no basis whatever in the gospels. Our authors combine John's Gospel, where John the Baptist publicly announces Jesus as God's Son, with Matthew, where John tries to dissuade Jesus from submitting to baptism but says not one thing to the crowd about him, and then they interweave the business about the crowd bowing before Jesus, which is nice, vivid detail but occurs in no gospel—except the Gospel according to Bill. Isn't this just the sort of funny business that cost former journalist Jayson Blair his job at the *New York Times*?

UNCLE JOHN WANTS YOU

O'Reilly and Dugard inform us that John's teachings are "radical" (p. 95) and that they "directly challenge the Roman Empire" (p. 96). Herod Antipas (as Josephus records) was fearful of John's great sway with the people, dreading that he might foment a popular uprising. Though O'Reilly and Dugard call John's message "nonviolent" (p. 99), there is reason to question that. Our authors quote John's counsel to various groups of penitents who had come to him for baptism: To tax collectors he says, "Don't collect any more than you are required." To soldiers he says, "Don't extort money and don't accuse people falsely. Be content with your pay" (p. 96). But Robert Eisler pointed out long ago that the Greek word is not στρατιωται, "soldiers," but rather στρατευομενοι, "those going off to war," in other words, about to ship out.[6] Eisler then compares the words of the Baptizer to the marching orders Josephus gave to his rebel soldiers some forty years later when preparing to fight Roman troops in Galilee.

> If you thirst for victory, abstain from the ordinary crimes, theft, robbery, and rapine. And do not defraud your countrymen; count it no advantage to yourselves to injure another. For the war will have better success if the warriors have a good name and their souls are conscious of having purified themselves from every offence. If, however, they are condemned by their evil deeds, then God will be their enemy and the aliens will have an easy victory.[7]

One can expect little support from the population one is fighting to liberate if one treats them no better than their current oppressors do. And, as is implied in Josephus' reference to the rebel troops purifying themselves before marching forth, John's baptism of repentance may well have been a ritual to make sure God was on the side of the Jewish freedom fighters. Even the question of the tax collectors would make sense in light of preparation for war. One of the main objects of the rebellion against Rome was the abolition of taxes, and that would likely result in putting the quisling tax collectors, working for Rome, to the sword. John's advice? Taxes will still be necessary, but would now be needed to supply and support the rebel forces, without defrauding one's own people.[8]

A saying in Matthew seems to ascribe revolutionary violence to the preaching of the Baptizer: "From the days of John the Baptist until now, the kingdom of heaven suffers violence, and violent men seize it by force" (Matt. 11:12). There have been many attempts to defuse the ticking bomb of this saying, but all of them seem like ad hoc products of theological desperation.

Raymond E. Brown drew attention to a saying that, in its present context in the Gospel of John, refers to Jesus as the sacrificial Passover lamb[9] (as in 1 Cor. 5:7), but that, before being thus Christianized, may have formed part of the preaching of John the Baptist: "Behold the Lamb of God who takes away [i.e., does away with] the sins of the world" (John 1:29). Brown suggests that John, without reference to Jesus, had been preaching the coming of a warrior king who would eradicate the forces of evil oppressing the world and Jews in particular. The same imagery of a warrior lamb or ram appears in two contemporary Jewish apocalyptic works, 1 *Enoch* 90:38 and the *Testament of Joseph* 19:8. This is certainly warlike imagery, implying an imminent military crusade against Rome.

Matthew, Mark, and Luke have it that John was arrested by Herod Antipas because the Baptizer persisted in publicly denouncing the Tetrarch as a scofflaw vis-à-vis the Torah: "It is not lawful for you to have your brother's wife" (Mark 6:18). Mark says Antipas had wooed Herodias away from his brother Philip. (Though Josephus says it was his brother Herod instead—it was hard to keep the Herodians straight without a scorecard. Still is.) Herodias could not stand the embarrassment, and we are told it was she who nagged Antipas into arresting John. Antipas was fascinated with John and did not wish him harm, but Herodias wanted the troublemaker dead. In a famous story, she used her daughter, Antipas' stepdaughter, Salome (as Josephus, but no gospel, names her) to trick Antipas into having John executed. This already sounds like something out of *One Thousand and One Arabian Nights*, but O'Reilly and Dugard decided the story would be even more exciting with a scene in which the manacled Baptist confronts Herod Antipas face to face, though the gospels do not provide one. So they save the line "It is not lawful for you to have your brother's wife" for this fictive scene instead of placing it back where Mark did, during the public activity of John. Admittedly, it might have happened this way, but there is no evidential basis for it. The gospel story may be a tissue of myth and legend already, but O'Reilly and Dugard have made it into literary fiction.

Chapter Three

HOW NOT TO BEHAVE IN CHURCH

LOUSY FIRST IMPRESSION

One of the most outrageous harmonizations of gospel contradictions offered by apologist spin doctors for biblical inerrancy is to say that Jesus overturned the tables of the money changers in the Temple not once but twice. All historical plausibility is against it. Common sense shudders at it. But the fact remains that in Matthew, Mark, and Luke, Jesus "cleanses the Temple" at the *end* of his ministry, while in John the event *opens* his career. Spin-meisters O'Reilly and Dugard side, as usual, with the fundamentalists. It happens twice in their gospel, er, I mean history.

Anyone ought to see the insurmountable problem here. In the Synoptics, it is this event that figures in Jesus' arrest a few days later. No one could get away with doing what Jesus did even once. He didn't get away with it. If he had done this at the beginning of his ministry, it would have been a mighty short one. There wouldn't have been time for a second Temple altercation. So you're really left with deciding whether the single Temple cleansing happened at the start or the finish. And it is obvious it would have to have been the latter. So then we must ask why John transferred it from its original and proper place. There is a good, though not historical, reason for it. As J. Ramsey Michaels notes, John has decided, in effect, to make the whole gospel into a Passion narrative.[1] It will culminate with the Triumphal Entry, the trials, the cross, and the resurrection, like the others, but he has the trial extend retroactively through the whole book.

This is why there are numerous scenes in which "the Jews" accuse Jesus of being a transgressor of the Torah and a blasphemer (John 5:16–

18; 8:59; 9:16, 24; 10:24–25,[2] 31–33, 39; 11:8) and even try to execute him on the spot (John 7:1, 19, 25, 30, 32, 44; 8:40, 45). This is why Jesus is constantly depicted as speaking of witnesses who testify on his behalf (John 1:7, 32, 34; 3:26; 4:39), of his own testimony (John 3:11, 22; 4:44; 5:31–35; 8:13–18), and so on. The whole gospel becomes one long courtroom drama, as if to say, "Everything points to this." This is also probably why there are no exorcisms in John, though the Synoptics fairly swarm with them. It is why the institution of the Eucharist happens not at the Last Supper but at an earlier Passover in John chapter 6. The presentation is thematic, not historical. Nor is this in any way a criticism. But we must criticize O'Reilly and Dugard for failing to see it and for treating it as history, and as even more historical than the Synoptics since they make John the chronological framework of *Killing Jesus*.

LIFE OF THE PARTY

If John is the template for the O'Reilly Gospel, it is not surprising that *Killing Jesus* includes the Wedding at Cana story, which transpires before the Temple cleansing in the fourth gospel. While at the wedding reception, Jesus changes hundreds of gallons of water into (presumably white) wine. If this is real history, then Lee Harvey Oswald assassinated Abraham Lincoln. O'Reilly and Dugard are discreet about miracles, committing only to saying that "rumors" or "reports" were circulating that Jesus had raised Lazarus from the dead or walked on water. O'Reilly says this is because he is merely reporting history and realizes the affirmation of miracles would cross the line from history to faith. That is a valuable point, but I get the feeling he is just being coy. Wink, wink, nudge, nudge, say no more. Well, here he doesn't say that anything out of the ordinary took place at Cana. But without the miracle, of course, there is no story. But *with* the miracle, there is no history. Let me explain why this should be. Historians do not claim to know with dogmatic certainty *what* happened in the past unless they happened to be on the scene to witness it. My father, Noel B. Price, was no historian, but he laughed off the claims of Holocaust deniers for the simple reason that he was present at the liberation of Dachau and saw for himself what had happened there. But we were not there to witness events of the remote past. So the historian can only weigh what evidence survives and make an assessment of the probability of some account being historically true.

And one of the most useful, indeed indispensable, tools for doing so is the Principle of Analogy.[3] Suppose you are studying a medieval chronicle that "reports" that one day a dragon flew into town and incinerated the whole populace. Well, technically, you weren't there and so do not know for sure that some dragon *didn't* show up. But you know that there are zero verifiable reports by contemporary, reliable witnesses of dragon attacks occurring today. And you know there are loads of fairy tales and myths in which dragons devastate villages. Which does your source's dragon story match: contemporary experience? No. Myths and legends? Yes. So you regard the story as no more than a story. Not a terribly difficult choice. But when you start treating biblical miracle stories the same way, then the outrage begins.

Samson kills a thousand Philistine soldiers with a sun-dried jawbone of a donkey (Judg. 15:14–15). Let's see: history or legend? You will look in vain through military history to find a story where something like this happens. No, it happens only in superhero comics. So wouldn't it seem inevitable that you are going to classify the Samson story as most probably a legend? It has nothing to do with your philosophical presuppositions or with a "naturalistic bias" against the miraculous. It's just a question of the way in which things happen, as far as we can tell. Those who protest such judgments of probability against miracles in the Bible have no interest in the way historians evaluate ancient evidence. Rather, their objections arise from the will to believe in the inerrant accuracy of the Bible. So O'Reilly is right: mixing miracles in alongside historical events is not possible in a pure work of history—or a book that wants to be regarded as history. I think O'Reilly and Dugard are just being cagey, though, especially since they do not hesitate to tell us, more than once, in a matter-of-fact way, that Jesus fulfilled this or that prophecy. (Someone ought to tell them that the verb corresponding to the noun *prophecy* is "to prophesy," *not* "to prophesize.")

So what about the water-into-wine miracle? Do you recall the last time you saw any such thing on the Food Network? I don't. But then there is Pausanias' account of the priests of Dionysus who used to impress the gawkers every year by setting out three empty kettles in the temple, sealing the doors, then "discovering" the receptacles full of wine the next morning (*Description of Greece* 6.26.1f.). It seems not unlikely that Dionysus' reputed feat inspired that attributed to Jesus in the Gospel of John. But that's not all.

Remember the story of the adolescent Jesus educating the scribes in the Temple? That was, I suggested, a specimen of the child-god stories with which the apocryphal Infancy Gospels swarm. This is another one, slightly adapted, as Raymond E. Brown observed.[4] It has all the classic features: Jesus is stuck amid a bunch of buffoonish (mortal) adults who have somehow underestimated how much wine they will need for a festive occasion, and now they are in danger of ruining it. Jesus' mother looks to him, as if she were Ma Kent knowing her son, Superboy, can save the day.[5] Jesus is impatient. "What fools these mortals be." He speaks to his mother in a supercilious tone, annoyed at being bothered. But she knows he cannot finally resist her and so assures the master of ceremonies that her son will take care of it somehow: "Do whatever he tells you." Jesus saves the day via an extravagant miracle, transmuting hundreds of gallons of water into wine—when everybody is already drunk (John 2:10).[6] It is a piece of apocryphal legend sneaking into the canon. Jesus has been made into an adult, and his disciples have been added to the story. We might wonder if perhaps the story of Jesus blasting the fig tree that disappoints him ("May no one eat fruit from *you* again," Mark 11:14), and even the story in which he rolls his eyes at the inability of the disciples (originally professional but incompetent exorcists?) to help the deaf-mute epileptic boy, are not more of the same. "O faithless generation. How long am I to be *with* you? How long am I to *bear* with you?" (Mark 9:19).

OCCUPY THE TEMPLE

O'Reilly and Dugard not only follow Jesus into the Temple; they show us through his eyes what any pilgrim to Jerusalem for Passover would have seen, which for them means Jesus, too, must have seen it and therefore *did* see it. And since typically pilgrims took a ritual dip in the baptismal *mikvah*, so did Jesus. He must have. O'Reilly once claimed on-air not to know the word "syllogism." This was probably self-deprecating humor. But he doesn't seem to know what a syllogism is in this case: All Jews visiting the Temple entered a *mikvah*. Jesus was a Jew headed for the Temple. Therefore Jesus entered a *mikvah*. That constitutes valid deductive reasoning, if, that is, the premises are true. But I suspect the major premise is a case of the Fallacy of Division, as if, for example, I were to infer from the statement "America is a wealthy country" that I, being an American, am personally rich. Oh, the rubber checks that would result! Isn't it a questionable assumption that Jesus was your typical Jew, or indeed, your typical anything? So much of Jesus scholarship today makes the same mistake: in order to promote ecumenical bridge-building between Jews and Christians (an excellent idea in itself), Christian[7] as well as Jewish[8] scholars rush to make Jesus a conventional Jew. "If it was good enough for Jesus, it's good enough for me." But this is very far from obvious, given the way Jesus is presented in the gospels as doing many things for which conventional Jewish authorities frowned on him. And one of those was "cleansing the Temple."

What precisely was supposed to be so bad about the Temple that Jesus felt he had to interrupt its operations? O'Reilly and Dugard do a good job sketching the spectacle one might have seen in the Court of the Gentiles, a forecourt, or outer ring, into which pious Gentiles might enter to observe Jewish worship at a distance, as they did back home in Gentile territories in the local Diaspora Jewish synagogues. What we know was wrong was that the authorities had allowed the sellers of livestock and the money changers to set up their pens and tables in this area, which would have made it pretty difficult for a Gentile to concentrate on the liturgy going on down front, as if you were trying to follow the plot of a movie standing at the popcorn counter. What were these functionaries doing there? As inconvenient as they were for visiting Gentiles, they were quite convenient for Jewish worshippers who could (and had to) offer animal sacrifices. The Torah stipulated three Temple festivals on high holy days throughout the year. You could drag your own sheep along with you from the hills of Galilee or wherever, but it was not unlikely that the poor beast, unaccustomed to such travel, might break a leg along the way. And if it did, you couldn't offer it, since the sacrifices had to be physically perfect, not a cast-off. You had to give God your best. So you get there with a defective animal: you're screwed, right? Why take the risk? Why not just go to the pens and buy a "government-inspected" animal from the priests who had already certified it?

But suppose all you had in your pocket were "idolatrous" Roman coins with portraits of Caesar on them? Images were forbidden to Torah-observant Jews. You couldn't use Roman coins to purchase animals in the holy precincts of the Temple. But you're in luck. There were currency exchange booths, just like in international airports today (I'm still stuck with a couple of Canadian quarters from my last trip). And there you could trade your pagan coins ("Mammon," good enough for everyday needs) for non-idolatrous Hebrew or Phoenician coins, unmarred by images of human beings. With these you could buy that perfect lamb.

What gets Jesus so riled up, as if he were Bill O'Reilly interviewing Barney Frank? Jesus says, "Take these things away. You shall not make my Father's house a house of trade" (John 2:16). It looks as if Jesus felt this buying and selling was allowing the profane to intrude upon the sacred, defiling the sanctity of the Temple. People ought to bring their own animals and trust God to keep them safe. After all, the Torah must have presupposed they would bring them from home. And if they still needed cash for the trip, they should have made sure they had the right money before they left.

But our authors surmise something more sinister than this. Invoking the invidious stereotype of Jewish Shylocks, O'Reilly and Dugard jump to the conclusion that the livestock dealers and money changers must have been skinning the pilgrims, since they had them where they wanted them, like movie theaters charging you ten bucks for a box of popcorn. But where does the text say anything of the kind? Sure, it's possible, but that's all you can say. I've never visited the Vatican, but I would not just assume that the sellers of souvenirs there were ripping me off.

O'Reilly and Dugard proceed with their shameless fictionalizing. They pretend to know that Jesus' actions in the Temple were the result of a spontaneous freak-out: "Something within him snaps" (p. 123). And his table-turning rage was uncharacteristic because "Jesus usually exudes a powerful serenity" (p. 123). How do our authors pretend to know this?[9] Or this: "Heavy as the tables might be, their weight does not bother Jesus—not after twenty years of hauling lumber and stone alongside his father. He places two hands beneath the nearest table and flips it over" (p. 124)? Somehow our authors know that Nicodemus was present to see all this transpire. Well, they must know more than any of the gospel writers. And on and on go the gratuitous embellishments. If anyone thinks he is reading a historical work, he has been deceived. We are reading a novel. And I don't think it even qualifies as a historical novel.

"Despite the commotion, soldiers do not run in to quell the disturbance. . . . No one blocks Jesus' path as he leaves the Court of the Gentiles" (p. 125). I will return to this matter when we accompany O'Reilly and Dugard to Jesus' "second" cleansing of the Temple later on. For now, suffice it to say that they casually glide right by a gaping historical implausibility: how on earth did the armed Temple police, especially on the watch for trouble during Passover, with the city and the Temple crowded with visitors, *not* arrest Jesus on the spot? The apologist might ask us to believe they wanted to avoid escalating the chaos, planning to have Jesus followed and arrested later, on the sly. While this makes some sense later, when we hear the Sanhedrin wants to prevent rioting by having Jesus apprehended away from the madding crowd, this is different. Surely the simple fact of stationing troops throughout the Temple means that they were on hand to intervene in the Temple *with armed force*. If it had been the policy to let Jesus go and to catch up with him later, then would this not also be the policy *all the time*? And then why would there be armed guards there at all? No, surely they would have swooped down on Jesus—in the real world. But that may not be where this scene is set. Or it may be that something more, *much* more, took place, and that we are reading a heavily redacted version of the story, just like mainstream media reports on Benghazi, or Eric Holder's account of Operation Fast and Furious.

NICK AT NITE

As usual, O'Reilly and Dugard are "omniscient narrators," pretending to know details they have actually fabricated, which would be perfectly fine if they admitted they were writing a novel.[10]

> Jesus has returned to the Temple time and again during his Passover stay, teaching from that Temple cloister known as Solomon's Porch. This is his favorite place in the Temple, and even when he is not listening to the scholars or joining in to offer his own teachings about the kingdom of God, he often lingers in that area, walking and soaking in the atmosphere. (p. 126)

Where does this "information" come from? Jesus' Facebook? His Twitter account? I guess a little bird (specifically a dove) told our authors.

The Pharisee Nicodemus sneaks out to see Jesus under cover of darkness. O'Reilly and Dugard earlier placed Nicodemus on the scene during the Temple cleansing, without any biblical grounding, in order to prepare for the present scene. He admits to Jesus that "we," presumably his fellow members of the Sanhedrin, supreme council of the Jews, recognize that he is the real thing: a teacher sent by God, since otherwise he would never be able to perform the miracles he does. What miracles would those be? Are we supposed to picture Nicodemus having been present at the Cana wedding feast? The reference is to John 2:23: "Now when he was in Jerusalem at the Passover feast, many believed in his name when they saw his signs which he did." These must be the ones Nicodemus refers to, so was he there to see these, too? Maybe so. But wait a second. "We," the Sanhedrin, all know Jesus is a teacher sent from God? Everywhere else in the Gospel of John the whole bunch of them, except for Nicodemus (this gospel does not make Joseph of Arimathea a member of the council), dismiss Jesus as the worst kind of heretic and blasphemer. It sounds more like the confessional "we" in 1 John, speaking on behalf of Christian believers in general: "That which was from the beginning, which we have heard, which we have seen with our eyes, which we have looked upon and touched with our hands, concerning the word of life—the life was made manifest, and we saw it and testify to it," and so on. Also in the Johannine Appendix (John 21:24): "This is the disciple who is bearing witness to these things, and who has written these things; and we know that his testimony is true." Even in the Nicodemus passage, the same author seems to be speaking through the mouth of the Jesus character: "We speak of what we know and bear witness to what we have seen" (John 3:11). Again, *we?*

O'Reilly insists on taking as historical reporting what is plainly written as edifying fiction. First, the very name "Nicodemus," an actual though uncommon name among Jews, seems to denote a type-character, what Tzvetan Todorov calls a "narrative-man," a character who amounts to no more than the embodiment of his function in the story.[11] He exists to typify a group, in this case, secret Christians among the Jewish leadership. No sooner are we introduced to him by name than we hear he is "a ruler of the people." What a coincidence; that is the meaning of the name "Nicodemus." *Nico* (Νικο) means "victor" or "ruler," while *demos* (δημος) means "people." As M. de Jonge made perfectly clear, Nicodemus typifies a certain group of intended readers for whom John is writing: Jewish leaders who privately assure Christians that they, too, believe in Jesus but who will not "come out of the closet" since they know they would be excommunicated from the synagogue and the Sanhedrin if they did.[12] This was all going on in the very late first century, after Christianity had taken form as a separate religious movement.[13] It is anachronistic for the time of Jesus, even though John 9:22 pretends this ban was already in effect in Jesus' day. John 16:1–4 makes it a future development to transpire after Jesus is gone. It is typical for John to read the conditions of his own day back into the career of Jesus as a literary device enabling him to let Jesus (fictively) comment on them. "What would Jesus do?"

So Nicodemus stands for crypto-Christians in the late first century. They are willing to go only so far as to admit Jesus was a teacher sent by God. Privately they believe more but dare not say so. And this is why John has Jesus abruptly confront Nicodemus with the demand "Unless one is born anew [or "from above," a double entendre in Greek], he cannot see the kingdom of God. . . . Truly, truly I say to you, unless one is born of water and the Spirit he cannot enter the kingdom of God" (John 3:3, 5). Protestants are surely wrong; Catholics are right: this refers to water baptism, believed by early Christians to convey the Spirit. John has Jesus tell the fearful Jewish believers in Jesus that they must take the crucial step and receive baptism if they wish to be saved. As in Romans 10:9–10, "If you confess with your mouth the Lord Jesus and believe in your heart that God raised him from the dead, you will be saved. For a man believes with his heart and so is justified, and he confesses with his lips and so is saved." "Anyone who is ashamed of me and of my words in this adulterous and sinful generation, of him will the Son of man be ashamed when he comes in the glory of his Father with the holy angels" (Mark 8:38).

When the apostles O'Reilly and Dugard quote John 3:16, they say Jesus "is expressing the predominant theology of his teaching. He has been telling all who will listen that a person must be spiritually reborn if he is to be judged kindly by God" (p. 127). What the . . . ? This is not a predominant theme even in the Gospel of John. Something like it turns up in Mark 10:15 (repeated in Luke 18:17), "Truly I say to you, whoever does not receive [i.e., welcome] the kingdom of God like a child shall not enter it," but this may either mean "welcome it as a child would" or "welcome it as he would welcome a child," which seems to be the point in the context. We can't say for sure. Matthew 18:3 rewrites the saying in a manner that seems to have caught John's eye, prompting him to rewrite it in the form we find in John 3:3. The Matthean version reads, "Truly I say to you, unless you turn and become like children, you will never enter the kingdom of heaven." But this statement is immediately interpreted by its continuation: "Whoever humbles himself like this child, he is the greatest in the kingdom of heaven" (Matt. 18:4). Thus the point is to encourage humility, not to teach spiritual rebirth. One must infer that being born again is our authors' favorite part of the teaching of Jesus in the gospels. But then they seem to be writing their own gospel.

Finally, are we even supposed to understand the greater part of John chapter 3 as Jesus' speech? There was no punctuation in the ancient manuscripts, and it sure sounds like someone talking about Jesus, rather than Jesus talking about himself. Some translations of the New Testament end the quote (and the speech of Jesus to Nicodemus) at the close of verse 15, making verses 16 to 21 commentary by the evangelist. These include the Weymouth,[14] Schonfield,[15] and Goodspeed[16] versions. William Barclay ends the quote even earlier, at the end of verse 13.[17] Thus it is not clear that O'Reilly is entitled to find in John chapter 3 Jesus' own declaration of his divine Sonship.

LOCAL BOY MAKES BAD

Back in the summer of 1974 I was visiting an innovative Evangelical congregation in hip Harvard Square. Everything had gone swimmingly until just before the benediction, when some church member surprised everyone by going up to the front and blurting out that the Reverend Sun Myung Moon was the true Messiah. Those near him hustled him out fast. Something similar is told of Jesus in Luke 4:16–30.

In Luke 4:16–30, Jesus has come home to Nazareth (though Mark does not supply this name), and his local congregation welcomes him home, asking him to read the scripture lesson for the day. He finds the appropriate passage in the Book of Isaiah and reads it, then begins to expound on it. As in Acts 13:14b–15, a visitor might be invited to give the sermon, an informal devotional on the prescribed reading, in this case Isaiah 61:1–2: "The Spirit of the Lord is upon me, and he has anointed me to preach good news to the poor. He has sent me to proclaim release to the captives and recovering of sight to the blind; to set at liberty those who are oppressed, to proclaim the acceptable year of the Lord." When he finishes, his sermonette is a doozy: "Today this scripture is fulfilled in your hearing." The reaction? "And all spoke well of him and wondered at the gracious words that proceeded out of his mouth, and they said, 'Is this not Joseph's son?'"

This is just the opposite of the reaction O'Reilly and Dugard attribute to the congregation: "The crowd is shocked . . . Jesus should remember his place. . . . He is the son of Joseph, and nothing more. In their eyes, Jesus exalting himself as the man sent by God to preach the good news is offensive" (p. 131). Uh, no it's not. By the end of the story, the crowd will have turned into an ugly lynch mob, but not because of this. What happened? As you can read for yourself in Luke 4, Jesus proceeds inexplicably to goad the crowd into enmity, mocking the enthusiasm they had expressed mere moments before. He says, essentially, "Oh, so now you're going to ask me to do some free miracles here, like I did in Capernaum. Well, I'm afraid a doctor doesn't treat his acquaintances. After all, Elijah didn't feed any of his fellow Israelites during the famine, only a foreigner. Elisha didn't heal any of the Israelite lepers, just a Syrian. Tough luck." This infuriates the crowd, one might add, understandably. But this is so crazy that O'Reilly and Dugard figure they can make it sound more reasonable by having the Nazarenes become affronted by Jesus' heroic, daring announcement of his Messiahship. That ought to be enough to set off those Jesus-hating Jews, right? Why did Luke make Jesus look like such a jerk?

Luke has rather extensively rewritten the scene as it appeared in Mark 6:2–6, but, typically, evangelists O'Reilly and Dugard ignore the fact that Luke's version is a product of literary art. They prefer this one, so, bingo, it's historical. Well, it looks like Luke was trying to improve Mark's underlying version, which does have its problems. Mark gives no idea of what Jesus may have said on the occasion (which is probably why Luke decided he had to expand it). Mark, too, had Jesus win the praise of the congregation, then turns on a dime and has them explode in unmotivated anger. "Many who heard him were astonished, saying, 'Where did this man get all this? What is the wisdom given to him? What mighty works are wrought by his hands! Is not this the carpenter, the son of Mary and brother of James and Joses and Judas and Simon, and are not his sisters here with us?'" But suddenly: "And they took offense at him." Why?

Just because Mark had another snippet he wanted to use, because it was sort of on the same topic, even though it contradicted the scene he had just written. We read the original version in the *Gospel of Thomas* (31): "No prophet is welcome in his own village; no physician cures those who know him." Like the opening scene in the hometown synagogue, the saying deals with the motif of a prophet in his own village, only in the proverb, the prophet gets a chilly reception, whereas in the story, he is warmly received. What was Mark to do? He just jammed them together.[18] First Jesus is applauded, and in the very next moment he is scorned, the result being that, à la the proverb, he proves unable to heal anybody because they do not believe in him. In Mark, there is no narrative motivation for the change, and this is what Luke sought to clarify. But he only made things worse by having Jesus *intentionally alienate* the crowd. In any case, the parallel between Elijah and Elisha spurning their needy countrymen and Jesus kissing off the Nazarenes serves Luke's larger agenda of God's offering the gospel to Gentiles once Jews reject it (Acts 13:46; 18:5–6; 28:25–29).

Luke's version is a much more exciting adventure than Mark's. Mark simply ends with Jesus surprised at the unbelief of the congregation and unable to perform many healings for them. The artificiality of that is evident. The ending note presupposes that several sick folks approach Jesus hoping to be healed. "Lord. I am affected by a bald patch."[19] But they have no faith to be healed? Then what were they doing standing in the healing line? Anyhow, the Markan scene concludes with a big fizzle. Not so Luke's new and improved version in which the crowd drags Jesus to the precipice on the cliffside on which Nazareth perched,[20] planning to execute him by the tried and true method of dropping the condemned man to his crashing death on the rocks below. But at the last moment, Jesus simply (and miraculously?) walks away through their midst. O'Reilly and Dugard feel their novelistic muse stirring.

> But at the last minute he turns to face his detractors. Drawing himself up to his full height, Jesus squares his shoulders and holds his ground. He is not a menacing individual, but he has a commanding presence and displays an utter lack of fear. The words he says next will never be written down [so how do O'Reilly and Dugard know there *were* any?], nor will the insults these men continue to hurl at him ever be chronicled. In the end, the mob parts and Jesus walks away unscathed. (p. 132)

This is Jesus as played by Jeffrey Hunter, who starred in the 1961 film *King of Kings*. Of course it is an almost plausible scene, but I suspect it is another "rationalistic paraphrase" (though even so it has the marks of fiction, even in Luke's terse version). It seems at least as likely that Jesus' ability to escape the crowd without effort reflects a popular early Christian heresy called Docetism, the belief that Jesus was too holy to possess a physical body of flesh and was instead a kind of divine phantom lacking substance and weight. He could merely drift through such a mob like a ghost. The gospels not infrequently toy with this idea, as in Mark 6:49 and Luke 24:36–43, though it is generally opposed (1 John 4:2). The *Killing Jesus* version is almost like the old rationalist reading of the walking on the water miracle, that he knew where the stepping stones were.

O'Reilly and Dugard sum up, informing us of something we would never know if we confined ourselves to what the gospels actually say. "Three times he has declared himself the Son of God, a blasphemous statement that could get him killed" (p. 132). The first, our authors imply, was during the cleansing of the Temple, when Jesus called the place "My Father's house." Too bad O'Reilly and Dugard did not take care to compare their favorite source, John's Gospel, with the earlier version of Mark, where Jesus simply quotes Isaiah 56:7, "Is it not written

'My house shall be a house of prayer for all the nations'?" (Mark 11:17). John has added the "My Father's." It is a theological embellishment, not a piece of historical reporting. The second declaration of his divine Sonship was that to Nicodemus in John 3:16, "For God so loved the world that he gave his only begotten Son, that whoever believes in him should not perish but have everlasting life." But this statement technically does not specify that the speaker is referring to himself. And who *is* the speaker? It sounds like the evangelist himself, putting a Christian creed into the mouth of Jesus, a character in his drama. The third declaration is supposed to be the application of Isaiah 62 to himself in the Nazareth synagogue. But this passage does not say anything about anyone being God's Son, only that the speaker has been anointed to free the captives, give sight to the blind, preach glad tidings to the poor, and so on. Here and elsewhere throughout *Killing Jesus* O'Reilly and Dugard blur the various Christian beliefs about Jesus into one another, regarding "Messiah" (anointed one), "Son of God," and "God on earth" as completely interchangeable. Like the old beer commercial with the Clydesdales: "When you say Bud, you've said it all."

So where are we? Mark's original was already a badly cobbled-together mess defying all psychological realism. Luke is a total rewrite, producing an even more grotesque result. O'Reilly rewrites Luke, much as Luke rewrote Mark. We are very far from any historical Jesus.

Chapter Four

FISHERMEN, PROSTITUTES, AND PHARISEES

One of the most fun features of novels based on the Bible is the clever and inventive ways the authors connect the dots left unconnected in the Bible. Also, the ways creative writers flesh out bit players in the biblical tales. It is the art of the docudrama: what might have been. *Killing Jesus* is such a novel. The trouble is that it presents itself as something else: a work of history, which it is very far from being. This chapter analyzes O'Reilly and Dugard's chapter 9 and shows how their narrative is the product of novelistic creativity and by no means of historical reconstruction. I don't think they know the difference.

PUMPKIN EATER

The material in the gospels about the Twelve is frustrating and tantalizing. I think that is because most of them are mere names on a list, only remotely connected, if at all, with real historical persons. The lists in the gospels and the Book of Acts do not even quite agree, though, as we will soon be seeing, defenders of biblical inerrancy have standard, if unconvincing, explanations at the ready, and O'Reilly and Dugard are happy to borrow them. The most developed character among the disciples is of course Simon Peter. This is not necessarily because anyone remembered the things he did and said. Rather, he is a literary foil. Peter plays the role of Ananda in the tales of the Buddha: he is well-meaning but a bit dense, and his dumb questions afford the opportunity for the storyteller to have the Buddha provide the true understanding for the readers' benefit.

Or think of Dr. Watson in Arthur Conan Doyle's adventures of the Great Detective, Sherlock Holmes. The reader can be privy to Holmes's feats of ratiocination only if Holmes has someone alongside him to whom he can explain them, and this he does by answering the questions of the baffled Watson, who is the intra-narrative counterpart of the reader. "I say, Holmes. How did you deduce that the IRS targeted conservative political groups for harassment?" "Elementary, my dear Watson . . ." That's what Peter and Jesus do. "Then Peter came up and said to him, 'How often shall my brother sin against me, and I forgive him? As many as *seven* times?' Jesus said to him, 'I do not say to you seven times, but seventy *times* seven'" (Matt. 18:21–22; cf. also Matt. 14:28–31; 15:15–20; 16:22–23; 17:24–26; Mark 9:5–6; 11:21–23; 14:29–31; Luke 8:45–46; 12:41ff.; John 13:6–11; 18:10–11; 21:21–22). The various gospel writers have used Peter wherever they needed a straight man, sometimes adding Peter's name when an earlier version simply had some unspecified disciple say or do something dumb.

The gospels are not completely consistent in their treatment of Peter, especially in the matter of when and how he met Jesus, became his disciple, and received the name "Peter" added onto his birth name Simon. Luke and John have major items regarding Peter that other, earlier, gospels lack. And by now you know what that means: they have been added to spruce up the story. Nor will you be very surprised to learn that this means nothing at all to O'Reilly and Dugard, who never met a gospel story they didn't like. And if they like it, it is ipso facto history, even if they have to tinker with it a bit.

To me, one of the most powerful gospel stories is that of the calling of the first disciples in Mark 1:16–20. Here these fishermen are, hard at work mending their nets, and a man suddenly appears on shore, someone they don't know from Adam, and he calls them to drop everything to follow him—on what mission, to what destination, who knows? And they do it. *One* thing they somehow know: destiny has just arrived and called their names. And they know they cannot turn away. Wow. Whether it happened or not, it is a perfect recruitment paradigm. And its power depends, I think, on Peter, Andrew, James, and John *not* knowing who Jesus is.[1] Nor does Mark give any indication that they do, so I don't think I am reading anything into this.[2]

We will see how Luke ventures to rewrite Mark's episode (Matthew figures it ain't broke, so he doesn't try to fix it). But John's Gospel lacks any version of this recruitment story. Instead, he places Peter and Andrew down in Judea with John the Baptizer. Andrew is lucky enough to be standing beside the Baptizer as the latter notices Jesus passing by, then points him out to Andrew, encouraging him to follow him and introduce himself. Andrew obeys, is impressed with Jesus, then goes to invite Peter, at this point called just Simon, to meet Jesus, too. Jesus welcomes Simon and, on the spot, bestows on him the name Peter (Greek equivalent to the Aramaic Cephas, "the Rock"). From then on Peter is numbered among the disciples. This version does not fit with the Synoptic Gospels. For one thing, no gospel tells both tales. For another, Mark 3:13–19a has Jesus christen Simon "Peter" when he chooses twelve assistants from the greater number of his followers. Matthew 16:18 seems to locate the naming at Caesarea Philippi in the wake of Peter's confession of Jesus' Messiahship.

John's version must be discarded as history if for no other reason than because it presupposes the fictive scene of the Baptizer publicly endorsing Jesus. In Mark and Luke, the Baptizer was and remained unacquainted with Jesus. In Matthew, in order to remove the stigma of Jesus submitting to the ministry of a superior, John is said to know Jesus as soon as he sees him, with the descent of the Spirit ensuing after the baptism. There is still no announcement about Jesus to the crowd. But in John, the Baptizer does not know Jesus as the Messiah until he sees the Spirit come down, and this is not even said to happen in conjunction with the baptism since Jesus is not said to have been baptized at all. John's Gospel makes the introduction of Peter and Andrew to Jesus a part of this complex, so, if the non-baptism sequence is the evangelist's own invention, the Andrew and Simon sequel goes down with the ship.

O'Reilly and Dugard try to solder the Synoptic and Johannine versions together, making nonsense of both. They want both versions to be true but wind up falsifying both. They figure that maybe Jesus did recruit Peter down in Judea in the days of John the Baptist, but then Peter had second thoughts and returned home to Capernaum in Galilee. When Jesus shows up there in Luke 5:1–11 (based on Mark's version), he is hoping to persuade Simon to come rejoin the team. While Luke does have Jesus already acquainted with Peter (Luke 4:38),[3] it is clear that he is recruited as a disciple only as of 5:10–11, after the miraculous catch of fish. O'Reilly and Dugard are trying to shoehorn John's recruitment story into the Mark-Luke version where it has no place.

O'Reilly and Dugard are trying to pass off this artificial synthesis of John and Luke as history, but it will not work. And even as fiction it is a blunder, since the notion of a previous acquaintance between Jesus and Peter totally saps the power of the Markan original. But, then again, Luke already ruined it. He apparently did not like Mark's version because it lacked any sensible motivation for Peter, Andrew, James, and John to pull up stakes and go off with a Jesus they did not know. It must have taken something pretty darn convincing to get them to make such a total break with the past. Luke knew of a miracle story in which Jesus caused a huge catch of fish for his disciples, a story seemingly borrowed from the lore of Pythagoras.[4] The same story appears in a variant version in the Johannine Appendix (John chapter 21). Luke decided, given the common element of Peter fishing just offshore, present in both Mark 1:16–20 and in the story of the miraculous catch of fish, he might as well take the opportunity to sandwich the latter into the former, with the result that now it is no big mystery why Peter and his buddies left their nets behind. And when a story can be dissected in this manner, we recognize it as a literary product, not a historical report.

O'Reilly and Dugard claim that they do not include gospel miracles except as (possibly true) rumors, but this is a major exception. With a straight face, they relate the essentials of the Luke 5 story, huge catch of fish and all. They don't actually say that Jesus *caused* the catch, but then neither does Luke. He doesn't have to. Do you think he figured it might be a coincidence? I assure you, O'Reilly and Dugard don't think so either.

Our authors once again transmute speculation into historical fact, just as Midas made lead into gold or Jesus turned water into wine, when it comes to Jesus' reasons for choosing fishermen for disciples. "Jesus has specifically singled out men from this calling [i.e., fishermen] because their job requires them to be conversant in Aramaic, Hebrew, Greek, and a little Latin, which will allow them to speak with a wider group of potential followers" (p. 139). This is sheer supposition, never even hinted at in the text. It is worth noting that the author of Acts must not have thought the disciples capable of such linguistic versatility, since when the time comes to declare the mighty works of God to an international audience on the Day of Pentecost, the same Holy Spirit who suggested to Bill that he write *Killing Jesus* became their translator. Who needs Rosetta Stone when you've got miracles?

Matthew suffers at the rude but dexterous hands of O'Reilly and Dugard, too. For one thing, they make him Peter's local tax collector in Capernaum. No gospel does this.[5] For another, they adopt the Gospel of Matthew's gratuitous identification of Matthew the disciple (Mark 3:18) with Levi the tax collector (Mark 2:14). Levi and Matthew are two separate characters in Mark, nor does Mark ever call the disciple Matthew a tax collector. But when we get to Matthew's Gospel, the two have been fused, though even here it does not say anything like "Levi who was also called Matthew" or "Matthew who was also called Levi." No, the evangelist Matthew (not the same man as the disciple character, by the way) simply changes the name from Levi to Matthew in the story where Jesus calls him to leave his toll booth to follow him (Matt. 9:9). And when we get to his list of the twelve disciples, suddenly we read what we never read in Mark: "Matthew the tax collector" (Matt. 10:3). Luke does *not* make Levi into Matthew, but this doesn't faze O'Reilly and Dugard, who assume Luke (and Mark?) hid Matthew's identity behind the pseudonym "Levi" because he was still alive at the time of writing (p. 144). What is that supposed to mean? The way they tell it, the "secret" had long been out, and Matthew must have gotten used to taking heat for his tax-collecting past. What a mess.

From some imaginary source our authors have pulled the "information" that Matthew "oversees all collections for Herod Antipas" (p. 139) and that the Jerusalem Pharisees "mock [Jesus] for selecting a much-despised tax-collector, Matthew, as a disciple" (p. 141). Oh, wait—they got it from the Gospel according to Bill.

JESUS' TALKING POINTS

Our authors are utterly without historical sense. If we didn't know that already, it would become clear enough with their summary of the Sermon on the Mount (Matt. chaps. 5–7). I think you can see one of the problems as illustrated in a famous scene from another gospel adaptation that is about as fanciful as *Killing Jesus*. Jesus is high atop the mountain in Galilee, preaching the Sermon. "Blessed are the peacemakers," he shouts. But listeners at the distant edge of the crowd cannot be quite sure what he says. A man opines, "I think it was 'Blessed are the cheesemakers.'" His wife replies, "What's so special about the cheesemakers?" Her husband, a skilled interpreter, says, "It's not meant to be taken literally. Obviously it refers to any manufacturers of dairy products."[6] Can we be sure that what Jesus may have said was correctly heard and transmitted in the first place, given the lack of amplification and recording equipment?[7] And that brings up another difficulty: it would be virtually impossible for anyone in the crowd to memorize the whole darn sermon while Jesus was speaking it, but that is exactly what O'Reilly and Dugard tell us happened.

And this sermon is no sermon, no speech given on one occasion. Luke has a shorter version in his sixth chapter. It does not look like an abridgment of the same one Matthew set forth, but it is so close to it that it is evident that both were using a common source, again, the Q Source. Both evangelists added material of their own from other sources, but Matthew certainly added more. You can pretty easily tell which one added what, as each writer leaves certain stylistic and thematic "fingerprints." But even the Q original was not the transcript of any single speech. The text is a compilation of self-contained sayings and maxims, strung together according to subject matter.[8] Even at that, there is no coherent line of thought. It is in these respects exactly like the *Dhammapada*, a Buddhist collection of sayings. Or like the Book of Proverbs in the Old Testament.

O'Reilly and Dugard would have us believe that these sayings were shocking and revolutionary. "And the words he speaks are like an emotional rejuvenation in the hearts of these Galileans, who feel oppressed and hopeless" (p. 142). "The crowd is stunned as Jesus finishes" (p. 143). No one audience heard this compilation at one time, so it is gratuitous for O'Reilly and Dugard to read the minds of imaginary listeners. (Of course, they are writing a novel here, so I guess they are free to do what they want.)

But would such preachments have shocked, stunned, and astonished first-century Galileans? I love these sayings, but I think the imagined audience reactions are based on our authors' ignorance of the fact that virtually the whole Sermon on the Mount is paralleled by well-known philosophical and religious wisdom freely circulating in those days. I am willing to bet that a lot more research about Roman road building and Herodian politics went into this book than study of Rabbinical, Stoic, Cynic, and other adjacent wisdom traditions. O'Reilly and Dugard are obviously laboring under the influence of a theological bias they don't even recognize as such. They repeatedly describe the Pharisees as obsessed with legalistic minutiae. The Pharisees made, we are told, Judaism into a spiritually bankrupt religion of rule keeping. "The folks" despaired because of such fanatical rigor and welcomed Jesus' radical vision of God's fatherly love. This stereotype will not survive a close look at the Mishnah, the Wisdom of Sirach, or other ancient compilations of scribal piety. Yes, there was plenty of careful attention to the commandments of scripture. But Jews appear to have viewed the Torah as a precious gift of God, an instruction manual written for our benefit by life's Designer. The notion of Judaism as stifling and oppressive legalism[9] arose as a polemical caricature by Christians who wanted to accentuate the need for their new faith.[10] Too bad O'Reilly and Dugard mistake it for historical fact and go on to perpetuate it.

> Who were those Jews who opposed the offer of grace to sinners? Where is there any indication that the parables were understood as blasphemy? Which Jews denied the fatherhood and mercy of God and held superstitious beliefs about his wrath? Where is the evidence that there was a connection between Jesus' parabolic teaching, the accusation of blasphemy, and the crucifixion? One marvels at the sentence which begins "those who nailed him to the cross because they found blasphemy in his parables": were the Romans offended by the "blasphemy" of the offer of grace to sinners? There is here an apparent loss of touch with historical reality.[11]

This single passage from E. P. Sanders's *Jesus and Judaism* might well stand as the epitaph for *Killing Jesus*.

O'REILLY AND DUGARD MAKE A CONVERT

Just a note here about a brief item our authors wedge in between the Sermon on the Mount and the next section.

> There, soon after entering the city [Capernaum], a most amazing thing happens: the Roman military officer in charge of Capernaum declares himself to be a follower of Jesus. Jesus is astonished. This admission could end the man's career or even get him killed. But Jesus turns to the centurion. "I tell you the truth," he says with emotion. "I have not found anyone in Israel with such great faith." (p. 143)

This is supposed to be a "historical" account of the episode of the healing of the centurion's slave from Matthew 8:5–10.

> As he entered Capernaum, a centurion came forward to him, beseeching him and saying, "Lord, my servant is lying paralyzed at home, in terrible distress." And he said to him, "I will come and heal him." But the centurion answered him, "Lord, I am not worthy to have you come under my roof; but only say the word, and my servant will be healed. For I am

> a man under authority, with soldiers under me; and I say to one, 'Go,' and he goes, and to another, 'Come,' and he comes, and to my slave, 'Do this,' and he does it." When Jesus heard him, he marveled, and said to those who followed him, "Truly I say to you, not even in Israel have I found such faith." . . . And to the centurion he said, "Go; be it done for you as you have believed." And the servant was healed at that very moment.

Notice anything missing from the *Killing Jesus* version? Where's the miracle? Oh, yes—O'Reilly and Dugard are clipping out the miracles lest readers catch on that they are writing a tale of devotional hero-worship. But the original story was told simply as the lead-in for the miracle. O'Reilly and Dugard leave the impression that the Roman just came up to Jesus and affirmed his faith, I guess, in Judaism, since there was not yet any Christianity to belong to. And he did it for no stated reason, at least not in this version. Of course, Matthew does not say the centurion has "declared himself to be a follower of Jesus." This is total fabrication on our authors' part.

But even if he had, would he have been risking his neck? Absurd. Many Roman soldiers embraced the religion of Mithras while on duty in eastern portions of the empire. Many Romans converted to Judaism as well. O'Reilly and Dugard are picturing the centurion as a character in such sword-and-sandal movies as *The Robe* or *Demetrius and the Gladiators*. The whole thing's ridiculous. Given the sales figures, about which Bill crows every night, I suppose *Killing Jesus* counts as the world's number-one source of misinformation about Jesus.

SACRED STING OPERATION

Who was the "sinner" woman who barged into the house of Simon the Pharisee and made a show of washing Jesus' feet with her weeping and of drying them with her long hair? Luke doesn't say. But O'Reilly and Dugard do. According to these gentlemen, she was none other than Mary Magdalene. How do they know this? Church tradition. That is a pretty weak link if you ask me. Ecclesiastical traditions of this kind are almost always no more than ancient guesswork, like that which identified Mary Magdalene with Mary of Bethany, the sister of Lazarus and of Martha in the Gospel of John chapter 11 (but just of Martha in Luke 10:38–42). The ancients combined all these characters as a way to harmonize three very different stories in which some woman anoints Jesus, but that's about all they have in common. The earliest version is found in Mark 14:3–9. The scene is the village of Bethany, in the house of Simon the leper.[12] A woman anoints Jesus' head with spikenard, and "some" present grouse that she has wasted the expensive ointment. She should have sold it and donated the cash to the poor (much like the scolding we hear from certain grumpy liberals today). Jesus replies, "Let her alone. Why do you trouble her? She has done a beautiful thing to me. For you always have the poor with you, and whenever you will, you can do good to them; but you will not always have me. She has done what she could; she has anointed my body beforehand for burying. And truly, I say to you, wherever the gospel is preached in the whole world, what she has done will be told in memory of her." The concluding sentence sounds anachronistic, speaking of the preaching of Christianity throughout the Roman Empire. I am guessing this addition originally contained the woman's name; it is mighty peculiar to say the story will be told to commemorate, ah, you know, what's her name. It has been omitted, probably because her name was eventually associated with "heresy." It would almost have to be Mary Magdalene, who was later made the patron saint of Gnosticism. But we don't know.

Matthew 26:6–13 hardly changes anything. Matthew just identifies the complainers as "the disciples." The rest is virtually identical to Mark.

John 12:1–8 sets the scene in Bethany, as before, but this time the occasion is a celebration in honor of Jesus and the newly resurrected Lazarus. It seems possible that John read Mark as recounting a banquet in honor of Jesus curing a man named Simon of leprosy, though no such cure is actually mentioned (though that little detail wouldn't have stopped O'Reilly if he'd thought of it). And perhaps he changed the guest of honor into Lazarus, the star of the miracle story he had just related (John 11:1–44). From leprosy to decomposition: not a big leap. Who anoints Jesus? This time it is Mary of Bethany, sister of Martha and Lazarus, and she anoints Jesus' feet, not his head, and dries them with her hair. And now the complainer is not just a bystander, not just a disciple, or rather a group of them as in Matthew, but—you guessed it: Judas Iscariot. His objection as well as Jesus' response are virtually the same as in Mark and Matthew. You can see why ancient readers decided Mary Magdalene was the same Mary as in John 12. But did they imagine Mary, Lazarus' sister, was a whore? Apparently not. It all hinges on what you think "Magdalene" means. I agree with John Lightfoot that "Magdalene" is based on an Aramaic term (*m'gaddla*) meaning "hairdresser," implying the madam of a brothel.[13] Hence the widespread characterization of Mary Magdalene as a reformed prostitute. But, as most do today, some ancient readers may have supposed "Magdalene" to denote Mary's home village, Magdala. We might wonder if John shared this assumption and so did not mean to portray Mary as a prostitute. But this doesn't help much, since she is, after all, located in Bethany, not Magdala. Granted, she could have been born in Magdala and moved subsequently to Bethany, but then why would her older sister not be called Martha Magdalene? Besides, the longer and more involved one of these explanations becomes, the less likely it becomes.

Now Luke: the feast takes place in the home of a man named Simon, all right, but this one is called Simon the Pharisee. Could he be the same Simon who was a (cured) leper? Could be. Pharisees were laymen, not clergy, and they held secular jobs, just like Hasidim today. But there is no hint in Mark that his Simon took a dim view of Jesus as Luke's Simon does. The use of the same name for the host implies that the two stories are variants of a single original. And it looks like Luke's is the later version, on account of its complications. If, like O'Reilly and Dugard, one wished to anoint Luke's version as the historical one, one has considerable explaining to do. Is it really plausible that no one stopped a known harlot from barging into the holy domicile of a pious Pharisee?

And if she had burst in, hell-bent on anointing Jesus, wouldn't she have been marched out before she could have done it? And Luke 7:44–46 describes her as anointing and washing Jesus' feet (not his head) for an extended period ("Ever since I came in, she has not stopped. . . ."). This just could not have happened. It is bad storytelling.

But our historians have a solution. Luke is an "omniscient narrator" and so knows what his characters are thinking even when he doesn't bother having them say it. He has Simon observe this risqué spectacle and muse silently, "If this man were a prophet, surely he would know what sort of woman this is" (Luke 7:39). Of course, he thinks Jesus is a false prophet. Well, O'Reilly and Dugard have decided that it is all a set-up, a sting operation, orchestrated by Simon to see if Jesus has prophetic powers of discernment—much like the Amazing Randi trapping a fake psychic. Let me get this straight: Simon the pious legalist sends out a servant to engage a local prostitute to visit his house, filled with similarly pious guests, all for a *Candid Camera* stunt with Jesus? Talk about eating with tax collectors and sinners! Wouldn't he be ruining his precious reputation for piety? And besides this, would a "plant," as O'Reilly and Dugard depict the woman, just happen to be gushingly repentant once she saw Jesus? Or was her repentance, too, part of the gag? Sorry, fellas. It just doesn't work.

Jesus' response to Simon's suspicions, totally unlike his reply to the carping of the bystanders (or the disciples or Judas) in the other three versions of the anointing story, takes the form of a parable, which O'Reilly and Dugard omit. Why? Commentators have always gotten headaches over it because it fits the scene so badly. "A certain creditor had two debtors; one owed five hundred denarii, and the other fifty. When they could not pay, he forgave them both. Now which of them will love him more?" Simon replies, "The one, I suppose, to whom he forgave more" (Luke 7:41–43). Then Jesus contrasts Simon's rudeness in failing to show Jesus the normal amenities due a dinner guest with the extravagant devotion shown him by the woman. She had been forgiven much more than the blue-nosed Simon and therefore was more loving. But then Jesus turns to the woman and says, "Your sins are forgiven." But surely the point of the parable was that the woman's enthusiasm demonstrated that she had *already* been forgiven and she knew it. What need, then, for Jesus to forgive her on the spot? Critical scholars suggest that Luke has inserted a parable about forgiveness of big-time sinners into a story about Jesus forgiving such a sinner, without noticing it didn't really fit, even though it was on the same subject. I'm guessing O'Reilly and Dugard noticed the difficulty and couldn't explain it, so they simplified the story, omitting the problem parable.

One last note. It is interesting to ask if Luke has preserved two fragments of the otherwise untold story (mentioned in Luke 24:34 and 1 Cor. 15:5) of Jesus' resurrection appearance to Simon Peter, one in this story, the other in the fish story in Luke 5. The version of that miracle that appears in John 21 makes it part of a resurrection appearance. Maybe Luke found it as a resurrection story, too, then transferred it over to the calling of the disciples. This would certainly give new meaning to Peter's lament in Luke 5:8, "Depart from me, for I am a sinful man, O Lord." In that case he would be referring to his denials of Jesus only a few days before. Similarly, some have suggested that the "Simon" of Luke 7 was originally Simon Peter on Easter morning, and that the parable of the two debtors was meant to assure a repentant Peter that his great sin of denying Jesus had been forgiven, and that he will love his Lord more because of it. That, too, would parallel the version in John 21 where the risen Jesus asks Peter to reaffirm his love for him three times to make up for the three denials. If this theory is true (and we can never know), Luke 5:8 would at first have been Peter's first words to the resurrected Jesus, and Luke 7:40–43 would have been Jesus' compassionate reply. Interesting. Who knows?

FOLSOM PRISON BLUES

Meanwhile, back in the Big House, John the Baptist is busy counting roaches and thinking about Jesus. Is he the Messiah after all? John was so sure before, but if Jesus were really the Anointed One, why the heck is John still languishing here, sitting in his own filth? So he dispatches a pair of his disciples to Jesus to ask him, "Are you he who is to come? Or should we keep looking?" (Luke 7:18–19; Matt. 11:2–3). Jesus lets them see a number of healings and tells the men to return to John with a report of what they have seen and heard. They do. O'Reilly and Dugard tell us that John is relieved by this news, his faith in Jesus happily restored. This is pretty much the standard Sunday school version of the story. But it is grossly erroneous.

As we have already seen, there is no reason to believe the Baptizer ever even knew who Jesus was until, while in prison, he heard reports about Jesus' miracles. Mark, followed by Luke, gave no hint that John knew Jesus when he baptized him. Matthew and John added the recognition in their tendentious retellings. This story about John sending his disciples to ask Jesus comes from the Q Source shared by Matthew and Luke (all the material the two share in common that they did not take from Mark). And the story presupposes the same version of Jesus' baptism we find in Mark and Luke. The Q Source did not assume John had recognized or endorsed Jesus at the Jordan. Thus when we get to this scene we are plainly supposed to understand that John is hearing of Jesus for the first time while John is behind bars, and it is these very reports that make him think, for the first time, "This man does miracles? Hey, maybe this is the Coming One!" D. F. Strauss put it well:

> Could John, then, believe Jesus to be the Messiah before he had performed any messianic works [i.e., at the time of the baptism], and be seized with doubt when he began to legitimatize his claim by miracles such as were expected from the Messiah? . . . But how could he become uncertain about the Messiahship of Jesus, if he had never recognized it? Not indeed in the sense of beginning to suspect that Jesus was *not* the Messiah; but quite possibly in the sense of beginning to conjecture that a man of such deeds *was* the Messiah.[14]

So where do people get the idea that John, once strong in his faith in Jesus, had begun to have second thoughts? Basically the notion is an attempt to harmonize the contradiction between the baptism stories of Matthew and John, in which John knows or endorses Jesus, and this story of the imprisoned John sending to ask Jesus if he is indeed the Coming One. If John the Baptizer believed early on, then has to ask later on, then somewhere in the middle he must have begun to doubt. But that won't work, since if, like O'Reilly and Dugard, you do take the Matthew/John version(s) of the baptism story as accurate, you have only shifted the problem, because now you have to square the Matthew/John baptism story with the very different Mark/Luke version. Good luck.

But there is also Jesus' parting shot as the Baptizer's men depart: "Blessed is he who does not take offense at me" (Luke 7:23; Matt. 11:6). It is not unreasonable to read this as implying that John will be blessed if he resigns his doubts and renews his faith in Jesus as the Coming One. But of course it doesn't actually say that. In fact it is a general blessing on all and sundry, whomever may hear it. It appears to be a general beatitude on Christians undergoing persecution and tempted to renounce Jesus in order to save their yellow hides, equivalent to Mark 13:13: "You will be hated by all for my name's sake. But he who endures to the end will be saved." And John is not in prison for his supposed faith in Jesus. He is in the can because he dissed Herod Antipas.

O'Reilly and Dugard add new material to the story when they state matter-of-factly that John the Baptist was relieved to hear his disciples' report. In fact, neither Matthew nor Luke gives us any idea of John's reaction. Why? For the same reason they leave it up in the air whether or not the rich young ruler (Mark 10:17–22) decided to sell his possessions and give the price to the poor.[15] Again, for the same reason Luke does not tell us if the Prodigal Son's older brother finally put aside his resentment, as their father pleaded with him to do (Luke 15:27–32), and joined in the Welcome Home party. In all such cases, the stories are meant as a challenge aimed at the reader: how would *you* react? How *will* you react? For O'Reilly and Dugard to tell us that John's supposed doubts were happily resolved is wholly gratuitous.

Chapter Five

THE AMAZING JESUS

MESSIAHS AND MISTAKES

The tenth chapter of *Killing Jesus* commences with a storm of contradiction and baseless surmise. It is my sad duty to recount them here. First we read that "many Galileans believe Jesus is the Christ—the anointed earthly king who will overthrow the Romans and rule his people as the king of the Jews, just as David did a thousand years ago" (p. 153). First, it is not clear that Galileans, who inhabited, along with the Samaritans, the northern portion of the Holy Land, corresponding to the ancient Kingdom of Israel (or Ephraim), would have had the slightest interest in any supposed Davidic monarch. Their ancestors had repudiated the Davidic dynasty and the Jerusalem monarchy centuries before: "What portion have we in David? We have no inheritance in the son of Jesse. To your tents, O Israel! Look now to your own house, David" (1 Kings 12:16). I suspect the Galileans would have been about as happy with Herod Antipas as with a new Davidic scion.

Later, O'Reilly and Dugard will get to the confession of Peter at Caesarea Philippi. There Jesus asks his disciples who the people in the crowd think he is. The disciples function as a buffer between Jesus and the crowds and so will be in closer contact with them and will have overheard their talk. We will see later in this chapter that there is good reason to believe the evangelist Mark has made up the Caesarea Philippi scene out of whole cloth, but at least it shows he did not think Jesus' fans believed him to be the Messiah. Notice, if you will, what *no one* in the crowd thinks of Jesus. Some think him to be the martyred Baptizer, others the prophesied second coming of Elijah (see Mal. 4:5), others regard him as some other of the biblical prophets returned

(Mark 8:28). What nobody seems to opine is that Jesus is the Messiah, though Peter dares to venture that opinion. So there is no particular reason to think many Galileans believed Jesus was the Messiah.[1]

But O'Reilly and Dugard assure us that they did. "Because of this, the Roman authorities are paying even closer attention to Jesus" (p. 153). Really? Where do the gospels even hint that the Romans had Jesus on their radar before the Sanhedrin approached them, at the end, to do their dirty work? I tell you, *Killing Jesus* is a novel.

"Knowing this [being aware of the increasing scrutiny of the Romans], Jesus takes great care no longer to proclaim publicly that he is the Christ" (p. 153). But he can't very well have been proclaiming it if the disciples have heard no one say they believe he is the Messiah. It is just impossible to believe that, if Jesus *had* been teaching that he was the Messiah, none *of his fans* would believe that but would cook up this stuff about Elijah and the Baptist instead. Not only that, but O'Reilly and Dugard, on the very next page, inform us that Jesus has not "told his vast audiences that he is king of the Jews" (p. 154). Well, which is it? Has he or hasn't he? And, if he has, why didn't anyone seem to have heard him? Oh, brother.

Speaking of John the Baptist, O'Reilly and Dugard have Herod Antipas believe that Jesus is "the reincarnation of John the Baptist" (p. 153). The, uh, *reincarnation*? Okay, there is some reason to believe that some contemporary Jews believed in reincarnation (John 9:1–2). But Antipas could not possibly have supposed Jesus was John reincarnated. Did he picture Jesus as the Holy Infant of Prague?[2] Of course, reincarnation means that the soul of someone now dead has returned to the world of the living via the birth of a new child. There wouldn't have been time for the grown-up Jesus to be the reborn John. Actually, what Mark has Antipas say to himself is "John, whom I beheaded, has been raised" (Mark 6:16). He is echoing the opinion of some of the people that "John the baptizer has been raised from the dead; that is why these powers are at work in him" (Mark 6:14). It is clear that some are seeing Jesus' deeds and inferring that John, slain by Antipas, has been resurrected. They think they are seeing resurrection appearances of a transfigured John. Why do O'Reilly and Dugard misrepresent resurrection as reincarnation? Why do they go on to say Antipas believes Jesus is the ghost of John returned to haunt him (pp. 153–54)?

What's the matter? Can't they read? Yes, but the trouble is that they are reading religious spin doctors like William Lane Craig who like to argue that Jesus must really have risen from the dead because, they say, contemporary Jews did not believe anyone would or could be resurrected within history, before the Last Day, when *all* the righteous would rise. They claim that, unless it had actually happened, there was no way first-century Jews could have come up with the idea that Jesus rose shortly after his execution since Jewish belief supposedly did not allow for that. They conveniently ignore Mark 6, where it plainly says that people thought John had already been resurrected. That verse undercuts their argument. I am guessing that O'Reilly and Dugard are following the lead of Craig and the rest and trying to disguise the fact that Mark says people commonly believed in the miraculous resurrection of a holy man executed by a tyrant. Sound familiar? The implication is that the belief in Jesus' execution by tyrants, followed by his resurrection into a superhuman form, may simply have been borrowed from recent preaching about John featuring the very same themes.

All of this assumes Jesus performed miracles, or at least that people commonly thought he did. You will recall that O'Reilly and Dugard claim they have spoken only of rumors and reports of miracles, because they dimly realize that miracle claims have no place in a properly historical presentation. Miracles are a matter of faith. But our authors seem to have forgotten this distinction in this chapter. They speak of the miracles of Jesus as objectively real events. They describe

> Jesus's ability to amaze the peasants of Galilee by seemingly performing supernatural acts. The Pharisees now hear that he transformed two fish and five loaves of bread into a feast that fed five thousand people in the mountains near Bethsaida early this spring. And even more fantastic is word that Jesus allegedly brought a dead girl in Capernaum back to life. Finally, the most astounding happening of all: Jesus's disciples claim to have seen him walk atop the Sea of Galilee in the midst of a violent

> storm . . . [and] a staggering number of witnesses are attesting to each and every one of these [miracles]. (pp. 155–56)

Let's take this a step at a time, shall we? First, the cagey business about Jesus "seemingly" performing miracles: what, pray tell, is *this* supposed to mean? That Jesus was a stage magician who took his audience's breath away by sleight-of-hand tricks? Did he saw Mary Magdalene in half on stage? Did he do voice-throwing stunts? Pull rabbits out of a turban? Or was he a hoaxer, flummoxing the naive? Of course O'Reilly and Dugard do not mean what their words would naturally suggest. They are covering their behinds as "historians," injecting a pretended element of doubt to hide their plainly religious partisanship. They sound too much like White House press secretary Jay Carney to me.

Second, there is no hint in the gospels that word of Jesus' multiplication of loaves and fish ever reached the Pharisees, nor is this just an argument from silence. In the gospel feeding stories, it is not even apparent that the crowd knew where the food came from. Few of them could even possibly have been close enough to the action to see what was going on. All they knew was that, so to speak, somebody was giving out free food stamps.

Third, the bad guys could not possibly have heard about the resurrection of Jairus' daughter, since Jesus strictly warned the girl's parents to tell no one about the miracle (Mark 5:43).

Fourth, there is nothing said in the gospel text to imply the disciples blabbed anything about Jesus walking on the water. Granted, it would not be too surprising for them to share the news of their experience, but how do O'Reilly and Dugard know they did? It is just a way of smuggling these miracle stories into the so-called history they are fabricating. You see, they know they can't get away with saying, "Jesus walked on the waves." They have to report that someone *heard* about it. But that's not what the gospels say.

Fifth, O'Reilly and Dugard conjure from thin air the "report" that huge numbers of eyewitnesses guarantee the truth of these reports. This is the wishful thinking of apologists. You can tell that our authors are merely bloviating as soon as you look at the miracle stories in question. Where were all these witnesses when Jesus walked on water? Were they stuffed into the boat with the disciples, like college fraternity pledges crammed into a Volkswagen? Were they peeking into the windows of Jairus' daughter's bedroom when Jesus raised her? Mark specifically says the only ones present were the girl's parents, plus James, John, and Peter. (And presumably the Holy Ghost, but he doesn't take up much space.) And again, though there were supposedly thousands present for the all-you-can-eat fish fry, there is no reason to think they even knew it *was* a miracle.

A LAMPOON UNTO MY FEET

The old Pharisees really come in for a drubbing in this chapter of *Killing Jesus*. We are almost in the audience of the Oberammergau Passion Play with its horn-sprouting and hook-nosed Jews. Get this:

> For as much as the Pharisees say they love God, most of them are arrogant, self-righteous men who love their exalted class status far more than any belief system. . . . They gained respect from the Jewish people by adding hundreds of new commandments and prohibitions to Moses's original ten, then passing them on through an oral history known as the Tradition of the Elders. (p. 157)

Surely O'Reilly and Dugard know that the Pentateuch already ascribes a total of 613 commandments to Moses, not just ten. But maybe they don't. It is true that later rabbis greatly elaborated these laws, trying to extrapolate how to apply the general principles of the Torah to new or more specific cases not actually mentioned there. But most of these traditions were in place a good bit later than the ostensible time of Jesus. O'Reilly and Dugard are following the anachronistic tendency of the Victorian-era scholar Alfred Edersheim, who simply assumed all of Rabbinical Judaism was in force in Jesus' day. Burton L. Mack puts it well:[3]

> The legal opinion [the Pharisees] generated may not have been inordinate. This point is important because of the traditional view among New Testament scholars, derived from a projection of the Mishna back into the time of Jesus, that Pharisees were casuistic legalists delighting in the application of hundreds of picayunish rules to throttle the performance of every natural activity.[4] Huge bodies of legal opinion did accumulate to fill the vacancy after the temple was gone.

They also hold to the baseless view that the Pharisees exercised some sort of tyrannical authority over other Jews who had no choice but to obey their oppressive stipulations. In reality, the Pharisees were a fellowship of pious laymen, not clergy. They followed the teachings of scribes who, in charge of making new copies of scripture, were hence the best versed in its teaching. But even the scribes were not clergymen. The Pharisees had hit upon the idea of undertaking to live every day according to the ritual purity regulations observed by the priests while on duty in the Temple. No one told them they had to do this. It was a self-motivated zeal to live in as sanctified a manner as possible. They began the formulation of detailed rules of holy conduct that would later be expanded into the Judaism of the Mishnah and the Talmud, but they did not pretend to order other Jews around. They fashioned a strict code of conduct that they rejoiced to follow. They do not seem to have disdained the common people who were in no position to live so strictly. What they were up to was what Roman Catholics call "works of supererogation," going above and beyond the call of duty to get as close to God as possible.

How on earth can O'Reilly and Dugard pass such a sweeping, damning judgment on "most" of the Pharisee sect? It reminds me of political commentator Chris Matthews slandering the Tea Party. It certainly seems that they are basing the whole thing on the worst polemical invective aimed by the gospel writers at the Jewish leaders who were their rivals for the allegiance of Jews toward the end of the first century. I think O'Reilly and Dugard are, like obedient fundamentalist proof-texters, taking their cue from a couple of passages such as we find in Matthew chapter 23, for example, "They bind heavy burdens, hard to bear, and lay them on men's shoulders, but they themselves will not move them with their finger. They do all their deeds to be seen by men . . . ; they love the place of honor at feasts and the best seats in the synagogues, and salutations in the market places, and being called rabbi by men" (23:4–7). But there weren't any synagogues in Galilee before the Jewish war with Rome (66–73 CE).[5] "Rabbi" did not come into usage as a title until the end of the first century.[6] But the fact that these verses are on the page of the Bible makes it factual information for "historians" O'Reilly and Dugard.

Our authors take as genuine historical reporting the dispute depicted in Mark chapter 7, which concerns the case of overzealous Jews deciding not to provide for their aged parents but to donate the money to the Temple treasury instead. Jesus maintains that no such vow is binding since filial duty takes precedence. But as far as our sources record, this was the *Pharisaic* view of the matter. Every time the question comes up, the rabbis whose opinions survive say just what Jesus said.

The Corban (offering) business treated in Mark 7 swarms with yet more difficulties standing in the way of taking the narrative as a historical record. For one thing, the complex purification laws Mark tells his readers that Jews must observe, ritually washing everything they bring home from the market, baptizing all sorts of kitchen utensils, and so on, applied only to Diaspora Jews, those living among pagans in other lands. That is why they were necessary: a faithful Jew could not be sure non-Jewish merchants and farmers had prepared everything in a kosher-compatible way as their Jewish counterparts back in the Holy Land would have.

For another, Mark has Jesus quote Isaiah 29:13 to Jewish scribes in the Holy Land, not exceptional in itself—or it wouldn't be except that Mark has Jesus quote the text of the Septuagint, the Greek translation used by Diaspora Jews, who did not read Hebrew. Jesus quotes as follows: "Well did Isaiah prophesy of you hypocrites, as it is written, 'This people honors me with their lips, but their heart is far from me; in vain do they worship me, teaching as doctrines the precepts of men'" (Mark 7:6–7). Jesus is attacking their extrapolated laws when these contradicted the literal laws of scripture, hence "precepts of men."

But this is not the wording of the Hebrew original, which has the last line as, "their fear of me is a commandment learned by rote," which is rather different and does not fit the point Mark wants Jesus to make. Jesus simply would not have been quoting the Greek Bible if he wanted his argument to be taken seriously by Palestinian Jewish scribes. Again, Mark is winging it, drafting a Jesus scene mistakenly presupposing a Diaspora setting, not a Palestinian one. Uh-oh.

O'Reilly and Dugard rival occult philosopher Rudolf Steiner in claiming to be able to read the minds of ancient people. They are sure that the Pharisees opposed Jesus because, if his teaching were to prevail, their cushy lifestyle (like that of fraudulent televangelists) would disappear. "Jesus is undermining their authority. If allowed to flourish, his movement will destroy their way of life, stripping them of wealth and privilege" (p. 156). Such a suspicion might be justified in the case of the aristocratic Sadducees, who controlled the Temple, but O'Reilly and Dugard amalgamate the two very different groups (p. 157) as if the Pharisees and the Sadducees were interchangeable. (They do rhyme, after all.)

Our authors are no doubt thinking of the scene in John 12:48, "If we let him go on thus, everyone will believe in him, and the Romans will come and destroy both our place and our nation." But if this is the passage they have in mind, O'Reilly and Dugard have garbled it badly. First, John is depicting the Sadducee-dominated Sanhedrin, not the Pharisees. Second, the danger they fear is Roman reprisals in case Jesus should decide to lead a popular uprising (cf. John 6:15), not the likelihood that Jesus, the new kid in town, will siphon off their precious customer base. Third, "our place" does not mean "our cushy position" but rather, as the Revised Standard Version renders it, "our holy place." They are shown anticipating the Roman destruction of the Temple forty years in the future.

TRUE CONFESSIONS

Now back to Caesarea Philippi. It is absolutely important for anyone looking into the history behind this episode to trace the development of the story from one gospel to another. It begins, oddly enough, in Mark 6:14–15: "King Herod heard of it; for his [Jesus'] name had become known. Some said, 'John the baptizer has been raised from the dead; that is why these powers are at work in him.' But others said, 'It is Elijah.' And others said, 'It is a prophet, like one of the prophets of old.'" These are the same options the disciples list as their survey results about popular opinions of Jesus in Mark 8:28. But there is an important difference. As Gerd Theissen pointed out, the first set of options are in the nominative case because they are direct discourse, and "John the baptizer" and "Elijah" and "a prophet" are all predicate nominatives.[7] They are not direct objects, in which case they would be in the accusative. But in 8:28 the three options are not presented as direct quotations of those who hold these opinions. Instead, they appear in indirect discourse: "Some say John, some say Elijah," and so on. Thus "John the Baptist," "Elijah," and "a prophet" should appear in the accusative, but only the first two do. The third remains in the nominative case. In other words, Mark has rewritten the earlier scene of 6:14–15 into that of 8:28, but he has forgotten to make the very last adjustment. It is a case of what Mark C. Goodacre calls "editorial fatigue."[8] So the scene does not represent any historical recollection or tradition. Mark composed it.

In all our versions of Peter's confession of faith, the words placed in his mouth represent whatever each gospel writer considers to be the truth about Jesus, and the formulas grow in the telling from each gospel to the next, as does Jesus' reaction to Peter's confession. In Mark 8, the true Christology is "You are the Christ," and Mark does not quote Jesus directly but says, "He told them not to tell anyone about it" (or "him," same thing in Greek). You can't even really be sure Jesus accepts what Peter says. In Luke 9:20, Peter says, "You are the Christ of God," which is pretty much the same thing, though expanded just a bit. And again,

Luke says he told them not to tell this to anyone. Matthew elaborates on the story more significantly. Rather than merely asking the disciples, "Who do men say that I am?" Matthew frontloads the right answer into the question: "Who do men say the Son of Man is?" And the answer? "You are the Christ, the Son of the Living God." I'd say that is quite a difference. If it had been known that Peter had said this, we would surely have read this version already in Mark. The fact that we don't shows the story and the confession (provided as an example for the reader to adopt) have been reworded and upgraded.

So which one do you suppose O'Reilly and Dugard chose for inclusion in their "historical" account? The least historical, most embellished version. Of course. By now that should be no surprise at all. And it only gets worse. How does Jesus react in Matthew's account? Remember, he was pretty much noncommittal in both Mark and Luke. Not so Matthew. Jesus is very pleased: "Blessed are you, Simon Bar-Jona. For flesh and blood has not revealed it to you, but my Father who is in heaven. And I tell you, you are Peter, and on this rock I will build my church, and the gates of Hades shall not prevail against it. I will give you the keys of the kingdom of heaven, and whatever you bind on earth shall be bound in heaven; and whatever you loose on earth shall be loosed in heaven" (Matt. 16:17–19). And only then does Matthew rejoin his predecessors: "Then he strictly charged the disciples to tell no one that he was the Christ" (Matt. 17:20). Do you think it likely that Mark and Luke, oh, I don't know, just left this part out because they were economizing on ink? No, Matthew is trying to reinforce the clout of Peter, or really the bishops who claimed succession from him. This is also obvious from the fact that Matthew has Jesus refer anachronistically to the "church." This is not history, except in the sense described by Collingwood: "Propaganda, too, has its history."[9] And that, I'm afraid, is the sort of history O'Reilly and Dugard are giving us.

ISCARIOT OF THE GODS?

Where would you guess O'Reilly and Dugard get the idea that Judas was the only non-Galilean among the twelve disciples? From his epithet "Iscariot." They simply take for granted one of the three leading theories about the derivation of this word, that it denotes "the one from Carioth" (or, better, "Kerioth"), which is actually part of several Old Testament place names. It just means "village," as in Kiriath-Arba or Kiriath-Jearim. The fact that "Iscariot," on this reading, would just mean "from the Village" makes this possibility seem remote to me. But some like it because it gives them a toehold to start psychologizing Judas as a misfit, someone not really "one of the guys" because he was the only Judean (or Edomite) among a bunch of back-slapping Galilean buddies (p. 161). Yeah, that ought to be enough to make a guy wind up selling out the Son of God. I would have to guess that our authors are aware of the still-open discussion (which can never be definitively settled) over the meaning of "Iscariot," but they give no hint of this uncertainty. No, they just pick the option they like best and sell that one to their unsuspecting readers as the historical fact.

The second major theory about the epithet "Iscariot" (and therefore about the bearer of it) is that it represents the name "Sicarius."[10] The Sicarii ("dagger men") were a subset of the anti-Roman Zealot party.[11] They were assassins who used the short-sword to stab their victims and then easily hid it up their sleeve while they joined in the ensuing melee, shouting like everyone else, then slipping away. Some important scholars have long held that at least three members of the Twelve could or should be understood as anti-Roman radicals based on their epithets.[12] Simon Zelotes, or Simon the Zealot, would qualify. Even Simon Peter might have had Zealot affiliations. His epithet in Matthew 16:17, "Bar-Jona," which does not quite work as a patronymic ("son of Jonah"), might instead be an Akkadian loanword, *barjona*, which means "extremist."[13] The Talmud (*Gittin*, 56a) says that, during the Roman siege of Jerusalem, there was a group of Barjonim led by one Abba Sikara, the Sicarius, who was Johanan ben Zakkai's nephew and who masterminded the rabbi's escape.[14] Here are plausible parallels to both Simon Barjona and Judas Iscariot understood as freedom fighters.

Since the Zealot party had not yet taken that name, it would seem to be anachronistic to make Simon a member. But this may easily be another use of the same noun in the same sense, albeit informally. On the other hand, the epithet may mean Simon was understood as a member of the Zealot party, but this identification was an anachronism on the part of the gospel writers, as when they have Jesus addressed as Rabbi and speaking in (nonexistent) synagogues. It would then be one more example of the phenomenon Burton L. Mack describes as the reading back of the conditions of the Jewish War into the time of Jesus.[15]

This understanding of the epithet and motivation of Judas goes unmentioned by O'Reilly and Dugard, but the way they describe Judas at one point implies something like it. "If Jesus is the Christ, as Judas believes, then he is destined one day to overthrow the Roman occupation and rule Judea. Judas's role as one of the twelve disciples will assure him a most coveted and powerful role in the new government when that day comes." (p. 162)

But with this notion O'Reilly and Dugard try to combine another characterization of Judas that is hardly consistent with Judas the Sicarius. From the Gospel of John they derive the pejorative depiction of Judas as a petty sneak thief. For John, Judas "was a thief, and as he had the money box he used to take what was in it" (John 12:6). The Synoptics give no hint of this kleptomania on Judas' part, nor does it make any sense. If Judas was looking to make some easy money via his sticky fingers, pilfering from the pittance held in common by an itinerant band of mendicants does not seem a very lucrative venue. And what would he have spent the money on? Something the other disciples would not have noticed? "Hey, Jude—where'd you come by that snazzy gold sundial? A Cracker Jack box?" It is all caricature and vilification.

The simplest explanation of "Iscariot" would seem to be that proposed by Bertil Gärtner, that the term represents the Aramaic *Ishqarya*, "man of falsehood," in other words, the Betrayer.[16] No one would think of calling Jesus "Mr. Christ" during his lifetime—though later it did become pretty much a last name for him. In the same was, Judas would not have been called "Mr. Iscariot" during his lifetime. It was only after he ratted out Jesus that he became known as "Judas the Betrayer." Finally, people were so used to it (and especially if they were Greek speakers) that they took it to be Judas' last name. At this point they began to use phrases like "Judas Iscariot, who betrayed him" (Mark 3:19), not realizing the redundancy, as if one should say, "Jesus Christ the Messiah." I suspect that O'Reilly and Dugard reject this option (assuming they are even aware of it, and I may be giving them too much credit) because it would count as another anachronism implying the gospel narrators were not particularly close to the events and that many matters were just as baffling to them as they are to us. No, like their apologist mentors, O'Reilly and Dugard want the evangelists to have been eyewitnesses. But they weren't.

Chapter Six

THEOLOGY HIDDEN IN PLAIN SIGHT

A CASE OF MISTAKEN IDENTITY

Occasionally, while working one's way through *Killing Jesus*, one actually has to wonder if its authors had read the gospels lately. There are some egregious errors, if that is what they are. My guess, though, is that they just took the liberty of rewriting the story like a movie adaptation of a book, in which the reader is warned in the opening credits that the film is merely "inspired by" or "suggested by" the original work. O'Reilly and Dugard, for instance, recount the carping of Jesus' smartass brothers from John 7:1–9, where they express surprise that Jesus is not packing up for the impending holiday in Jerusalem. If he is so eager to gain a reputation,[1] surely he can't be intending to pass up an opportunity like this. And he tells them the time is not right, so he is giving this one a miss. He is fibbing to them, because, as soon as they depart, he sneaks out to make the trip separately. Well, O'Reilly and Dugard are not above a bit of fibbing themselves, because they switch this incident from the brothers of Jesus to his disciples:

> The disciples are so eager for Jesus to come with them and publicly announce that he is the Christ that they try to give him a piece of advice, something they've never done before.
>
> "Go to Jerusalem." They beg before setting out. "No one who wants to become a public figure acts in secret. Since you are doing these things, show yourself to the world."
>
> "The right time for me has not yet come," Jesus answers. "For you any time is right. The world cannot hate you, but it hates me because I testify

> that what it does is evil. You go to the feast. I am not going, because for me the time has not yet come." (p. 171)

You can see that the whole scene is drawn, virtually verbatim, from John 7, only the sarcastic brothers (much like Cinderella's nasty sisters) have been changed to the overenthusiastic disciples. Strangely, no reason is ever provided, either in John's Gospel or in *Killing Jesus*, for Jesus' deception. It would make plenty of sense if he had actually stayed behind, knowing that any visit would lead to his crucifixion, and that it is not the proper time for that yet. But, of course, he goes after all.

THE UNRESOLVED PROBLEMS SEGMENT

Up to this point, *Killing Jesus* has told us both that Jesus has publicly taught that he is the Christ, though he decided to cool it for a while when he saw it ruffling some feathers, *and* that he hasn't spilled the beans. Now we are told that his fans are eager for him to come out of the Messianic closet and that "Jesus is on the verge of admitting that he is the Christ" (p. 173). Rudolf Bultmann[2] and others have cogently pointed out that Jesus cannot very well have been "admitting he is the Christ" if early Christians believed he had become the Messiah and Son of God only as of his resurrection. Jesus "was descended from David according to the flesh and designated Son of God in power according to the Spirit of holiness by his resurrection from the dead" (Rom. 1:3–4). "God has made him both Lord and Christ, this Jesus whom you crucified" (Acts 2:36). "This [prophecy] he has fulfilled to us . . . by raising Jesus; as also it is written in the second psalm, 'Thou art my Son. Today I have begotten thee'" (Acts 13:33). These astonishing theological fossils imply that Christians first believed that Jesus' Messiahship dated only from Easter, not before.

But eventually Christians came to believe that Jesus had been the Messiah all along, some thinking the office was bestowed upon him at the Jordan baptism (Mark 1:11), others as of his miraculous birth (Matt. 2:2; Luke 1:35), still others from before creation itself (John 1:1,

18; Heb. 1:2). Raymond E. Brown shows how Christology developed backward. Three major motifs—the divine declaration of Sonship, the agency of the Spirit, and a display of miraculous power—were pushed back every step of the way, from the resurrection to the Transfiguration, to the baptism, to the Nativity, and finally to Creation.[3] Once the Messiahship had been retrojected into the lifetime of Jesus, storytellers felt free to have Jesus speak of it openly, as if it were already in effect. But some remembered the days when the Messiahship was believed to be coincident with Easter, not before. And to iron out this inconsistency,[4] some began to tell the story as if Jesus did act and speak as Messiah already but simultaneously warned people not to tell anyone else what he had said or done until the resurrection. Maybe that would explain it, though it was not clear why he should have kept it under wraps. But that was okay: the theory was mainly retrofitting, an ad hoc exercise in juggling the disparate elements in the gospels, something Christian apologists have raised to a fine art today.

WAKE UP CALL

I remember one Sunday when John's story of Lazarus (chap. 11) was one of the lectionary readings, along with Ezekiel 37:1–14 (the valley of dry bones) and other texts with the same theme: resurrection. The rector made what I considered an embarrassing mistake, explaining to the congregation that he did not plan to make Lazarus' resurrection the text for his homily since many scholars believed the story was not historically true. So he went for one of the others. He had confused two different universes of discourse. The historical accuracy of a biblical text has nothing to do with whether or not to preach it. Even if it is a fiction, obviously it was written to teach some lesson, and Lazarus' story certainly was, issuing in the great declaration "I am the resurrection and the life. He who believes in me, though he die, yet shall he live. And whoever lives and believes in me shall never die" (John 11:25), one of the most powerful spine-tinglers in the New Testament.

Well, O'Reilly and Dugard have made the same mistake my priest did, only the other way around: they imagine it is history. Oh, they try to look like they are being objective and impartial, but once again it is perfectly obvious that they believe (and want you to believe) Jesus raised the rotting carcass of Lazarus from the dead. Why isn't it historical? Right off the bat, you have to wonder why, if this really happened, it doesn't show up in any other gospel, especially since it is so much more spectacular even than the resurrection stories the others do have.[5] Mark 5:22–24, 35–43 (paralleled in Matt. 9:18–19, 23–26; Luke 8:40–42a, 49–56) tells of the raising of Jairus' daughter, while Luke 7:11–17 has him raise up the son of the widow of Nain. It is not quite clear that Jesus is supposed to be actually raising the dead in these two stories once you compare them with a number of similar stories from the Hellenistic world.

> Here, too, is a miracle which Apollonius worked: A girl had died just in the hour of her marriage, and the bridegroom was following her bier lamenting, as was natural, his marriage left unfulfilled, and the whole of Rome was mourning with him, for the maiden belonged to a consular family. Apollonius then witnessing their grief, said: "Put down the bier, for I will stay the tears that you are shedding for this maiden." And withal he asked what was her name. The crowd accordingly thought that he was about to deliver such an oration as is commonly delivered as much to grace the funeral as to stir up lamentation; but he did nothing of the kind, but merely touching her and whispering in secret some spell over her, at once woke up the maiden from her seeming death; and the girl spoke out loud, and returned to her father's house, just as Alcestis did when she was brought back to life by Hercules. And the relations of the maiden wanted to present him with the sum of 150,000 sesterces, but he said he would freely present the money to the young lady by way of a dowry. Now whether he detected some spark of life in her, which those who were nursing her had not noticed,—for it is said that although it was raining at the time, a vapour went up from her face—or whether life was really extinct, and he restored it by the warmth of his touch, is a mysterious problem which neither I myself nor those who were present could decide. (Philostratus, *The Life of Apollonius of Tyana*, 4.45)[6]

Once, when [Asclepiades the physician] returned to the city from his country house, he saw a great funeral pile in the outskirts of the town, and around it a vast multitude, who had followed the funeral, all in great grief and soiled garments. He went up to the spot, as is the nature of the human mind, that he might know who it was, since no one answered his enquiries. Or, rather, he went that he might notice something in the deceased by means of his art. At all events, he took away death from that man who was stretched on the bier and nearly consigned to the tomb. The unfortunate man's body was already bedewed with perfumes, and his face was anointed with odorous ointment. Having carefully contemplated the man thus anointed and made ready for the funeral banquet, he noticed in him certain signs, handled the body again and again, and found life latent in it. Instantly he cried out that the man was alive, that they should take away the torches, put out the fire, pull down the pile, and carry back the funeral banquet from the tomb to the table. Meanwhile, a murmur arose, some saying that the physician should be believed, others making a mock of medicine. Finally, against the will of all the relations, whether it was that they were disappointed of the inheritance, or that they did not believe him, Asclepiades, with great difficulty, obtained a brief respite for the defunct, and so, in the end, he took him back to his house, snatched from the hands of the undertakers, and as it were from the infernal regions, and immediately revived his spirits, and called forth, by some medicine, the vital breath that was lurking in the recesses of his body. (Apuleius, *Florida* 14)[7]

"I gave him no poison, but a soothing drink of mandragora, which is of such force that it will cause any man to sleep as though he were dead. . . . But if it be so that the child hath received the drink as I tempered it with mine own hands, he is yet alive and doth but rest and sleep, and after his sleep he shall return to life again. . . ." The opinion of this ancient physician was found good, and every man had a desire to go to the sepulchre where the child was laid: there was none of the justices, none of any reputation of the town, nor any indeed of the common people, but went to see this strange sight. Amongst them all the father of the child removed with his own hands the cover of the coffin and found his son rising up after his death and soporiferous sleep: and when he beheld him as one risen from the dead he embraced him in his arms and he could speak never a word for his present gladness, but presented him before the people with great joy and consolation, and as he was wrapped and bound in the clothes of his grave, so he brought him before the judges. (Lucius Apuleius, *The Golden Ass*, 44)[8]

So saying, he ordered that a pyre be constructed immediately. But while the pyre was being carefully and expertly constructed and assembled, a medical student of youthful appearance but mature judgment arrived. When he saw the corpse of the girl being placed on the pyre, he looked at his teacher and said, "What is the cause of this recent unexplained death?" The teacher said: "Your arrival is timely; the situation requires your presence. Take a jar of unguent and pour it over the body of the girl to satisfy the last rites." The young man took a jar of unguent, went to the girl's bier, pulled aside the clothing from the upper part of her body, poured out the unguent, ran his suspicious hands over all her limbs, and detected quiescent warmth in her chest cavity. The young man was astounded to realize that the girl was only apparently dead. He touched her veins to check for signs of movement and closely examined her nostrils for signs of breathing; he put his lips to her lips, and, detecting signs of life in the form of slight breathing that, as it were, was struggling against false death, he said, "Apply heat at four points." When he had had this done, he began to massage her lightly, and the blood that had coagulated began to flow because of the anointing.

When the young man saw this, he ran to his teacher and said: "Doctor, the girl you think is dead is alive. To convince you, I will clear up her obstructed breathing." With some assistance, he took the girl to his bedroom, placed her on his bed, opened her clothing, warmed oil, moistened a woolen compress with it, and placed the compress on the upper part of the girl's body. Her blood, which had congealed because of severe cold, began to flow once heat was applied, and her previously obstructed breathing began to infiltrate to her innermost organs. With the clearing up of her veins, the girl opened her eyes, recovered her breath, and said in a soft, indistinct voice, "Please, doctor, do not touch me in any other way than it is proper to touch the wife of a king and the daughter of a king."

When the young man realized he had discovered with his skill what his teacher had failed to observe, he hurried joyfully to his teacher and said, "Come, teacher, and witness your student's skill." The teacher, on entering the bedroom, saw that the girl he thought was dead was alive and said to his student, "I commend your medical knowledge, I praise

> your skill, and I admire your care. But I don't want you to be deprived of the rewards of your medical expertise; take as your payment the money that accompanied the girl." And he gave him ten thousand gold sesterces and prescribed for the girl a nourishing diet and a regimen of fomentations. (*The Story of Apollonius King of Tyre*)[9]

In all these tales what the hero does is to save someone from premature burial. The victims were believed dead and were about to be disposed of. Luckily, the hero detected some obscure sign of life and prevented a real death. Suddenly we have to take a second look at Mark 5:39: "Why do you make a tumult and wail? The child is not dead but sleeping." It starts looking like Mark was depicting Jesus as rescuing the girl from waking up in a coffin. I don't mean Mark hyped up the story to make it into a resurrection; rather, he did not mean for us to read it as a resurrection. In the story of the widow's son, it is a bit less clear whether the lad is supposed to be truly dead, but perhaps he is not, since the story seems to be a rewrite of 1 Kings 17:8–24, the story of Elijah raising up the only son of a poor widow. Like Elijah (1 Kings 17:10), Jesus encounters the widow "at the gate of the city" (though archaeology shows that Nain, now called the village of Ain, did not have a city gate). And the story ends the same way: Elijah, in 1 Kings 17:23, raises the boy, and then "he gave him to his mother," just as in Luke 7:15.[10] And in verses 21–22 we read that Elijah performed something like artificial respiration to bring the lad back to consciousness, so this one may not have been intended as an actual resurrection either. Why the pantomime? Why not just speak a divine command if you were miraculously restoring life to a genuine corpse?

O'Reilly and Dugard again use gospel characters as their ventriloquist dummies so they can continue to claim they do not actually say Jesus performed miracles. "Witnesses [not just rumor mongers] say he is performing miracles once again. In one startling account out of the town of Bethany, a man named Lazarus came back from the dead. And Lazarus was not recently deceased. He was four days dead and already laid in the tomb when Jesus is said to have healed him before a great crowd" (pp. 175–76). Is *said* to have healed him, huh? This is like the scene in the 1939 movie *The Son of Frankenstein*, in which the villain Ygor tells Baron Wolf von Frankenstein why he was hanged: "I stole bodies . . . they *said*."[11] Okay, I'm glad we got *that* cleared up. "Lazarus's body already reeked of decomposition when Jesus ordered that the stone covering the tomb entrance be rolled away" (p. 176). Or so they assumed. I have to wonder if the original story, before John got hold of it, was yet another of these tales of rescuing a comatose person from premature burial.[12] Notice that, in John 11:11, having received the news of Lazarus' illness, Jesus tells the disciples, "Our friend Lazarus has fallen asleep, but I go to awake him out of sleep." By the time they reach Bethany, Lazarus has been entombed. Jesus, as O'Reilly says, orders the removal of the stone. Martha protests, "Lord, by this time there will an odor, for he has been dead four days" (John 11:39). But suppose that he was simply comatose. They only *assume* he was decomposing.[13] Suppose that, as in these other stories, Jesus somehow knows the man is "not dead but sleeping." No stench. And Jesus rouses him. On this reading, John has done to the story what Mark did *not* do to the story of Jairus' daughter: he has heightened the miraculous element by adding this brief exchange between Jesus and the disciples. "'Lord, if he has fallen asleep, he will recover.' Now Jesus has spoken of his death, but they thought that he meant taking rest in sleep. Then Jesus told them plainly, 'Lazarus is dead'" (John 11:12–14).

But there is probably a still earlier version of the story in Luke 16:19–31, the story of, ahem, *Lazarus* and the rich man. In this well-known parable, Lazarus is a destitute beggar lying in the gutter right outside the palatial estate of an unnamed rich man, who takes no notice of him at all. Poor Lazarus would be thrilled to get the scraps that fall from the rich man's banqueting table, but he doesn't. Not surprisingly, he soon expires, only to awaken to the welcoming embrace of Father Abraham in Paradise. Not long after, the rich man dies (choking on an "imperialist tidbit," perhaps?[14]). He is awakened by the smell of his own charring flesh, down in the pit of Hades. Calling out to Abraham across the great cosmic chasm, the rich wretch begs Father Abraham to send Lazarus to him with a wet finger for him to lick. Tough luck, replies the glorified patriarch. No mercy missions allowed. The rich man then asks if Lazarus might be permitted to go haunt his brothers, à la Jacob Marley, to warn them away from this disastrous destiny. Abe is honest with him: scripture ought to be sufficient to tell them how to avoid hell. But the rich man says they'll never heed what the Bible says. "No, Father Abraham; but if someone goes to them from the dead, they will repent" (Luke 16:30). But Abraham tells him he is kidding himself; Lazarus stays where he is.

Hmmm . . . in Luke, a character named Lazarus kicks the bucket, and the option is raised that he might return from the dead to provoke repentance, but the option is ignored, and nada. In John, a character named Lazarus actually *does* rise, causing some to repent and believe in Jesus (John 11:45), while others still do not get the message and are only reinforced in their opposition to Jesus. Coincidence? Which is more probable (and remember, probability is the historian's stock-in-trade): that one man raised another from the dead by shouting into his tomb, or that a man rewrote a parable into a miracle?

There is much beneath the surface here, in depths where O'Reilly and Dugard do not care to delve. They pretend to be deep divers, but they are only water-skiing.

PROFESSING PROPHECY

Is it a purely historical work or a religious one that flatly informs us that "Jesus has led a life that is a continual fulfillment of Jewish [i.e., biblical] prophecy" (p. 176)? "In order, these prophecies are Psalms 27:12 and 35:11; Micah 5:1; Isaiah 50:6; Psalms 22:18; Psalms 22:16, Zechariah 12:10, and Deuteronomy 21:23; Numbers 9:12, Psalms 34:20, and Exodus 12:46; and [a second time?] Zechariah 12:10" (p. 177). Nowhere is O'Reilly and Dugard's distortion of scripture more flagrant than here. Nowhere is it clearer that they intend to set forth orthodox Christian doctrine as if it were sober history. I do not mean to accuse them of duplicity; it is almost worse than that. I have to think they don't know the difference between the two. Certainly they have not given so much as a fleeting thought to the original context of any of the Old Testament texts they cite. Let's take them one by one.

Psalm 27:12 reads as follows: "Give me not up to the will of my adversaries; for false witnesses have risen against me, and they breathe out violence." This is not a prophecy of anything, much less of Jesus. Many of the Psalms (hymns sung in the Temple) are what scholars call "individual laments," prayers in musical form for people to sing (or more likely to pay Levitical singers to sing on their behalf) in a time of crisis.[15] Since they were for anybody and everybody, the nature of their predicaments is not specified in detail. Others are written for the reigning king of Judah, whoever that may be at a given time.[16] This one seems to be one of the latter, and the occasion envisioned seems to be the eve of warfare. The king is in distress (as Saul is in 1 Samuel 28:4–5) and calls on God to grant him triumph on the morrow, not to let him fall into the hands of his adversaries who threaten him (cf. Ps. 27:12's "they breathe out violence" with Acts 9:1, "But Saul, still breathing threats and murder against the disciples of the Lord," etc.) and slander him so as to justify their military actions. What on earth do O'Reilly and Dugard see here that pertains to Jesus? The mere fact that there were false witnesses at his trial? If that counts as "prophetic fulfillment," there are loads of Messiahs in every courtroom.

Psalm 35:11 ("Malicious witnesses rise up; they ask me of things that I know not.") looks like another royal psalm for the same sort of occasion, though some scholars interpret it as a lament psalm on behalf of anyone being sued or threatened by personal or business rivals. But in any case, this text is not a prediction of anything. Are O'Reilly and Dugard reading a different Bible than I am? I daresay they are hoping none of their readers are planning to look up these passages.

Micah 5:1 ("Now you are walled about with a wall; siege is laid against us; with a rod they strike upon the cheek the king of Israel.") also sketches a scene of national and royal emergency. The capital is surrounded by siege engines, and the king has been captured and beaten (cf. King Zedekiah's treatment in 2 Kings 25:6–7). Of course, our authors are thinking of Jesus getting cruelly slapped and beaten by soldiers and guards in Mark 14:65 and 15:18–19, but, again, how is Micah, who is explicitly talking about events in his own day, predicting anything about Jesus? What does the one have to do with the other? Just because the same things happened to Jesus? That's like saying a newspaper report about Lincoln's assassination is a prophecy of Kennedy's.

Isaiah 50:6 says, "I gave my back to the smiters and my cheeks to those who pulled out the beard; I hid not my face from shame and spitting." This is all in the past tense, and it recounts something that happened to the speaker. This not even as much of a prophecy as Janice Dean's FOX News weather forecasts. To claim this for a prophecy fulfilled in the life of Jesus is like saying that some poor guy's diary entry from decades ago mentioning his getting audited by the IRS is a prediction of when the same thing happened to me. If I have to get a wisdom tooth extracted, is a report of someone undergoing the same procedure last week a prophecy of my surgery?

Psalm 22 is not framed as a prediction of anything either. It is another individual lament psalm. But I will wait till chapter 12, which discusses the crucifixion, to discuss that one.

Zechariah 12:10 says, "And I will pour out on the house of David and the inhabitants of Jerusalem a spirit of compassion and supplication, so that, when they look on him whom they have pierced, they shall mourn for him, as one mourns for an only child, and weep bitterly for him, as one weeps for a first-born." This one is set in a context of victorious battle in which a besieged Jerusalem turns the tables on the invading troops, utterly steamrolling them. The passage itself is not clear in its reference, but the point would seem to be that, having triumphed, the victors turn and mourn for the victims of their triumph, weeping at their loss. But if one makes it some sort of a prediction of the crucifixion of Jesus Christ (as in John 19:37), one does so at the cost of making the Zechariah text into complete nonsense. What, pray tell, does the scenario just described possibly have to do with the circumstances of Jesus' execution and the general aftermath? Did all Jerusalem mourn his passing? Did Jesus die in the course of a Judean victory over pagan armies? No, with the whole Christian tradition, O'Reilly and Dugard have no scruples about plucking the verse out of its historical and literary context.

Deuteronomy 21:22–23 is no prophecy but rather a clear-cut regulation applying to its own day and in perpetuity. "And if a man has committed a crime punishable by death and he is put to death, and you hang him on a tree, his body shall not remain all night upon the tree, but you shall bury him on the same day, for a hanged man is accursed by God; you shall not defile your land which the Lord your God gives you for an inheritance." Joshua 10:26–27 records an instance of the application of this law. The Israelite practice was not to kill by crucifixion but rather to display the already dead bodies, hanging them on a tree for all to see and take a lesson. The gospels have Jesus crucified by the Romans, who did suspend the living from trees or crosses, leaving them to die from exposure or asphyxiation. But Jews insisted on at least removing the bodies as their own ancient law required. So in what sense was Deuteronomy 21:23 a prediction of Jesus? It was simply the rule that his executioners followed in disposing of his body. Were all the other men the Romans crucified "predicted" by this verse, too?

Numbers 9:12 deals with the disposal of the Passover lamb each year: "They shall leave none of it until the morning, *nor break a bone of it*; according to all the statute for the Passover they shall keep it." The same rule occurs in Exodus 12:46, "In one house shall it be eaten; you shall not carry forth any of the flesh outside the house; and *you shall not break a bone of it*." Prediction of anything at all? No. Regulation still observed in Jesus' day? Sure. But that's all. O'Reilly and Dugard are thinking of John 19:31–36, where the evangelist tells us that the Roman soldiers had to remove the bodies of the crucified criminal, before sundown in consideration of Jewish Sabbath customs. Crucifixion usually took days to kill its victims, so the Romans had to hurry the Grim Reaper. They broke the legs of Jesus' two neighbors so they could no longer hoist up their chests to inhale. They died quickly. But Jesus had already expired, so there was no need to break his legs. Nor was this an accident. "For these things took place that the scripture might be fulfilled, 'Not a bone of him shall be broken'" (John 19:36). John regards Jesus as the Passover lamb (John 1:29), so it makes sense that he should apply the Numbers passage to Jesus, but even that does not make a regulation into a prediction.

Psalm 34:20 occurs in the middle of an affirmation of God's protection of his favorites: "Many are the afflictions of the righteous; but the Lord delivers him out of them all. He keeps all his bones; not one of them is broken." Is this a prophecy of anyone? Jesus or Joe Schmo? It is something of a promise made to all the righteous, so presumably it would apply to Jesus, a pretty righteous guy. But that's just not the same thing. Why do O'Reilly and Dugard include Numbers 9:12, Exodus 12:46, and Psalm 34:20? Simply because no one knows which of the three passages John intended as the prophecy of Jesus not having his legs broken. Not one of them makes any sense as a prediction of it, though. Why do our authors call these rag-tag scraps of Old Testament texts predictions of Jesus?

They are following the practice of the New Testament writers and those of the Dead Sea Scrolls, all of whom meant something quite different by "fulfilled prophecy" than we do. Even if we do not believe in such things, we understand prophetic fulfillment to mean a prediction that so-and-so event is going to happen, as when psychic Jeane Dixon predicted the assassination of President Kennedy. But that is not what is going on in the Dead Sea Scrolls and the gospels. These ancient authors operated according to the *pesher* ("puzzle solution") technique, whereby one sniffed out (by the use of certain key words important to one's sect's theology) esoteric meanings supposedly hidden in scripture.[17] They knew that Isaiah, Jeremiah, and their colleagues had issued predictions about the future, things their contemporaries would sooner or later witness (national victory or defeat, famines, exiles, etc.), but these things had long since come to pass. Did that mean the scriptures containing those predictions were dead letters, museum relics with no further relevance? They couldn't believe that. Scripture must continue to speak. It had fresh revelations to impart if only one knew how to listen. These new messages were not to be found by a literal, straightforward reading of the old texts. Since the scriptures had been composed under the inspiration of the Holy Spirit, and by no mere human creativity, there must be deeper levels of meaning.

Thus when Matthew says that the Holy Family taking refuge in Egypt was the fulfillment of Hosea 1:1, "Out of Egypt have I called my son," quoted in Matthew 2:15, he knew darn well that this was not what the prophet Hosea had in mind. No, as any fool can see, Hosea chapter 11 is all about the Exodus of Israel, God's beloved child, and how the people have been disobedient ever since that time. Nothing about any Messiah. Certainly nothing about Jesus Christ. Likewise, Matthew knew as well as modern scholars do that Isaiah 7:14, quoted in Matthew 1:23, is talking about the birth of a child, likely Isaiah's own son, whose name would remind the wavering people that "God is with us" and will defeat our pagan adversaries. And so he had. But had God nothing else to say through this sacred text? Sure he did, and Matthew saw in the passage an esoteric prediction of Jesus' conception.

The ancient writers were not appealing to these alleged prophecies in the manner of modern apologists. They did not claim that an unbeliever ought to be convinced of Christianity by these amazing predictions coming to pass.[18] No, these esoteric prophecies were visible only to the eye of faith. One had to be in the fold already for this hindsight hermeneutic to make any sense. One viewed the texts through new lenses provided by Christian faith. Thus no one could have known these prophecies *were* prophecies until after the secretly predicted events had occurred. Since the meanings they sought were esoteric ones, it did not matter whether the Christian reading made any sense in the original context. What they were doing was much like the Kabbalistic technique of Gematria,[19] even like the modern "Bible Code" manner of reading the scriptures.

This is clearly the approach taken by O'Reilly and Dugard. But this approach is completely out of place in a book that purports to abstain from theology and just to tell the history of Jesus. You just can't try to palm off as secular history a method of interpretation that is only supposed to make sense from a particular religious perspective. The authors of *Killing Jesus: A History* see themselves as intrepid explorers in search of truth about the past, but in their desperate wanderings they are satisfied with a mere mirage, and, tragically, they don't know the difference between the two.

Chapter Seven

LIAR, PINHEAD, OR LORD

Theology obtrudes in a big way in chapter 12 of *Killing Jesus*, as we will shortly see. So does our authors' tendency to turn myth into history by means of the sleight-of-hand trick of rationalistic paraphrase,[1] smoothing out some of the jarring supernaturalism by substituting more naturalistic motivations and explanations so as to save the miraculous element for the payoff. It is basically little different from H. P. Lovecraft's technique for writing convincing horror stories: you have to fill the lead-up narrative with meticulous and mundane detail to lull the reader into a false sense of this-worldly complacency so that, when the supernatural intrudes, it will seem to have erupted into the reader's own world.[2] That is also why *Killing Jesus* is filled to the bursting point with otherwise superfluous background matter like what Herod Antipas had for breakfast and what sort of toothpaste Julius Caesar used (what's he even doing in a book about Jesus Christ, except that both share the initials "J. C."?). All of it is aimed at historicizing a character who plainly belongs to the never-land of epic and myth.

ROUGH SAILING AHEAD

A clear case of rationalizing paraphrase meets us with the Passion predictions, derived ultimately from Mark, though the other gospels repeat them. Here is the version of them in *Killing Jesus*.

> "We are going up to Jerusalem," Jesus tells his disciples as they prepare to depart for the Passover. "The Son of Man will be betrayed to the chief priests and the teachers of the law. They will condemn him to death and

> will turn him over to the Gentiles to be mocked and flogged and crucified. On the third day he will be raised to life." But if those words disturb the disciples, they don't show it. (p. 183)

Three times, Jesus has told his disciples that he will die this week. But his followers refuse even to contemplate that. (p. 187)

Once again, Jesus is predicting his own death. And yet the disciples are so focused on the glorious moment when Jesus will reveal that he is the Christ that they ignore the fact that he is telling them he will soon die. . . . The adoration being bestowed upon Jesus makes any talk of death incomprehensible. (p. 184)

Okay, that's sort of plausible. But O'Reilly and Dugard are "psychologizing,"[3] "naturalizing,"[4] the narrative. It does not appear with such polish in the gospels. Here are the original predictions:

> And he began to teach them that the Son of man must suffer many things, and be rejected by the elders and the chief priests and the scribes, and be killed, and after three days rise again. And he said this plainly. And Peter took him, and began to rebuke him. But turning and seeing his disciples, he rebuked Peter, and said, "Get behind me, Satan. For you are not on the side of God, but of men." (Mark 8:31–33; cf. Matt. 16:21–28; Luke 9:22–27)

> And as they were coming down the mountain, he charged them to tell no one what they had seen, until the Son of man should have risen from the dead. So they kept the matter to themselves, questioning what the rising from the dead meant. And they asked him, "Why do the scribes say that first Elijah must come?" And he said to them, "Elijah does come first to restore all things; and how is it written of the Son of man, that he should suffer many things and be treated with contempt?" (Mark 9:9–12; cf. Matt. 17:9–13; Luke 9:36)

Matthew pointedly omits the disciples' bafflement over the meaning of "rising from the dead," while Luke reduces the Markan scene simply to "And they kept silent and told no one in those days anything of what they had seen."

> "The son of man will be delivered into the hands of men, and they will kill him; and when he is killed, after three days he will rise." But they did not understand the saying, and they were afraid to ask him. (Mark 9:31–32; cf. Matt. 17:22–23; Luke 9:43–45)

Matthew changes their reaction to "they were greatly distressed," while Luke replaces the dialogue with

> "Let these words sink into your ears; for the Son of man is to be delivered into the hands of men." But they did not understand this saying, and it was concealed from them, that they should not perceive it; and they were afraid to ask him about this saying.

The Greek word for "that" in Luke 9:45, ινα, means "in order that," not "so that," in other words, "intentionality," not just "result." The idea is the same as later in Luke, 24:16, during the walk to Emmaus: "But their eyes were kept from recognizing him." Kept by *whom*? This is pretty odd, because it looks as if Jesus means to communicate something to his disciples, but God is blocking their comprehension.

> And they were on the road, going up to Jerusalem, and Jesus was walking ahead of them; and they were amazed, and those who followed were afraid. And taking the twelve again, he began to tell them what was to happen to him, saying, "Behold, we are going up to Jerusalem; and the Son of man will be delivered to the chief priests and the scribes, and they will condemn him to death, and deliver him to the Gentiles; and they will mock him, and spit upon him, and kill him; and after three days he will rise." (Mark 10:32–34)

Matthew 20:17–19 omits the fear of the disciples. In the list of Jesus' humiliations he substitutes "scourging" for "spitting," making the torment much more severe. Interestingly, he also changes Mark's "after three days" to "on the third day," even though elsewhere Matthew, too, has the dead zone scheduled for three days and three nights (Matt. 12:40). In the previous Passion predictions he retained Mark's "on the third day." Luke 18:31–34 has extensively rewritten this last prediction.

> And taking the twelve, he said to them, "Behold, we are going up to Jerusalem, and everything that is written of the Son of man by the prophets will be accomplished. For he will be delivered to the Gentiles, and will be mocked and shamefully treated and spit upon; they will scourge him and kill him, and on the third day he will rise." But they understood none of these things; this saying was hid from them, and they did not grasp what was said.

We notice at once that Luke has introduced one of his favorite themes, that the sufferings of Jesus were prophesied, as in Luke 24:26–27, 44–46. Even more important, he has again depicted the disciples as being prevented by God from understanding what Jesus was attempting to tell them. Why? The reason is not, I think, hard to find.

In all the gospels, when Jesus is actually apprehended by the Sanhedrin's goons in the Garden of Gethsemane, the disciples appear to be totally flummoxed, completely unprepared, as if they had received no hint of what was going to happen. The same is true of the resurrection narratives: it is as if the disciples have never been given any reason to suspect it might happen. How can this possibly be, if Jesus had repeatedly spelled out the coming sequence of events in plain terms and in such detail, reminding all to "stay tuned for scenes from next week's episode"? Robert M. Fowler explains what is happening.[5] The gospels are setting their narrative stage with characters who will say various things for the benefit of the reader, though they have to be depicted as if speaking to one another. There are very few explicit asides to the audience. Once Mark has Jesus say something to the reading audience, anticipating the action, he cannot have the story characters, to whom the words were ostensibly addressed, understand them, or the plot would be ruined. In this case, Jesus has to go to the cross, but the disciples cannot be allowed to realize that because the prophecy must be fulfilled: "You will all fall away; for it is written, 'I will strike the shepherd, and the sheep will be scattered'" (Mark 14:27).

The evangelists recognize the problem this creates, so they try to erase the contradiction by simple and arbitrary authorial fiat. The disciples are depicted as stupidly scratching their halo-clad heads over what on earth "rising from the dead" might mean, even though we have already heard them telling Jesus that many people believe him to be John the Baptist risen from the dead (Mark 8:28, abbreviating Mark 6.14). The idea simply could not have been that strange to them. And they do not ask Jesus to elucidate his words because, if they did, they would understand what is to come, but we cannot have that. They must be taken by complete surprise by both the arrest and the resurrection. Luke really pours it on, as we have seen, by having God jam the transmission Jesus is trying to send: "Oh no, you don't." Again, the whole thing is arbitrary, and all because Mark felt the reader needed to be reassured that events were not spinning out of control. Jesus was not being overwhelmed by events. God had his providential hand on the rudder all the time. Everything was under his control, playing out according to the predetermined purpose of God.

This means that the Passion predictions are editorial comments, not anything a historical Jesus may have said. But O'Reilly and Dugard want to leave as little as possible of the gospel texts on the cutting room floor. Jesus therefore must have said these things. And so they try to massage the passages by making it look psychologically natural for the overenthusiastic disciples to tune out all negative vibes. Again, that might not be inherently implausible; people hear what they want to hear. But the gospels don't present it like that. The disciples are just made impenetrably stupid, or God prevents Jesus from getting his message across, something so ludicrously contradictory we can't help but recognize it as a clumsy literary device. Why do O'Reilly and Dugard leave the predictions in? For the same reason the gospel writers *put* them in: to depict Jesus as a man of destiny, fully in charge. The reader must be assured that the plan proceeds inexorably. The Passion predictions serve exactly the same purpose as the numerous chapter endings in *Killing Jesus*: "Jesus has less than a year to live," and so on.

DOUBLE-BLIND STUDY

Mark (10:46–52, repeated in Luke 18:35–43) has Jesus, on his way into Jerusalem, encounter a blind beggar named Bartimaeus, whom he gladly heals. Of course most readers of the gospel stories are already pious believers who take for granted that Jesus is a divine incarnation. If they were to take a step back, they might notice the intrinsically fictive nature of a scene in which Jesus (or anyone—and that's the point) effortlessly cures a man of blindness just as a casual favor, like Superman swooping down to rescue a cat from a tree. And O'Reilly and Dugard, good Catholics, have no problem with it. They cannot really disengage from the spell their beloved scriptures have over them.

But it gets stranger than that, for our authors follow Matthew in going Mark one better. Matthew has this odd propensity to double things he found in Mark. Where Mark had Jesus exorcise a single demoniac (Mark 5:2, followed by Luke 8:27), Matthew suddenly makes it a tag team of demoniacs (Matt. 8:28). I guess he figured two heads are better than one, like that two-headed dragon in the old *I Love Lucy* episode. And it doesn't stop there. Matthew even has Jesus ride two donkeys into Jerusalem (Matt. 21:1–3), whereas all three other gospels agree on a single beast. Matthew repeats Mark's Bartimaeus incident, adding a second blind man (Matt. 9:27–31), and then tells the same story a second time (Matt. 20:30–34). Which version do you suppose O'Reilly and Dugard use in their "history" of Jesus? You guessed it, Matthew's. At least they use only one of Matthew's versions.

THE SWEET RIDE

O'Reilly and Dugard have several times commented that it would be a dangerous thing for Jesus to ride into Jerusalem on donkey back because the crowds would explode with Messianic fervor. For Jesus' enemies, this would constitute the last straw, the straw that broke the donkey's back, as it were. And this notwithstanding that donkeys were the mode of transportation for many entering the city for the Passover. Would Jesus even have been noticeable in such a crowd? Of course, the gospel writers are not concerned with Jesus' superfluous fellow pilgrims, so as far as they are concerned Jesus might as well be entering the Holy City in a vacuum, like a cordoned-off city block where a movie scene is being filmed. But as O'Reilly and Dugard are pretty much engaged in the same enterprise, they don't notice the implausibility either.

As they go on to paint the scene, grabbing pieces of various gospels as they proceed, they provide a scenario in which Jesus is hailed by adoring fans as the Messianic king and the fulfillment of the prophecy of Zechariah 9:9: "Rejoice greatly, O daughter of Zion. Shout aloud, O daughter of Jerusalem. Lo, your king comes to you; triumphant and victorious is he, humble and riding on an ass, on a colt, the foal of an ass." Let's pause to get a few things straight here. First, even a glance at the immediate context in Zechariah will make clear that, though this text is in fact a predictive prophecy (unlike all the others our authors claim Jesus fulfilled), it is not like the prophecy that whoever is able to pull Excalibur from the stone will qualify as the true king of England. That is not the point of it. Rather, Zechariah 9:9 is predicting a definitive victory of Judah over her threatening foes from adjacent countries. How does the king come into the picture? The battle having been successful, the king has stabled his war horse and exchanged it for a peacetime mount, a humble donkey. The crowd will rejoice in victory and the ensuing peace, being "at ease in Zion." But both the gospel writers and O'Reilly and Dugard have completely lost sight of this. It is not that Jesus performs some kind of amazing feat by riding a donkey into the city, and thus everyone recognizes him as the Messiah. "Hey, did you *see* that guy? By God, he's riding on a *donkey*! He must be the Messiah!" Instead, it is only in the light of faith in Jesus as the Messiah that Christian writers projected Zechariah onto the scene of Jesus' entry. And John 12:14–16 actually makes this explicit: "And Jesus found a young donkey and sat upon it; as it is written, 'Fear not, daughter of Zion; behold, your king is coming, sitting on an ass's colt.' His disciples did not understand this at first, but when Jesus was glorified, then they remembered that this had been written of him and had been done to him." Yikes. This is a definite fly in the O'Reilly ointment.

Matthew 21:4–5 similarly quotes Zechariah 9:9 at the Triumphal Entry, but he gives no hint that anyone saw the prophecy playing out in front of them. Mark and Luke do not even mention the Zechariah prophecy. So the way O'Reilly and Dugard repeatedly make the passage central to an alleged Messianic gambit on Palm Sunday, as well as a red flag to his enemies, is utterly without support in the gospels even if you want to take them as literal history.

But don't the gospels at least show the crowds hailing Jesus as the Messianic king, whether or not Zechariah had anything to do with it? It does at first seem that way, but upon closer scrutiny there may be less there than meets the eye.

> "Hosanna to the Son of David! Blessed be he who comes in the name of the Lord! Hosanna in the highest!" (Matt. 21:9)

> "Hosanna! Blessed be he who comes in the name of Lord! Blessed is the kingdom of our father David that is coming! Hosanna in the highest!" (Mark 11:9–10)

> "Blessed be the King who comes in the name of the Lord! Peace in heaven and glory in the highest!" (Luke 19:38)

> "Hosanna! Blessed be he who comes in the name of the Lord, even the King of Israel!" (John 12:13)

Notice first that Matthew, Luke, and John do have Messianic, or at least royal, acclamations, but *not the same one*. All of them seem to be based on Mark, the earliest version, in that Matthew and John repeat Mark's Hosanna. Luke omits it in accordance with his tendency to cut Semitic words he found in Mark.[6] All three have retained Mark's acclamation "Blessed be he who comes in the name of the Lord," though with significant alterations.

O'Reilly and Dugard correctly note that the acclamations derive from the entrance liturgy of Psalm 118, in other words, an antiphonal chant sung back and forth between the crowds entering the gates of Jerusalem for festival and those already inside. But they do not see the implication of this. Psalm 118:26 reads, "Blessed is he who enters in the name of the Lord! We bless you from the house of the Lord!" This is the standard, formulaic greeting for any and every pilgrim coming to the holy festival. Again, for the gospels (and *Killing Jesus*) the spotlight falls on Jesus alone, so as we read the story, this greeting is for him only, and it reminds us of John the Baptist's talk about "the one who is to come." But that is to read an alien notion into the entrance liturgy, which was by no means a welcome extended only to the Messianic king.

And this is why Matthew, Luke, and John have to change Mark at this point. They want the Triumphal Entry to have been a Messianic acclamation of Jesus by the adoring crowd, so Matthew changes Mark's "Blessed is the kingdom of our father David that is coming" into "Hosanna to the Son of David." Mark's crowd celebrated the prospect that the Davidic dynasty and Jewish independence would one day come, perhaps even during this Passover season, but Matthew makes them welcome Jesus as the Davidic heir, quite a difference.

Luke likewise changes Mark's acclamation, substituting "the king" for Mark's "he" who comes in the name of the Lord. John adds "the King of Israel" as a gloss, an explanatory afterthought. The upshot is this: Mark, the earliest version, did not portray the crowd lionizing Jesus as their Messiah, only as one more pilgrim in this season of Messianic hopes for liberation from Rome. If we are looking for history, as O'Reilly and Dugard say they are doing, the house of cards collapses right here: the impression that Jesus was hailed as Messiah on Palm Sunday turns out to be a later embellishment, not even part of the original story.

DID JESUS TEACH THE NICENE CREED?

To hear O'Reilly and Dugard tell it, the essence of Jesus' message was that he was the very incarnation of God on earth. "He has been very specific with the disciples that he is more than just an earthly Christ. . . . He has told them again and again that he is a divine being, the Son of God" (p. 187). "But will they make that incredible leap to believe that Jesus is God in the flesh?" (p. 189). No one could possibly get this impression from reading Matthew, Mark, or Luke. No hint of it in the Sermon on the Mount. Nothing about it in the parables. No sign of it in any of the aphorisms and proverbs. Where, then? Of course, from the Gospel of John, which does give conflicting signals but certainly seems to ascribe this belief to Jesus: "I and the Father are one" (John 10:30). "He who has seen me has seen the Father" (John 14:9). "I have been since before Abraham came to be" (John 8:58).[7] "I proceeded and came forth from God" (John 8:42).[8]

Unfortunately for O'Reilly and Dugard, there is just no way the Gospel of John can be taken seriously as a genuine record of the teaching of Jesus, any more than the Gnostic *Pistis Sophia* or *The Dialogue of the Savior* can be. I have already summarized the reasons critical scholars have long ago come to this conclusion. So what is going on in that gospel? I think David Friedrich Strauss put it best, discussing the passages I have just quoted, as well as the numerous sayings: "I am the light of the world" (John 8:12), "I am the true vine" (John 15:1), "I am the resurrection" (John 11:25),[9] "I am the good shepherd" (John 10:11), "I am the bread of life" (John 6:35). Strauss says: "The speeches of Jesus about himself in this Gospel are an uninterrupted Doxology, only translated out of the second person into the first, from the form of address to another, into the utterance about a self."[10] They form a kind of litany of devotion, Jesus in effect inviting Christian readers to "abide" in him by enfolding them into his own divine essence as illustrated in these sublime predicates. In this respect the Gospel of John is much like the *Bhagavad Gita*, in which it is Krishna who proclaims his divine qualities and invites worship. The Gospel of John is a unique masterpiece in the New Testament, but, alas, it is nothing the historical Jesus ever said. These spiritual treasures represent the reflections of the evangelist, who elsewhere (John 16:12–14) broadly hints that he is placing in Jesus' mouth deeper teachings for which Jesus' contemporaries were not ready and which they never heard.

O'Reilly and Dugard seem to forget a crucial fact: as they themselves earlier reminded us (pp. 104–105), "Son of God" didn't necessarily denote anything more than "Davidic monarch" (as in Psalm 2). Now they make it denote "second person of the Trinity," which is quite the jump. "To claim he is the Son of God would make Jesus one of three things: a lunatic, a liar, or a divinity who fulfills Scripture" (p. 189). Here our authors are borrowing a famous argument advanced by C. S. Lewis:

> I am trying here to prevent anyone saying the really foolish thing that people often say about Him: "I'm ready to accept Jesus as a great moral teacher, but I don't accept His claim to be God." That is the one thing we must not say. A man who was merely a man and said the sort of things Jesus said would not be a great moral teacher. He would either be a lunatic—on a level with the man who says he is a poached egg—or else he would be the Devil of Hell. You must make your choice. Either this man was, and is, the Son of God; or else a madman or something worse. You can shut Him up for a fool, you can spit at Him and kill Him as a demon; or you can fall at His feet and call Him Lord and God. But let us not come with any patronizing nonsense about His being a great human teacher. He has not left that open to us. He did not intend to.[11]

This spurious line of reasoning (rather typical of Lewis' facile urbanity) is often laid down like a trump card by popular apologists who fail to see the grossly fallacious nature of it. It is a perfect example of the fallacy of Bifurcation, or oversimplification. It is a classic propaganda technique to lead one's audience to believe that only two (or in this case, three) alternatives lie before them, and then to seek to disqualify the ones you have mentioned, ignoring the choices you have not. "My friends, two alternatives face you today: anarchy or totalitarianism. So remember, on Tuesday, vote Nazi." In the present case, we are asked to believe that no one who believes himself to be God could be sane or honest, so that if Jesus did not appear to be either a madman or a charlatan, why then, by process of elimination, Jesus must be God incarnate. Several things are wrong with this argument. For one thing, it ignores the fact that there have been numerous gurus and mystics who believed themselves to be divine beings and were, as far as we can tell, both sincere and sane.

What Lewis forgot was what Albert Schweitzer remembered.[12] In his dissertation, *The Psychiatric Study of Jesus*, Schweitzer refuted academics who alleged that Jesus must have been crazy for believing himself to be the Messianic Son of man. He pointed out that Jesus shared the assumptions to which the people of his generation were accustomed: that a man might be chosen by God to bear the Messianic mantle and to be exalted to heaven. In our world, even among orthodox Christian believers, such a person would be suspected of paranoid delusions of grandeur. But in a world thoroughly imbued with apocalyptic supernaturalism, such ambitions did not seem outlandish. For Jesus to have regarded himself as God's destined Messiah would be less like someone thinking himself to be Napoleon and more like young Bill Clinton believing he would one day become president of the United States. It is not as if C. S. Lewis were to have believed himself to be King Arthur.

Lewis was arguing for Jesus as lawyer Fred Gailey argued for Kris Kringle in the 1947 version of *Miracle on 34th Street*. The prosecution alleged that "no one who believes himself to be Santa Claus is sane."[13] But Gailey countered that if he or the prosecutor or the judge believed himself to be Santa, then he must be deemed insane for the simple fact that none of them actually *is* the jolly old elf. But if Mr. Kringle is really and truly Old Saint Nick, then it is no delusion for him to believe it. Gailey is able to "prove" that Kris really is Santa by appealing to the authority of the federal government. Since the US Post Office identifies Kris Kringle as Santa Claus by delivering all their "Dear Santa" letters to him, then, before the law, the old man must indeed be the real thing. For all I know, that tactic might work in the courtroom. But as a syllogism in logic, it fails. It is vitiated by the fallacy of Appeal to Authority. Some big name says so, and we take his word for it—instead of being able to demonstrate it.

Lewis seems to be assuming that belief in one's own divine identity must be incompatible with a normal, healthy human psyche. It is too much of an enormity, like believing oneself to be a poached egg. But if that is so, then the implication would seem to be that Jesus must have been insane to believe in his divinity *even if he were correct*. Why? Because orthodox doctrine posits that Jesus, while truly and fully God, was also completely and truly human, only without sin. Doesn't this mean that Jesus' mind, as a real human mind, would be short-circuited even by the *true* belief in his own Godhood? For example, can we picture a mind staying sane if it was omniscient, constantly aware of everything going on throughout the universe? Can Jesus have been conscious of the shifting surface temperature of every foot of ground on all the planets of the solar system? The current position of every bird on Earth, whether perched on a limb or falling from it (Luke 12:6)? The number of follicles on every human head (Luke 12:7)? No human mind could stand it. Nor could that of Jesus if he were a real man. So, even if Jesus were the divine Lord, he would still have to be a lunatic, wouldn't he?

The classic answer of theologians is that God had temporarily set aside his prerogatives for the duration of the incarnation,[14] just as his imperishability and changelessness had to be placed on hold if he were to exist as a human being. I'm not sure if we could still say he was God if he did that, but suppose we could. Then we would be able to posit that Jesus did not experience the mind-blowing fullness of deity (Col. 2:9). He, too, must have believed in the doctrine of *kenosis*, or self-emptying. He would not have been *experiencing* himself as God but rather *believing* he was God, and this would place him on the same level as a number of other ostensible God-men and indeed with every Nondualist Hindu. He needn't be insane, any more than any Protestant fundamentalist who expects to be "raptured" into the sky at the Second Coming of Christ. That's pretty extravagant, too, but you don't have to be a lunatic to believe in it.

But the real Achilles' heel of Lewis's argument (and that of O'Reilly and Dugard) is the false premise that the historical Jesus claimed to be God. That assertion is founded on the unstable sand of the Gospel of John. This is a serious flaw in *Killing Jesus*, for it drastically skews the message of Jesus, making him a mouthpiece of fourth-century Trinitari-

Chapter Eight

TEMPLE TANTRUM

THAT FRIGGIN' FIG TREE

After the Triumphal Entry, Mark presents us with a lame anticlimax: "And he entered Jerusalem, and went into the temple; and when he had looked around at everything, as it was already late, he went out to Bethany with the twelve" (Mark 11:11). We imagine Jesus glancing at his wrist sundial and saying, "Gee, I guess we should have gotten an earlier start. Peter, I *told* you we should have skipped that brunch buffet." Next day, the group is retracing their steps to Jerusalem when Jesus (hungry, since they *did* skip the buffet this time) walks over to a fig tree, looking to munch a couple of figs. "When he came to it, he found nothing but leaves, for it was not the season for figs." So he flies off the handle, blaming the tree for spiting him: "May no one ever eat fruit from *you* again" (Mark 11:11–14). The next morning, as they pass the place, they see the recalcitrant tree has withered down to the roots. Matthew, seeking to heighten the impact, rewrites the scene so that the tree withers as soon as Jesus reads it the riot act (Matt. 21:18–19). *Zap*. I'll tell you what the real miracle is here: O'Reilly and Dugard accept this tall tale as historical fact, I know not how. But surely at this point, if not before, any reader hoping for a historical account of Jesus had better drop *Killing Jesus* and head back to the bookstore.

Let's take a look at the rings of the poor fig tree. It belongs to that genre of extravagant tales of the super-powered and petulant Kid Jesus, just like the story of young Jesus outclassing the elders in the Temple (Luke 2:41–52) and the one about him changing water into wine to bail the host out of an embarrassing jam (John 2:1–10). Like the latter, the fig tree tale has been transferred to the adult career of Jesus, but its origins are nonetheless clear. The story is a gross embarrassment to Christians today, but it already made Mark cringe. He didn't feel at liberty to omit it, so he tried to redeem it by tacking on a superfluous stock saying about faith and forgiveness.

> Have faith in God. Truly, I say to you, whoever says to this mountain, "Be taken up and cast into the sea," and does not doubt in his heart, but believes that what he says will come to pass, it will be done for him.[1] Therefore I tell you, whatever you ask in prayer, believe that you receive it, and you will. And whenever you stand praying, forgive, if you have anything against any one, so that your Father also who is in heaven may forgive you your trespasses. (Mark 11:22–25).

It sounds like somebody is trying to change the subject. One can imagine the disciples answering, "Uh, yeah, great. But what happened to the fig tree?" The unintentional comedy is the result of Mark trying to dilute the effect of the grotesque original.

But he is not done with it. Mark has split up the story (I think Matthew decided to restore the original unity, having the curse and the withering up occur all at once) so that its two halves (Mark 11:12–14 and 20–21) now bracket the episode of the Temple cleansing (Mark 11:15–19). That way, Mark makes the fig tree story into a symbolic comment on the Temple: it has failed to produce the fruit of repentance and righteousness when God came looking for it (Mark 12:1–3, etc.), so the Temple is doomed (Mark 13:1–2). One has to marvel at conservative scholars[2] who manage to convince themselves that the tree blasting actually occurred, but that Jesus did it as "an acted parable." I'm afraid that's not much help.

Luke lacks the whole incident. He seems perhaps to have rewritten it into a couple of sayings: "If you had faith as a grain of mustard seed, you could say to this sycamine tree, 'Be rooted up, and be planted in the sea,' and it would obey you" (Luke 17:6) and

> A man had a fig tree planted in his vineyard; and he came seeking fruit on it and found none. And he said to the vinedresser, "Lo, these three years I have come seeking fruit on this fig tree, and I find none. Cut it

> down; why should it use up the ground?" And he answered him, "Let it alone, sir, this year also, till I dig about it and put on manure. And if it bears fruit next year, well and good; but if not, you can cut it down." (Luke 13:6–9)

This is what I think happened, because the parable has Lukan fingerprints on it; it features dialogue in which a man in a tight spot manages to think quickly and find a way out (as in Luke 15:16–18, etc., 16:2–5, etc., 18:4–5), as well as the key Lukan motif of a delay of the Day of Judgment (as in Luke 17:22, 19:11ff., 21:8, 23–24). So Luke very likely decided to get rid of Mark's embarrassment by splitting it up into a saying and a parable, each of which looks suspiciously reminiscent of the Markan fig tree story. On the other hand, it is quite possible that Luke had access to two earlier bits that eventually got combined to form Mark's version, and for obvious reasons Luke preferred the original versions. Impossible to say.

GOD'S MAN CAVE OR MAN'S GOD CAVE?

O'Reilly and Dugard's fixation on the Johannine God-man Christology permeates even the Temple cleansing story. "The Temple guards are tense. They know that arresting Jesus is now completely justifiable. He has interfered with the flow of commerce and called the Temple his home—as if he were God" (p. 193). As usual, this represents an outrageous twisting of the text. As our authors know quite well, "'My house will be called a house of prayer,' Jesus says, quoting Isaiah, the prophet who predicted so much of the Nazarene's life" (p. 193). Who did *what*? Here we are again, with theology being dumped full strength into this ostensible history book. You just state flat-out as a matter of fact that Isaiah clairvoyantly outlined Jesus' biography in advance? As we have already seen, this is an exegetical mirage. Even a cursory look at any of the supposed prophecies shows that claims like O'Reilly and Dugard are making here are complete misreadings of the Old Testament texts, without any regard for the historical contexts. O'Reilly and Dugard do not even supply any specifics. It is obvious they are simply proof-texting John 12:41, "Isaiah said this because he saw his glory and spoke of him." That's what fundamentalists do. It's enough for them.

But besides this, how stupid do O'Reilly and Dugard think the Temple police were (or that their readers are)? Jesus is not shown claiming the Temple is his own bachelor pad. He is quoting Isaiah speaking for God.[3]

It is significant that O'Reilly and Dugard quote from Luke, who has Jesus say, "It is written, 'My house shall be a house of prayer'" (Luke 19:46). But Luke has abridged Mark at this point, leaving out a crucial portion of the Isaiah passage. Mark has: "Is it not written, 'My house shall be called a house of prayer *for all the nations*'?" (Mark 11:17). This is important if we want to know how the earliest version, Mark's, understood Jesus' motivation. Remember where this scene is supposed to be taking place: the Court of the Gentiles, the only portion of the huge sanctuary non-Jews were allowed to enter. Mark implies that Jesus is angry over the livestock trading and currency exchange because the chaos made it impossible for the pious Gentiles to follow the Jewish worship.[4] Matthew and Luke have clipped this portion of Mark's Isaiah quote, perhaps unwittingly obscuring Mark's point. John has omitted the Isaiah quote altogether. We will soon see that even Mark's version may be an attempt to whitewash a still earlier version of the Temple incident.

What about the Jeremiah quote? Understandably, O'Reilly and Dugard take the phrase "you have made it a den of robbers" (Luke 19:46b) to imply that the Temple authorities were ripping off the pilgrims, inflating both the price of sacrificial animals and the exchange rates. But not so fast. Looking at the Jeremiah passage, we find that "robbers" does not intend literal monetary abuse but rather general hypocrisy and corruption:

> Will you steal, murder, commit adultery, swear falsely, burn incense to Baal, and go after other gods that you have not known, and then come and stand before me in this house, which is called by my name, and say, "We are delivered."—only to go on doing all these abominations? Has this house, which is called by my name, become a den of robbers in your eyes? (Jer. 7:9–11).

Jeremiah doesn't even seem to be speaking to the priests but to the people, whose defeat at the hands of Babylon he predicts will soon fall on the nation for these sins. The Temple has become a hideout for the "pious" villains who gather there to pray. We see the same scenario in Isaiah 1:10–20. It is reasonable to assume that Jesus or Mark understood the point of the original passage and meant the same thing by quoting it.[5] And in this case, O'Reilly and Dugard's nasty vilification of the Temple priesthood collapses: Jesus overthrowing the tables is "something [the crowd] wanted to do every time they stood in that long line to change their money, watching corrupt men siphon off a significant piece of their earning" (p. 193).

TURNING THE TABLES

Even if we disregard the wholly implausible move O'Reilly and Dugard have made in retaining the Johannine Temple cleansing at the beginning and the Synoptic cleansing toward the end, we still choke on the bone of the restraint shown by the Jewish Temple police and the Roman troops. It just does not compute that armed troops who were posted about the Temple to deal with emergencies just like this one would have done nothing to stop Jesus from creating havoc.[6] Again, if we rationalize the story as O'Reilly and Dugard do, "explaining" that the authorities gave a Benghazi-style "stand down" order to their troops, we would have to ask why there are such troops there in the first place. Why wouldn't the *general policy* be to let trouble-makers get away and then apprehend them later by stealth? They even leave him at liberty to teach for the next few days? It just doesn't make any sense. If these guys had itchy trigger fingers, something like Jesus' cleansing of the Temple would be just the kind of action they had been waiting for. They would have, they *must* have, nabbed him on the spot. So we have to wonder if we are reading a severely edited version of the events.

S. G. F. Brandon argued that if we are to justify key details of the narrative, even as it now stands, we must posit a much larger-scale disturbance fomented by Jesus, and a violent one.[7] Consider the vast size of the Court of the Gentiles. Mark tells us that once he had made a mess of the tables, and so on, Jesus "would not allow anyone to carry anything [literally, "any vessels," i.e., sacrificial implements] through the temple" (Mark 11:16). Now how could he have managed *that*? "Hey, *you*. I *told* you not to bring that stuff back *in* here." "Oh, sorry, sir. What was I thinking?" No, Jesus would absolutely have to have secured all the doors in this huge expanse with his own armed men. And then we just cannot picture the Temple guards letting them get away with it. Mustn't there have been a pitched skirmish? Later we will read about Barabbas, who was "among the rebels who had committed murder in the insurrection" (Mark 15:7). Wait a second . . . *what* insurrection? Maybe the one that Jesus ignited right there in the Temple? It had to be pretty recent, in any case, right? It seems most plausible to picture Jesus being arrested in the Temple along with Barabbas and the others. Maybe the scene that we now read as set in the Garden of Gethsemane, where Jesus' men defend him with swords and violence, was originally located in the Temple, on the very day Jesus "turned the tables." The two men crucified along with him at Golgotha are called *lestai*, "robbers," the very term Josephus uses for the anti-Roman fighters in the Jewish-Roman War of 66–73 CE. Jesus is said to be crucified by the Romans as "the man who would be king," King of the Jews.

Brandon reasoned that Jesus had been executed by the Romans for their own good reasons, not merely as a favor to their Jewish allies.[8] If they had simply been accommodating Caiaphas and his buddies ("Sure, we can take care of it for you, old man"), why wouldn't Pilate have granted the Sanhedrin permission to stone him as a blasphemer, which was supposedly the crime for which they had condemned him? The answer always offered at this point is that the Sanhedrin feared rioting among the people if they were to have their own men execute Jesus. But this brings us back to the question: why have armed Temple troops at all, if not to control and disperse angry crowds? And why would the Romans not be similarly hesitant to execute Jesus and spark violent unrest? Because they had armed troops? Well, again, so did the Sanhedrin. In fact, the gospels place a large crowd of them at Gethsemane to arrest Jesus. They could use them. They *did* use them. Apologists are trying to steer us into the same neighborhood they occupy when they defend the plausibility of the scene where a crowd of roustabouts intimidate Pilate into condemning Jesus and releasing Barabbas. It's just as ridiculous.

If the story of Jesus' arrest by Temple guards (now set at Gethsemane) was originally the direct response to the Temple incident, we would have to posit that all the intervening material we now read in the gospels has been sandwiched in. Some of it may have been fictionalized, some of it transferred from elsewhere in the original plot line, as we shall see. For instance, it would be natural for the Last Supper to have preceded the Temple incident.

Brandon suggested that the role of the Jewish authorities seems superfluous, since the Romans would have had their own reasons for killing Jesus.[9] So why are the Jews part of the story? To shift the blame from the Romans, whose favor the gospel writers were hoping to curry. On Brandon's hypothesis,[10] Christianity has mutated from a failed revolutionary movement (though also religious, just as the Taliban is religious) into a quietistic, Rome-accommodating faith community and sought desperately to hide their now-repudiated anti-Roman roots. As Christians were being marginalized within Judaism and well on their way to emerging as a separate religion with an increasingly non-Jewish membership, they chose to downplay Rome's role in their founder's death, making the Jewish leaders, then the Jews collectively, primarily responsible for the execution. Jewish objections to Christian doctrines were retrojected into the lifetime of Jesus, with the result that, at the Sanhedrin trial, Jesus is condemned for teaching what was really subsequent Christian doctrine (Jesus as God's Son, seated beside him in heaven, etc.).[11] Even at that, though, traces of the original charges can still be seen when "false" witnesses at the trial say they recall Jesus threatening to destroy the Temple (something John 22:19 admits he said, though John reinterprets it). This reframing of the charges against Jesus allows Mark to have the Jews condemn Jesus for a religious offense, blasphemy (reflecting Jewish estimates of Christian belief as blasphemy and heresy). But since much had been made (and still is) not simply of the death by whatever means but specifically of the *crucifixion* of Jesus, it was impossible to erase any and all Roman involvement. The solution of Mark (or of his predecessors) was to have the Jewish Sanhedrin engineer Jesus' death and then manipulate the Romans into doing their dirty work. The story portrays it as the result of the Jewish authorities wanting to avoid popular displeasure for doing away with a popular prophet, but the underlying reality was the Christians' motivation to shift blame to the Jews while not being able to eliminate Roman involvement completely.

SEAMLESS GARMENT OR WHOLE CLOTH?

And yet, if, à la Brandon, there may be much more to the Temple story than appears on the surface, there may also be much less. Burton L. Mack thinks that there *was* no Temple incident in the first place.[12]

> The temple act cannot be historical. If one deletes from the story those themes essential to the Markan plots, there is nothing left over for historical reminiscence. The anti-temple theme is clearly Markan and the reasons for it can be explained. The lack of any evidence for an anti-temple attitude in the Jesus and Christ traditions prior to Mark fits with the incredible lack of incidence in the story itself. Nothing happens. Even the chief priests overhear his "instruction" and do nothing. The conclusion must be that the temple act is a Markan fabrication.

Christian readers are too close to the text and take too much for granted. It is simply unthinkable for Jesus to have gotten as "O'Reilled up" as he did and to have disrupted the sacred and inviolable ritual of the Temple, upon which the continual spinning of the world depended—with no on-the-spot repercussions, nor any for days after.[13] Let me give an analogous example from the other end of the Bible. There are several stories in Genesis that do not fit with the Flood story of Noah. For one, Noah's very name is punningly explained (as typical for the

Bible) as deriving from the "rest" he brought to toiling humankind (Gen. 5:28–29) by inventing wine (Gen. 9:20). Such a naming pun always seeks to make the name anticipate the great thing for which the character will be remembered. Obviously whoever originated this etymology for "Noah" had never heard of him building an ark and surviving a universal cataclysm. Similarly, there are ancient culture heroes venerated as the founders of certain arts and lifestyles: Jabal, "father of those who dwell in tents and have cattle" (Gen. 4:20) and Jubal, "father of all those who play the lyre and the pipe" (Gen. 4:21). The present tense implies that the writer assumes that all nomad herders of his day can trace their way of life back to Jabal, while all musicians of his day are continuing the playing begun by Jubal. That means the writer envisioned an unbroken cultural continuity between these primordial culture heroes and his own day. And that means he knew of no world-erasing flood in the meantime. Everything would have had to be rediscovered, reinvented. After all, there's nothing about God telling Noah to go around recruiting one of every profession or talent to get aboard the ark so as to preserve the gains of culture. No, Genesis combines variegated sources, snippets, and traditions into one vast and colorful patchwork quilt, and a marvelous one it is. But it is not consistent. And the same is true for the gospels. Mack is pointing out how the whole section of Mark (and his successors) in which Jesus teaches in the Temple makes better sense without the cleansing of the Temple, which would have made the rest impossible. So Mark has either created the Temple incident or dropped a story of it into the middle of a sequence that had no place for it. Nor would this be any new thing for Mark, who elsewhere seems to group things together as long as they share the same basic topic even if they contradict one another on how they deal with it.[14]

One of the strengths of the Brandon "Zealot hypothesis"[15] is how strikingly similar the scenario it envisions—Jesus leading a raid against the Temple—is to various events of the Jewish War as described by Josephus, who lived through those events some forty years later. For instance, with the Triumphal Entry on Palm Sunday we may compare the grand entrance of Simon bar-Giora. He was an anti-Roman rebel who had also been fighting a rival Jewish faction, the Zealots (i.e., the ones who actually "copyrighted" the name), who in turn were allied with a group of Idumeans. Simon's opponents, led by one John of Gischala, had successfully occupied Jerusalem. But then their Idumean allies turned on John's Zealots, cornering them in the Temple compound. Then the tricky Idumeans, now having sided with the Temple priests, hit upon the scheme to call upon Simon, who had remained with his men outside the city walls. With these reinforcements, they could crush the Zealots.

> In order to overthrow John, they voted to admit Simon, an olive branch in hand, to bring in a second tyrant to be their master. The resolution was carried out, and they sent the high priest, Matthias, to implore Simon to enter, the man they so greatly feared! The invitation was supported by those citizens who were trying to escape the Zealots and were anxious about their homes and property. He in his lordly way expressed his willingness to be their master, and entered with the air of one who intended to sweep the Zealots out of the city, acclaimed by the citizens as deliverer and protector. (Josephus, *The Jewish War*, 5, 9, 11)[16]

So let's take stock: here is a would-be Messiah entering Jerusalem to the acclaim of crowds who pin their hopes for deliverance on him. He is to cleanse ("sweep") the Temple of Zealots, whom Josephus habitually called *lestai*, "robbers," who were holed up inside. And Josephus even mentions the figurative waving of an olive branch, the sign of peace and reconciliation, recalling the palm fronds waved at Jesus by the adoring Jerusalem crowd.

At first, the parallels seem to support Brandon's version of the Temple event, that it was one more act of revolutionary religion. But on second thought, perhaps the two stories are rather *too* similar, too close for comfort. It begins to look as if the gospel sequence of the Triumphal Entry and the cleansing of the Temple has been borrowed and rewritten from Josephus, or at least is a reflection of the same events Josephus describes. They must have been common knowledge, after all. And we will see that other incidents in the Passion narrative are uncannily paralleled in contemporary sources, with the same implications of borrowing and fictionalizing.

Whether Brandon or Mack is right (and they both seem to have pretty strong arguments to me), either one of them is to be preferred to the way the ancient evangelists Matthew, Mark, Luke, and John, or their modern successors, O'Reilly and Dugard, tell the tale.

TURN DOWN THAT NOISE

Matthew 21:14 shows a party of indignant priests and scribes buttonholing Jesus in the Temple, but they are not calling him on the carpet for overturning the tables and general hell-raising, but only for accepting the acclamations of children. Again, the Temple ruckus looks like a bomb going off without making a noise. *This* is what they complain about: kids singing? Of course, this episode does not presuppose the Temple cleansing.

> And the blind and the lame came to him in the temple, and he healed them [just like *that*]. But when the chief priests and the scribes saw the wonderful things he did, and the children crying out in the temple, "Hosanna to the Son of David," they were indignant; and they said to him, "Do you hear what these are saying?" And Jesus said to them, "Yes; have you never read, 'Out of the mouths of babes and sucklings thou hast brought perfect praise'?"

O'Reilly and Dugard think this happened and that Jesus' opponents took his scripture quoting to be a declaration of his own divinity, since, in the quoted passage, Psalm 8:2, "thou" is addressed to God. But this is to read a bit too much into a text that, as usual, is quoted for its own sake, purposely indifferent to the original context. How do O'Reilly and Dugard (who merely attribute their own inference to the priests and scribes) know Mark and/or Jesus do not mean that, in this instance, God has enjoined that children bring forth "perfect praise" *to*

Jesus, not to himself? What is the point of Psalm 8:2 in context? Look at the verse just before it.

> O Lord, our Lord,
> how majestic is thy name in all the earth.
> Thou whose glory above the heavens is chanted
> By the mouths of babes and infants.

The point of the psalm seems to be, almost pantheistically, to say that the whole creation shows and magnifies God just by doing the things he created it to do. Thus every coo and cry of every baby is perfect hymnody. It is reminiscent of Mark 10:13–16, where Jesus complains that the disciples cannot see that they must welcome children and not think them a bother, because the little ones are the angels of God's kingdom. Maybe Matthew, who repeats the children's saying from Mark, is trying to rebuke the high-and-mighty religious elites in the same way as he and Mark rebuked the self-important disciples.

But does this charming scene reflect actual events in the life of Jesus? It looks like an alternative version of a scene we find over in Luke 19:37–40, at the climax of the ride into Jerusalem, where it makes a bit more sense.

> As he was now drawing near, at the descent of the Mount of Olives, the whole multitude of the disciples began to rejoice and praise God with a loud voice for all the mighty works that they had seen, saying, "Blessed is the king who comes in the name of the Lord! Peace in heaven and glory in the highest!" And some of the Pharisees in the multitude said to him, "Teacher, rebuke your disciples." He answered, "I tell you, if these were silent, the very stones would cry out."

In both stories some are praising Jesus in similar terms for miracles they had seen him perform, and some of Jesus' sour-pussed adversaries urge him to put a stop to it. Jesus' rejoinders look different, but I think they boil down to the same thing, as both of them look to me like Matthew's and Luke's attempts to make sense of a fragmentary Aramaic/Hebrew original. The word for "sons" is *beni*, while that for "stones" is *ebeni* (as in

Eben-ezer, "stone of help"). The words of John the Baptist in Matthew 3:9 and Luke 3:8, "God is able from these stones to raise up children to Abraham," use a pun based on this similarity between the words. I am suggesting that Luke's chorus of "children" represents the *beni*, while Matthew's speaking "stones" come from what he read as *ebeni*. If the original had read clearly one way or the other, both evangelists would probably have had it the same way, so, as it stands, I think both are independent attempts to plug the holes in a fragmentary source and to find an appropriate spot to place it in the timeline, someplace where Jesus is being praised, and somebody doesn't like it. Thus, neither one can be trusted as a historical report.

Chapter Nine

MESSIAHS AND MATCHSTICK MEN

VERSUS THE PINHEADS

In a couple of chapters of *Killing Jesus*, O'Reilly and Dugard adoringly portray their hero Jesus (oh, I'm sorry—for a second there I forgot *Killing Jesus* is a purely factual piece of sober, historical repor-*tazh*) as a great intellectual, easily making fools of the best point men in the Judaism of his day. We might as well be hearing the *Hosannas* in passages like these: "Word of Jesus's intellectual victory spreads through the Temple courts" (p. 203). "The brilliance of Jesus's words will last throughout the ages" (p. 204). "Jesus has now defeated the sharpest minds in the Temple" (p. 205). Alas, such superlatives are never going to be showered upon *Killing Jesus*.

In the present chapter I propose to survey the issues over which O'Reilly and Dugard have Jesus lock horns with Jewish leaders, with a view to assessing how fairly the gospels depict the latter, as well as how impressive Jesus' reasoning is. And I want to give some attention to a couple of the disputes O'Reilly and Dugard skip, looking at why they did so.

These gospel episodes are variously classified by scholars[1] as "pronouncement stories" and "controversy stories."[2] The main difference is what one imagines was the original reason for telling (or creating) them. Did they function to define the Christian position on issues like fasting, almsgiving, and divorce? And if so, do they reflect debates between Christians and non-Christian Jews in the early days when the two faith communities were drifting apart? Many scholars think so.[3] Others, pointing out that a bottom-line pronouncement by Jesus was not likely to carry much weight with anyone who did not already believe in his divine authority, suggest that these anecdotes addressed issues of controversy between Christians.[4] Others[5] believe that the substance, at least in some or most of them, was not really the point, that the tales were told pretty much as O'Reilly and Dugard tell them: to delight in the spectacle of "our guy" whipping the behinds of his opponents in public. "No man ever spoke like this man" (John 7:46). In these cases, it is not only the subject matter but also quite possibly the cogency of Jesus' reasoning that is secondary. Burton Mack comments: "If one . . . tried to assess the persuasive power of the pronouncements from the objectors' points of view, Jesus' responses did not appear all that enlightening."[6] How cogent are Jesus' replies? And is he really talking to Jewish leaders as known to history?

HEALING ON THE SABBATH

In Mark 3:1–6 some Pharisees know Jesus' habits well enough to suspect he will heal a man's withered hand on the Sabbath, in the synagogue, which he does. This constitutes a violation of the holy day of inactivity. Was this the view of the Pharisees? It doesn't seem so. What the Sabbath law forbade was professional physicians working for payment on the Sabbath. Explicit exception is made (in the Mishnah, the compilation of rabbinical traditions) for "healing by word," that is, divine healing such as Jesus practiced. So the Pharisees are portrayed as fictional straw men. It looks like the gospel writers are giving Jesus easy wins against opponents who did not actually exist.[7]

Not only that, but the response of Jesus seems to assume that it was an urgent, life-or-death case: "Is it lawful on the Sabbath to do good or to do harm, to save life or to kill?" But this man is only handicapped. There is no necessity to heal him on the spot. Even if there had been, no one forbade healing on the Sabbath in a case like that. And who is proposing "to do evil" on the Sabbath? (O'Reilly and Dugard rewrite Jesus' lines to "It is always lawful to do good on the Sabbath," presumably in order to make Jesus seem to have avoided this absurdity. And why would it be absurd? Because Jesus is shown blatantly committing the Bifurcation fallacy. "Well, if I have to decide whether healing on the Sabbath is doing good or doing evil, then I guess it's good." Jesus wins. But does he?

Luke 13:14 has a similar case. During the synagogue service, Jesus spots a woman who has suffered with a bent spine for all of eighteen years. Jesus heals her. "But the ruler of the synagogue, indignant because Jesus had healed on the Sabbath, said to the people, 'There are six days on which work ought to be done; come on those days and be healed, and not on the sabbath day.' Then the Lord answered him, 'You hypocrites! Does not each of you on the sabbath untie his ox or his ass from the manger, and lead it away to water it?'" Well, we don't know if they did or not. More than likely, strict Sabbatarians would have provided a double portion of food and water for their animals before the Sabbath arrived. In any event, the cases are not analogous, since neglect of one's livestock would be inflicting suffering and should be avoided, while making the woman "bound by Satan for eighteen years" wait one more day is a minor inconvenience. (For the analogy to be valid, Jesus should have told *Satan* to give the old lady a day off.) And this takes us back to the synagogue ruler's rebuke. Isn't he right? Why make an exception if there's no emergency? Only for convenience? The fact that Luke has the crowd delighted that Jesus has put the elites in their place doesn't make Jesus right, as anyone who has heard the applause for each side's favorite candidate in a debate knows perfectly well.

Another one awaits us in John 5:1–18ff. Jesus heals a lame man on the Sabbath. "The Jews persecuted Jesus because he did this on the Sabbath. But Jesus answered them. 'My Father is working still, and I am working.' This was why the Jews sought all the more to kill him, because he not only broke the Sabbath, but also called God his Father, making himself equal to God" (verses 16–18). Is that what John's Jesus meant? I would say so, though with a bit of hesitation, since sometimes John seems to be telling us that Jesus' critics had misunderstood what he said. If he was pulling rank, though, we do not have an argument at all, only an assertion of divine prerogatives that wasn't winning Jesus any friends in this crowd. But perhaps he is offering a theological argument that would have legitimatized anyone working on the Sabbath. We know some rabbis traded learned opinions on whether or not the Almighty really rested from his work on the seventh day (Gen. 2:2–3). What about Divine Providence? Wasn't God maintaining creation pretty much nonstop every day since he made it? Some said yes, he was. Jesus appears to share that opinion. If the rabbis were trying to say that God is exempt from the Sabbath rest commandment, and Jesus is appealing to that, then he is saying he has the same exemption, thus making himself equal to God. But if he means to say everyone is entitled to follow God's precedent, then he is in effect repudiating the Sabbath commandment. And thus he is removing himself from the game of legal deliberations. And that is not exactly winning the argument.

There is more of a legal, scriptural argument in play elsewhere in John 7:22–23, where the same healing seems to be in view. Jesus defends himself: "Moses gave you circumcision . . . and you circumcise a man upon the Sabbath. If on the Sabbath a man receives circumcision, so that the law of Moses may not be broken, are you angry with me because on the Sabbath I made a man's whole body well?" Jesus is shown employing the *qal wahomer* type of argument familiar from rabbinical arguments, reasoning that the same principle that applies in a lesser case mentioned in scripture must also apply to a more important matter that scripture does not explicitly mention.[8] If you can circumcise a baby boy's penis even though it is the Sabbath, how can it be wrong to heal a whole body on the Sabbath? But no one should accept this reasoning for the simple reason that the Torah mandates that a baby boy must be circumcised on the eighth day after his birth, whenever in a week it happens to fall. Thus the circumcision commandment supersedes the Sabbath commandment. That was no news to anyone. But there is no requirement that a chronically sick man, in no acute danger, must be healed on any particular day. It doesn't work.

Jesus comes out a bit better in a Sabbath controversy in Mark 2:23–28.

> One Sabbath he was going through the grainfields; and as they made their way his disciples began to pluck ears of grain. And the Pharisees said to him, "Look, why are they doing what is not lawful on the Sabbath?" And he said to them, "Have you never read what David did, when he was in need and was hungry, he and those who were with him: how he entered the house of God, when Abiathar was high priest, and ate the bread of the Presence, which is not lawful for any but the priests to eat, and also gave it to those who were with him?" And he said to them, "The Sabbath was made for man, not man for the Sabbath; so the Son of man is lord even of the Sabbath."

So human need takes precedence over Sabbath observance. And Jesus buttresses his reasoning with an apt scripture precedent. The only trouble is that all the ancient rabbis on record share the opinion ascribed to Jesus here. In the Mishnah we read the same thing several times: "The Sabbath is delivered unto you; you are not delivered unto it."[9] So it looks again as if Jesus' opponents are cardboard cut-outs, caricatures of the real thing.

The appended comment is perhaps originally a parallel saying from a different occasion: "So the Son of man is lord even of the Sabbath." In a Jewish context it would seem to mean that the dominion over the whole earth granted human beings in Genesis 1:26 extends even to the Sabbath, hence the discretion exercised by the scribes to decide how strictly or loosely it is to be observed. "Son of man" originally meant only "humanity," as in Psalm 8:4 and Ezekiel 25:2, and others.

If, however, Mark intended "Son of man" in a Christian sense as a Messianic title for Jesus, then we would have another case of Jesus simply pulling rank, which is no argument at all. And that would seem to make the preceding scriptural argument beside the point. But Morna D. Hooker notes that David was not setting aside the Sabbath and that the disciples are criticized, not for eating, as David did, but for plucking the grain.[10] She thinks that Mark means the David precedent to prepare the way for Jesus, the Messianic heir of David, being above the law. Again, this would cut no ice with the scribes whom Jesus is depicted as debating.

BY WHAT AUTHORITY?

O'Reilly and Dugard make Mark 11:27–33 a prime case for Jesus' intellectual superiority over his foes (p. 203). The Temple officials demand to know what right Jesus has to do what he does in the Temple. Who gave him permission? Jesus answers a question with a question: "Answer me, and I will tell you by what authority I do these things. Was the baptism of John from heaven or from men?" They go into a huddle and decide that any answer they give will be wrong. If they say John had no divine authorization, they take a risk of reprisals from John's fans. If they admit John acted under orders from God, then Jesus will demand to know why they boycotted him. So they say the jury is still out on the matter. Jesus replies, "[Then] neither will I tell you by what authority I do these things." Is he just stonewalling? "If you won't be straight with me, then I won't be straight with you." Could be. But it seems more likely he means that they can answer their own question. If they think John was a false prophet, as they no doubt do, then they must think Jesus is just as much a charlatan. If they think John was the genuine article, then Jesus is, too. As Joachim Jeremias suggested, the silent premise here seems to be that Jesus is claiming a kind of "apostolic succession" from John and to have inherited his legitimacy.[11] But that's not much of an argument, either. Early Christians believed that the heretics Simon Magus and Dositheus the Samaritan were disciples of John, too. Were they sent from God? Was Judas Iscariot divinely ordained because Jesus commissioned him as a disciple?

IHS AND IRS

The question put to Jesus in Mark 12:13–17 is said to be a pretext for getting Jesus to say something incriminating—or discrediting. In any case, Jesus' reply is no rhetorical ploy or evasion but shows genuine insight into the issue.

> "Is it lawful to pay taxes to Caesar, or not? Should we pay them, or should we not?" . . . [Jesus replied:] "Bring me a [denarius], and let me look at it." And they brought one. And he said to them, "Whose likeness and inscription is this?" They said "Caesar's." Jesus said to them, "Render to Caesar the things that are Caesar's, and to God the things that are God's." And they were amazed at him.

As well they might be. It is a brilliant answer. The issue was an important one. In the year 6 CE, the formerly and formally independent kingdom of Judea, ruled by Herod the Great and his son Archelaus, became officially a Roman province. Everyone knew Judea had been a client state, even a puppet state, dependent on Rome, but, as it had been technically independent, Judea had paid no taxes to Rome. Eventually Rome decided to end the legal fiction. To Rome, this might have seemed a mere adjustment on paper, but not to the Jews. The loss of even nominal independence placed them back under pagan rule, as their ancestors had endured for centuries. Some Jews believed that God was their only proper king and that therefore paying tribute to any mortal king not ruling under the aegis of the Jewish deity amounted to a compromise with idolatry. They thought of paying taxes to Caesar much the same as later Christians regarded the requirement to offer a pinch of incense in sacrifice to the divine Caesar. Just a pledge of allegiance in Rome's eyes, idolatry in the eyes of Christians who risked life and limb refusing to do it. It was such opposition that prompted Judas of Galilee to raise up a Jewish revolt against Rome in 6 CE. Decades later, the issue continued to fester: by paying Roman taxes, were Jews receiving the mark of the Beast?

This is why the question put to Jesus was a particularly loaded one. And it need not have been a trick question. But the answer could be controversial, that's for sure. If Jesus said not to pay, this put him in sympathy with seditionists. If he said the opposite, some would consider him, so to speak, a JINO (Jew in name only). So what was so special about Jesus' reply? O'Reilly and Dugard do not tell us. They just quote it and praise it. One wonders what they think he meant. Most Christians seem to think it means separation of church and state, but I think that is an application of Jesus' answer to a modern issue (and as such, it is a good and fair one).

Jesus seems to be saying that even devout, especially nationalistic, Jews need have no qualms of conscience about giving Caesar's coins back to him if he wants them. It entails no compromise, since this money, bearing "graven images" (Exod. 20:4), is "filthy lucre" (1 Peter 5:2), unclean by Jewish standards. That's why there were exchange tables in the Temple. Roman denarii could not be used to purchase sacrificial animals in the Temple or to pay one's annual Temple dues. They had to be traded in for good Jewish and Tyrian coins that lacked "idolatrous" images and therefore could be "rendered to God" (Mark 12:17). So what religious compromise could there possibly be in giving Caesar's stinking coins back to him? Bravo.

ONE RULE TO RULE THEM ALL

O'Reilly and Dugard think that the request for Jesus to choose the greatest commandment of the Torah (Mark 12:28–34) was another trick question. One might argue that such a question was near-blasphemous. If all the Commandments were ordained by God, how could any of them be less than ultimately important? "Whoever keeps the whole law but fails in one point has become guilty of all of it. For he who said, 'Do not commit adultery,' said also, 'Do not kill.' If you do not commit adultery but do kill, you have become a transgressor of the law" (James 2:10–11). But in fact, the question was a common one. The great first-century BCE rabbi Hillel had said that the entire Torah was summed up in the so-called Silver Rule, "What you do not want done to you, do not do to another." Rabbis have historically ranked service to one's fellow man above the obligations of worship. You should choose good deeds over worship if you had to choose, though in fact you don't.[12] Good works may not be sufficient to please God, but they are necessary. So it was a real and fair question. Jesus names the Shema, the great creed of Israel, as Commandment number one:

"Hear, O Israel. The Lord your God is one, and you shall love the Lord your God with all your heart, and with all your soul, and with all your mind, and with all your strength" (loosely quoting Deuteronomy 6:4). But he cannot leave it at that. A close second, equally important in its own way, is "You shall love your neighbor as yourself" (Lev. 19:18).

O'Reilly and Dugard tell us it is a trick question, but Mark has a scribe congratulate Jesus on the wisdom of his answer (Mark 12:32–34). Our authors seem to think that only the Ten Commandments were ascribed to Moses. "Under the teachings of the Pharisees, there are 613 religious statutes" (p. 205). No, all these are given in the Torah of Moses, the Pentateuch (Genesis, Exodus, Leviticus, Numbers, Deuteronomy). O'Reilly and Dugard have somehow confused the 613 Commandments of the Torah with the centuries-later Traditions of the Elders (which they mention on p. 157).

DIVORCE IS DIVORCE, OF COURSE, OF COURSE

We come across what at first looks like another piece of legitimate *halakhic*[13] dialogue in Mark 10:2–9, though on closer inspection it appears it has been skewed a bit by being placed in a later Christian context.

> And Pharisees came up and in order to test him asked, "Is it lawful for a man to divorce his wife?" He answered them, "What did Moses command you?" They said, "Moses allowed a man to write a certificate of divorce, and to put her away." But Jesus said to them, "For your hardness of heart he wrote you this commandment. But from the beginning of creation, 'God made them male and female.' [and] 'For this reason a man shall leave his father and mother and be joined to his wife, and the two shall become one flesh.' So they are no longer two but one flesh. What therefore God has joined together, let not man put asunder."

We know that the Pharisees were debating the matter of divorce. But they did not question whether divorce was permitted by the Law of Moses. It is impossible to imagine them even asking the question they are depicted asking here. The contemporary debate was over what constituted adequate grounds for divorce. The school of Hillel took a liberal perspective: a husband might send his wife packing for so trivial an offense as burning supper. The rival school of Shammai, by contrast, insisted that there had to be some sexual irregularity, mainly adultery. The evangelist Matthew, himself a Jewish scribe (Matt. 13:52), had a more secure grasp of scribal thought and so corrects Mark at this point. He has the Pharisees ask Jesus, "Is it lawful to divorce one's wife for any cause?" (Matt. 19:3). They are in effect asking Jesus if he agrees with Hillel's more liberal stance.

Jesus' reply is quite interesting. He grants that Deuteronomy allows for divorce, so it is certainly legitimated in the Torah, but that doesn't make it God's will. For that, one needs to turn some pages and look at the Genesis creation account, which shows God's original blueprint for human life. And there one finds that God has united husband and wife, virtually organically, and that it is not the prerogative of mere mortals to surgically separate these "conjoined twins." Does Genesis, then, contradict Deuteronomy? No, because the two texts are not on the same level. Genesis gives us God's original intent, his perfect will, while Deuteronomy is a concession offered in view of human stubbornness.[14] (We see an analogous distinction in 1 Corinthians 7:6.) Some marriages, obviously, just do not work out in the real world, and maybe that is due to human sin, but that sin and its consequent abuses are only going to get worse if the couple is imprisoned in the toxic relationship. As Tony Soprano would say, "Whadda y'gonna do?"

This does not really sound like a legal opinion, at least not until we get to the third-person imperative in the concluding sentence: "let not man put asunder." Without that, it sounds like a sadly wise comment on an unavoidable state of affairs. After all, we are given no hint that Jesus thinks the human heart has become less hard since Moses. So it seems odd that he would go on to reject divorce as an option, even as the lesser of two evils in a fallen world. We may suspect that someone has made this observation into a law for Christians.[15]

We also detect a heightening of Christology in Jesus' reference to Moses having given "you" the divorce commandment, not "us." He is either speaking as a non-Jew or as a divine being. Or as the Marcionite Jesus, the son of a different God than the one who gave the Law to Moses. Forgive a momentary digression, but it will be useful to explain this just a bit. Marcion of Pontus,[16] the first great Paulinist, read Paul as teaching the existence of two Gods: the Creator and giver of the Law, a righteous but severe judge, and the hitherto-unknown Father of Jesus Christ. He sent Jesus into the world to make it possible for the creatures of the Hebrew God to jump ship and swim over to him, becoming the adopted children of the Father. Marcion's Jesus revealed the existence of his Father and his gracious offer. He died to purchase us from the Hebrew God, like paying for the freeing of a slave. Marcion was an ascetic who discouraged marriage because it only led to the production of new souls trapped in the sinful, fleshy bodies made by the Creator. However, if one were already married, one ought not try to undo the damage by dissolving the marriage, given the hardships involved. Best to wait for freedom from the flesh after death. If the divorce saying attributed to Jesus came originally from Marcionite Christians, this would neatly explain why Jesus says Moses gave "you," the hapless creatures of the Hebrew God, the divorce commandment as well as why Jesus would forbid divorce: you poor wretches are already in too deep.

There is another such passage that first circulated independently of any gospel text, finally preserved by Christian copyists who recognized it as too good to risk losing and added it to the Gospel of John as John 7:53–8:11,[17] the famous story of the woman caught in adultery. Again Jesus is asked an impossible question: "Teacher, this woman has been caught in the act of adultery. Now in the law, Moses commanded us to stone such. What do you say about her?" Do they have any reason to suspect Jesus will say, "Verily, I don't give a damn *what* the law says. I say let her go"? Or "Let her off with forty hours of community service"? It has to be a Christian creation, presupposing that, Christianity having split off from Judaism, all bets are off and we have to rethink everything. "Are we bound to keep the regulations of Judaism? What would Jesus say?" Even so, in Mark's divorce passage, Jesus says, "Moses wrote *you* the commandment," referring to Jews, as opposed to Christians.

KINKY RESURRECTION

One of the most fascinating exchanges between Jesus and the Jewish authorities (Mark 12:18–27) pits him against not the Pharisees, the usual gospel whipping boys, but the Sadducees. O'Reilly and Dugard characterize them as some sort of philosophical demythologizers of Judaism, having absorbed too much influence from the Hellenistic world around them.[18] This, supposedly, was why they could be said to reject beliefs such as the end-time resurrection of the dead, like Modernist Protestants.[19] The Sadducees were the Jerusalem nobility and dominated the Sanhedrin and the Temple priesthood. Their name comes from the word *Syndikoi*, Greek for "Syndics," meaning "councilmen."[20] They were probably arch-traditionalists who rejected as theological innovations the doctrines of the Pharisees and the Essenes, who had borrowed a great deal from the Zoroastrian religion of Persia. These beliefs included angelology, a virgin-born end-times Savior, an apocalyptic end to history, the resurrection of the dead, and the idea of an evil anti-God. The Sadducees scoffed at these ideas as foreign corruptions of Judaism, and thus they dubbed the partisans of these notions "Pharisees," denoting "Parsees," "Persians," in other words, Zoroastrians.[21] Sadducees viewed the Jewish adoption of the resurrection doctrine as traditionalist Christians regard suggestions that reincarnation be worked into Christian theology.[22]

So the Sadducees are depicted as posing a hypothetical question to Jesus that they had probably also asked the Pharisees. Given the law of Levirate marriage, if a man dies without an heir, his brother must try to impregnate his widow. If successful, the son would be considered the dead man's son and heir. Well, suppose such a husband dies, and his widow marries her brother-in-law, but he dies, too, without impregnating her. He had a lot of brothers, but, between them, they had a lot of bad luck. She marries each of them, one after the other, but each husband proves sterile and dies. Finally, she's had it and joins them in the grave. When the trumpet sounds on Resurrection Morning and they are all united in a joyous reunion, uh, which one of the brothers is she going to be married to? Judaism tolerated polygyny, usually when a man's original wife proved infertile, but there was no way Jews were allowing polyandry, one woman with a harem of husbands, though some cultures do. If they had, there would have been no problem. But they didn't.

How is Jesus, himself a believer in the doctrine of resurrection, supposed to get out of this one? He does some fast thinking and says that all earthly marriage bonds will be dissolved in the age to come. Sex will be a thing of the past, because inheritance will be a thing of the past because death will be a thing of the past. Not a bad answer. But, as Morton Smith put it, "That the resurrected are not married is not a legal principle, but an *ad hoc* revelation."[23] Again, we cannot picture anyone not already believing Jesus is a divine revealer taking this bit of "information" seriously. Not even O'Reilly and Dugard make this a win for Jesus, and it is thus no surprise that they skip it.

But it gets worse. Jesus takes the fight to the Sadducees, seeking to prove from scripture that they are wrong about the resurrection. "And as for the dead being raised, have you not read in the book of Moses, in the passage about the bush, how God said to him, 'I am the God of Abraham, and the God of Isaac, and the God of Jacob'? He is not God of the dead, but of the living; you are quite wrong.'" How's that again? Jesus seems to be resting the whole weight of the resurrection doctrine on the slim reed of a verb tense. Abe, Ike, and Jake were all dead by Moses' day. But here is God announcing that he is *still* their God, which Jesus says implies they are still alive and available for him to *be* their God. Hm.

Obviously this is pretty lame. The present tense only implies that God is the same God that Abraham, Isaac, and Jacob once worshipped. And any idiot knows that.

Jesus wasn't the only one to argue this way. The Talmud records a defense of the resurrection belief by quibbling that, because the Hebrew imperfect tense is variously taken as past *or future* depending on the context, we should really read Exodus 15:1 not as "Moses and the children of Israel sang this song to the Lord," but as "Moses and the children of Israel *will sing* this song to the Lord," in other words, in the distant future of the resurrection.

Apparently this sort of nonsense was enough to convince some people, so maybe it sounded good to some of Jesus' contemporaries, too. But that hardly entitles us to call Jesus a brilliant dialectician. Some may have thought so, but then some people today take politicians' cant seriously. I think we can guess why *Killing Jesus* conspicuously skips this particular bit of Jesus' "intellectual brilliance."

Incidentally, why didn't Jesus just appeal to the two Old Testament passages that actually *do* seem to refer to the end-time resurrection, Daniel 12:2–3 and Isaiah 26:19? Simply because, as traditionalists, the Sadducees did not accept the recent addition of these books to the Hebrew canon. So they were off-limits in a debate like this.

APOCALYPSE NO

Another conspicuous omission, and another easily explained, is Jesus' apocalyptic discourse in Mark chapter 13 (repeated in rewritten form in Luke 21 and Matthew 24). O'Reilly and Dugard set the stage, having Jesus sit with an inner circle of disciples atop the Mount of Olives. He had startled them earlier by quipping that the impressive architecture of the Temple would soon wind up a thin coating of crushed rubble on the ground. They want to know when. In Mark, they ask, "When will this be?" In reply, Jesus embarks on a lengthy list of calamities leading to the Abomination of Desolation, culminating in the Great Tribulation, the end of the age and the advent of the Son of man. And there is a very definite timetable: "Truly, I say to you, this generation will not pass away before all these things take place" (Mark 13:30). But of all this we read not a word in *Killing Jesus*. Instead, we read this:

> With the disciples sitting at his side, Jesus summarizes his short life. Darkness is falling as he tells his followers to live their lives to the fullest, speaking in parables so that they will comprehend the magnitude of his words. The disciples listen in rapt fascination but grow concerned as

> Jesus predicts that after his death they, too, will be persecuted and killed. Perhaps to lessen the impact of this, Jesus shares his thoughts on heaven and promises the disciples that God will reveal himself to them and the world. (pp. 206–207)

Well, this is a bunch of gibberish that bears no relation at all to the Olivet Discourse, as it is called, of Mark 13. It seems to reflect, albeit very distantly, the Farewell Discourse at the Last Supper in John's Gospel, but it is really a banal and pedestrian substitute for both gospel passages. O'Reilly and Dugard seem to have discarded the gospel material altogether, though they have nothing of any substance to substitute for it. This passage is an insult to both their readers and the gospels. One can only surmise that they wanted to bypass, really to censor, the monumentally embarrassing prediction of Jesus that the world would end in his own generation. Looked at the calendar lately? The statute of limitations has long ago run out.

Jesus is supposed to be a revealer of hidden realities that our senses could never otherwise know. And here is the single one of them that is subject to verification. He predicted the Second Coming to occur in the next thirty or forty years, so we can verify or falsify that "revelation." And it simply didn't materialize. So what reason is there to believe any of the other "revelations" he bequeathed us? It is like Edgar Cayce predicting that Atlantis would rise from the ocean in 1971. No sign of it. Tough to get around that. Better to ignore it, eh? That is what Christianity has done for two millennia. And that is surely why O'Reilly and Dugard completely omit any mention of these difficulties. Is this impartial history or faith propaganda? We report, you decide.

Chapter Ten

THE IMP ACT SEGMENT

AND ONE OF YOU IS A DEVIL

How does a man become a devil? First we must ask, how does a verb become a man, a "word made flesh"? For that seems to be just what happened in the case of Judas Iscariot.

Did you ever notice anything strange about the story of Jesus getting arrested in the Garden of Gethsemane? We are told that the authorities wanted desperately to eliminate Jesus. They feared his influence among the people, and they feared it so greatly that they judged it too dangerous to arrest him publicly for fear that the crowds would not permit it. They might rise up and lynch anyone who tried to make away with their favorite. This is why the Sanhedrin engages Judas Iscariot. They want to know where they can find him out of the public eye. But why would they need a man on the inside for that? Luke 22:39 says Jesus and his band habitually retreated to the Mount of Olives. That must have been easily known. There is no hint of Jesus trying to keep his whereabouts a secret, nor of how he might have succeeded in the endeavor if he had wanted to.

And then, once the arresting party arrived in Gethsemane, why do they need Judas or anyone else to identify Jesus? Isn't the whole point of the exercise to seize Jesus on the sly since he is known to everybody? O'Reilly and Dugard have some inkling of the problem, since, as they describe the scene, they "explain" that the soldiers' torches were not bright enough for them to distinguish faces (p. 223). Then why in Sheol did they bring them in the first place? Were they as discombobulated as poor Jimmy Carter, who failed to send enough helicopter gunships to rescue the American hostages in Tehran? If their flashlights were running out of juice, then surely they would have simply drawn their swords and approached the group of disciples, shining the fading light in each face. John 18:4–5 does not even have Judas point Jesus out, unlike in the Synoptics: "Then Jesus, knowing all that was to befall him, came forward and said to them, 'Whom do you seek?' They answered him, 'Jesus of Nazareth.' Jesus said to them, 'I am he.'" Naturally, O'Reilly and Dugard hybridize John and the Synoptics, having Judas kiss Jesus to point him out *and* having Jesus ask who the soldiers are looking for, unwittingly underlining the superfluity of Judas in the scene. He seems to be a fifth wheel, of as little use as most of Michelle Obama's hundred-plus staff assistants.

You have to begin to wonder if Judas has been artificially inserted into the story. Where did the Judas character come from? We have already seen that perhaps the best guess as to the meaning of "Iscariot" is *ishqarya*: "Man of Falsehood," "the False One," or "the Betrayer." This marks him as one of Tzvetan Todorov's "narrative-men,"[1] a character who is identical with his function in the narrative, no more, no less. "We need someone to betray Jesus, so let's add Mr. Betrayer."[2] And such was the zygote for the Judas Goat.

POGROM'S PROGRESS

The New Testament epistles know nothing of Judas Iscariot or even of any betrayal of Jesus. Not even in 1 Corinthians 11:23: "The Lord Jesus on the night he was betrayed took bread and broke it," and so forth. The word translated here as "betrayed" is παρεδιδετο, *paradideto*, which can just as easily mean "handed over" or "delivered up," as in Romans 8:32, "He who did not spare his own Son but gave him up [παρεδωκεν, *paredoken*] for us all." There is no reason, unless we insist on reading the gospel accounts into 1 Corinthians 11:23, not to translate the verse as "the Lord Jesus, on the night he was delivered up," in other words, by the providence of God. But once someone thought to read the word as "betrayed," the question arose to which Judas became the answer.

We need a betrayer, so how about Mr. Betrayer? Judas the False One, Judas Iscariot.

Why the name "Judas"? Isn't it obvious? Judas stands for the Jews collectively, who rejected Jesus.[3] He is exactly the same sort of fictionalized personification we see a bit later in the tradition (after the New Testament) as the Wandering Jew,[4] the wise guy who heckled Jesus as the Savior painfully made his way to Golgotha. The legend has it that Jesus, not in a very forgiving mood, turned to him and muttered, "Tarry thou till I come again."[5] The poor jerk was condemned to live on and on, drifting through the wide world like the murderer Cain (Gen. 4:12, "You shall be a fugitive and a wanderer on the earth"). He witnessed terrible suffering and adversity, longing for surcease but doomed to this role until Christ should come again to reprieve him in death. The Wandering Jew was a symbol of Jews, Christ-rejecters sentenced to wander through the Gentile world until the end of the age. He was essentially a second Judas. Judas Iscariot was the first Wandering Jew, only his sojourn was not to last that long, finishing at the end of a length of rope.

The first thing on Judas' rap sheet is his unmotivated visit to the Sanhedrin to offer information on Jesus. "Then Judas Iscariot, who was one of the twelve, went to the chief priests in order to betray him to them. And when they heard it they were glad, and promised to give him money" (Mark 14:10–11). Compare this with Matthew's rewrite: "Then one of the twelve, who was called Judas Iscariot, went to the chief priests and said, 'What will you give me if I deliver him to you?' And they paid him thirty pieces of silver" (Matt. 26:14–15). Notice that, while Mark had Judas volunteer to turn Jesus over to the authorities, with no strings attached, Matthew has Judas mention money right up front. He has Judas offer to sell out Jesus if they will pay for his services.

Matthew even names a figure, and he is the only gospel writer who does. Where do you suppose he got that bit of "information"? From Zechariah 11:12: "Then I said to them, 'If it seems right[6] to you, give me my wages; but if not, keep them.' And they weighed out as my wages thirty shekels of silver."[7] But Matthew mines even more "historical" data from Zechariah, which he regarded as a fruitful source of "facts" about Jesus, if only one knew how to read scripture esoterically (Matt. 13:52). What does Judas eventually do with his ill-gotten gains? He finds they are burning a hole in his conscience, so he rids himself of them. He goes back to the priests, who have neither sympathy for nor any further interest in him, so the betrayer pitches the money to the floor of the Temple treasury and leaves. The priests then deliberate on what to do with it. As it is bounty money, they cannot put it back into the treasury, so they decide to use it for a charitable act, the purchase of the potter's field to use as a cemetery for indigents (Matt. 27:3–10). How did Matthew "know" any of this? An educated scribe, Matthew draws on three different versions of scripture, Hebrew, Syriac, and Greek, as it suited his purposes. The Syriac version of Zechariah 11:13 says, "Then the Lord said to me, 'Cast it into the treasury, the lordly price at which I was paid off by them.'" But the Hebrew has, probably because of some transcriptional error, "Cast it to the *potter*." Matthew decided to harmonize the two, having Judas dump the money in the treasury (a place to which he could not have gained access in real life), whence it is recovered and given to the potter.[8]

THE FUNCTION OF UNCTION

Mark may have meant to imply that Judas was disgruntled at Jesus welcoming the Bethany anointing, thus violating his usual policy of telling rich would-be followers to cash in their possessions and give to the poor (Mark 14:4–5), and this was the last straw. Disillusioned with Jesus, he sneaks off to the Sanhedrin to conspire with them. Could be, I guess. But then Mark does not even specify that the carpers were among the disciples, though Matthew drew that inference (Matt. 26:8). And if Judas had decided to drop out of the disciples, convinced that he had backed the wrong horse—would his natural reaction be to engineer his former master's *death*? That seems a bit extreme. Why not just shake his head and go back home, like the disillusioned disciples in Luke 24:13–

21? So it is not clear that Mark assigned any particular motive for the betrayal. And that is what we might expect. Hyam Maccoby comments on "Judas' motive in betraying Jesus. In view of the fact that he is the vehicle of a cosmic purpose, a necessary actor in a drama of sacrifice, we should expect to find that any personal motives ascribed to him are flimsy, ad hoc, or contradictory; and this is just what we do find."[9] That is because these motives will be secondary attempts to historicize the original myth. If one is trying to make the story look like an account of historical events, one requires psychological, or at least narrative, motivation. And different authors will posit different motives, just as the gospel writers do.

As we have seen, Mark does not offer us a motive for Judas' actions. It is enough that Judas' epithet tells him what to do: Iscariot, the Betrayer. Again, Matthew felt he needed to make more sense of it, so he makes Judas venal and greedy: he sells Jesus out to make a few extra bucks. John carries this particular theme a step further: Judas was embezzling from the disciples' petty cash fund the whole time (John 12:6). But even that is not as bad as it (and as Judas) gets. Luke has a different anointing story (7:36–50), in which it is a character called Simon the Pharisee who criticizes Jesus for putting up with the woman who anoints him. So he does not even hint that this episode might have goaded Judas into betraying Jesus. Nor does he ever intimate that Judas was a greedy man (though he does not hesitate to vilify the Pharisees in this manner, Luke 16:14). No, when it comes to Judas, Luke loads the big guns: "Then Satan entered into Judas Iscariot, who was of the number of the twelve; he went away and conferred with the chief priests and captains [of the Temple police] how he might betray him to them. And they were glad and engaged to give him money. So he agreed, and sought an opportunity to betray him to them in the absence of the multitude" (Luke 22:3–6). So Judas was possessed, and not even by some subordinate demon like Wormwood, but by Satan himself, "Our Father Below."[10] John, as we have seen, makes Judas the prototype for modern televangelists, skimming off the ministry receipts, but he also echoes Luke as well as *Saturday Night Live* comedian Dana

Carvey's Church Lady: Who could have gotten Judas to betray Jesus? "Oh, I don't know . . . could it be . . . *Satan?*" John says, "The devil had already put it into the heart of Judas Iscariot, Simon's son, to betray him" (John 13:2).

O'REILLY AND DUGARD: FALSE WITNESSES

What do our intrepid historians (that's Syriac for "novelists") make of Judas' motivation? They drop the devil-possession business. I guess even they felt queasy about bringing Satan onstage as a character. Keep in mind, in general, they are trying to make the Jesus story look like it could have happened in the real world, and Satan would make the thing start looking like *The Exorcist*. But they do retain John's picture of Judas as a coin-pinching Jew—and this, even though it doesn't fit very well with another version they like: Judas as enthusiastic for Jesus but impatient to see him do his thing.

> "What are you willing to give me if I hand him over to you?" Judas asks. [There's Matthew.] . . . "Thirty silver coins," comes the reply. This is 120 denarii, the equivalent of four months' wages. Judas has lived the hand-to-mouth existence of Jesus' disciples for two long years, rarely having more than a few extra coins in his purse, and very little in the way of luxury. Now the chief priest is offering him a lucrative bounty to select a time and place, far from the Temple courts, to arrest Jesus. Judas is a schemer. He has plotted the odds so that they are in his favor. He knows that if he takes the money, one of two things will happen: Jesus will be arrested and then declare himself to be the Christ. If the Nazarene truly is the Messiah, then he will have no problem saving himself from Caiaphas and the high priests. However, if Jesus is not the Christ, he will die. Either way, Judas' life will be spared. (pp. 210–11)

It doesn't seem to occur to Judas, or to O'Reilly and Dugard, that, if Jesus is the Messianic Superman, and even if he does cast aside his Clark Kent disguise and kick Caiaphas' sanctimonious butt, he is going to know that Judas set him up. No hard feelings? I wouldn't bet on it.

Nor is the Judas of *Killing Jesus* worried about reprisals from the other disciples if Jesus dies. The whole implausible scenario is the product of O'Reilly and Dugard treating the various gospel motivations of Judas as jigsaw puzzle pieces and trying to make a unified picture out of them, even if they have to shave some of the pieces and toss others off the table altogether. To borrow their comment about Caiaphas, "All these details . . . can be massaged" (p. 207).

Note also that our authors do not hesitate to include as a piece of their puzzle Matthew's thirty pieces of silver, derived from no one's memories, but from Zechariah. Matthew was not writing history, and neither are O'Reilly and Dugard.

They make a salad of the gospels' various anointing stories, too. Their first maneuver is to resort to the oldest and most ridiculous trick in the harmonist's playbook. If there are contradictory versions of the same event, biblical inerrantists blithely conclude that the event happened two or more times. They want to be able to say that each account is accurate. Thus all must have happened. We have already seen O'Reilly and Dugard pull this stunt by having two different Temple cleansings. Now we are told that Jesus has been approached and anointed by devoted women *several times*—presumably much like Elvis, everywhere bombarded by female fans. This allows them to preserve as accurate the very different Mark/Matthew story of an unnamed woman in Bethany anointing Jesus' head, the Lukan tale of an unnamed prostitute anointing Jesus' feet, and John's episode of Mary of Bethany anointing Jesus' feet at a dinner for Lazarus. And yet they combine elements of them anyway. We already saw that they identify the woman in Mark and Matthew (perhaps Mary Magdalene) with Luke's prostitute just because Catholic tradition says so. And now we are told that the feast in Lazarus' honor was held not in Lazarus' own home, as in John 12, but in the house of Simon the leper from Mark.

I suggested that Mark just might have assumed that it was the anointing (deemed an extravagance by some) that pushed Judas over the edge, though it seems unlikely. John makes Judas the complainer but does not make the incident part of Judas' motivation. O'Reilly and

Dugard, however, do. And they do not present this as a speculation. No, they are mind readers. "Judas has decided to force Jesus' hand. Judas made his decision moments ago, during dinner, when Jesus and the disciples were eating at the home of a man named Simon the leper" (p. 209). One might as well ask how Mark knew what Jesus said in the Garden as he prayed, since he had excluded any possible witnesses (they were at a good distance, a-snooze). Simple: Mark "knew" what Jesus said because Mark made it up. He was writing fiction. And so are O'Reilly and Dugard.

I'M AT THE END OF MY ROPE

I mentioned how Matthew embellished Mark's Judas sequence by borrowing the thirty silver pieces from Zechariah 11:12, then spun the story out further into Judas' attempt to return the money, and so on, based on the very next verse of Zechariah. Matthew extends the story even further, concluding with Judas' suicide by hanging, probably modeled on the hanging death of David's betrayer Ahithophel (2 Sam. 18:9–10). O'Reilly and Dugard chose this version over the very different account in the first chapter of Acts (which they refer to as "the first book of Acts," a minor but symptomatic sign of their unfamiliarity or carelessness regarding the Bible).[11] O'Reilly and Dugard include a colorful piece of trivia from ancient legend, namely that Judas hanged himself with a horse's halter, but they admit it might not be historically true (p. 265). That's too little, too late. The whole Judas story, including Judas himself, is legend, as we can tell by tracing its gestation in the womb of the early Christian imagination.

Chapter Eleven

CHECK, PLEASE

The only way I can account for the shabby treatment accorded the Last Supper in *Killing Jesus* is to suggest that its authors are interested only in the plot to execute Jesus to the exclusion of everything that does not directly bear upon it. But the rest of the book has plenty that does not directly concern this theme. And the Last Supper itself, one would think, seems to have a great deal to do with the death of Jesus, else we would not be calling it the Last Supper, reminiscent of a convicted murderer's "last meal." So what gives? Because what the authors do to the Supper is to gut it. They give no real idea of the significance of the event in either John or the Synoptics, and the significance is vastly different between them. It is true, as we will see, that much of what appears in the Last Supper narratives of all the gospels cannot be considered historical in nature. But that hasn't stopped O'Reilly and Dugard up to now.

Let's begin with the three matters that do interest our authors before we examine what they left out.

VENUE AND MENU

Was the Last Supper of Jesus with his disciples supposed to be a Passover seder? Believe it or not, this is very far from clear. The stages of a typical Passover meal are not recorded in any of the gospels, but that might simply be because the point is not to depict the ritual meal for its own sake, but rather to use it as the setting and vehicle for something else. Suffice it to say that there are not enough details to confirm the Paschal nature of the occasion. What other evidence is there?

Mark and Matthew place their Last Supper material in a framework according to which the meal must be a Passover seder, but, as with most of the material in the Synoptics, the connection between one narrative unit and those adjacent to it may well be artificial. And the beginning and end of each episode may be a secondary embellishment intended to spin the main portion in this or that direction, interpreting it for the reader. That looks like what we find in Mark and Matthew. Mark 14:12–16 appears to be a self-contained narrative about the providential or miraculous provision of the Passover feast for Jesus and his disciples who have no home or possessions. There is no hint, despite O'Reilly, that Jesus has made prior arrangements and then tells the disciples about them. *These* are the only arrangements. He is *talking* to the men whom he would have had *make* any prior arrangements, but this is all new to them.

And the story looks like it is based on 1 Samuel chapter 9. Jesus corresponds to Kish, who dispatches two men, his son Saul and a servant (1 Sam. 9:3), just as Jesus sends two disciples (Mark 14:13). When Saul and the servant arrive in the city, they see a young woman coming out to draw water (1 Sam. 9:11), just as Jesus' disciples are told to keep an eye out for a man carrying water (Mark 14:13). All transpires as predicted (1 Sam. 9:6; Mark 14:16). Saul asks, "Where is the house of the seer?" (1 Sam. 9:18), while Jesus directs the disciples to ask, "Where is my guest room?" (Mark 14:14). In 1 Samuel 9:19, Samuel oversees the preparation of a feast, while in Mark 14:16, the disciples prepare the Passover feast. "Everything works together for the good of them that love God" (Rom. 8:28). The story did not necessarily lead into an account of the feast for which these providential preparations had been made. The point may have been simply to depict God's provision for his Son. And if we imagine that the episode of the Last Supper itself was another independent cameo, there is no internal evidence of it being a Passover meal. This is, then, the case with Mark and Matthew.

In Luke it is different. He seems to have noticed, in Mark, the loose fit between the preparation story and that of the Supper. To knit them together more firmly he has added an initial remark of Jesus as the Last

Supper begins: "I have earnestly desired to eat *this passover* with you before I suffer" (Luke 22:15). Luke makes other adjustments to Mark's original, but they will concern us a bit later on.

Does John's Gospel understand the Last Supper as a Passover meal? John 13:1 sets the scene "before the feast of the Passover" and goes on to open the scene thusly: "during supper" (verse 2), so it would be natural, if this is all John said, to infer that it was the Passover supper. But it does not explicitly connect the two. And the meal is not described, only the feet-washing and the prediction of imminent betrayal, which are the only two items O'Reilly and Dugard recount. But if we widen our focus to the rest of John's Passion narrative, we can see that the Last Supper is not supposed to be a Passover at all.

First, when Jesus tells Judas to go and do his business and get it over with, and Judas does get up and head for the door, John says none of the others lifted a finger to stop him because they assumed "that, because Judas had [charge of] the money box, Jesus was telling him, 'Buy what we need for the feast'" (John 13:29). This by itself is enough to prove that it cannot have been the seder that they were then sitting down to eat. If the scene took place on Passover eve, that is, the evening commencing Passover (in accord with the Hebrew calendar whereby each day officially begins at sunset), then we must picture them sitting down to (actually reclining around) a bare table. A little late for buying the food and wine if they were right then sitting down to a Passover meal. And what Jewish merchant would have been open for business? The Torah required every Jew to be in his home on that holy night. No, this is just the evening meal on the night *before* Passover.

O'Reilly and Dugard assume the meal was a Passover supper and recognize there is an apparent contradiction between John and the Synoptics on what day of the week it took place, for John implies it was on a Wednesday evening, while the Synoptics set it on Thursday. They tell us in a footnote that Pope Ratzinger (Benedict XVI) has resolved the problem by positing that Jesus and his men observed a different ritual calendar, the solar calendar, like the Qumran sect of the Dead Sea Scrolls. The Pharisees and Temple priests followed the lunar calendar, with the result that different Jews celebrated Passover a day apart, just as Eastern Orthodox Christians celebrate Christmas a week later than Roman Catholics and Protestants today. This harmonization, by the way, must not be credited to Ratzinger. He merely borrowed it from Annie Jaubert, who proposed it back in 1965.[1] But it will not work, despite its ingenuity, because John 13:29 makes it clear that Jesus and his men planned to celebrate the Passover the next night, the same night everybody else did.

In John 18:28 we read that the priests requested Pilate to emerge from his palace to talk with them because to enter a Gentile's home would render them ritually polluted. They might have done this otherwise, but not this night, desiring to remain pure so that "they might eat the Passover," which therefore had not yet arrived. In 19:14 it is explicit that Jesus' scourging and crucifixion were taking place before Passover: "Now it was the day of Preparation for the Passover." But there is more. For this evangelist, the death of Jesus is that of the new Passover Lamb, "the Lamb of God who takes away the sin of the world" (John 1:29). John's chronology is theologically, not historically, based. He has arranged it to have Jesus crucified on the day the Passover lambs were being butchered.

In summation, it is not clear that the pre-Markan tradition knew the Last Supper as a Passover celebration. Mark juxtaposed the scene with another depicting the providential provision for Jesus and his disciples to observe the Passover, the result being that the latter story introduced the former and made the Last Supper *into* a Passover seder. Matthew took this over from Mark. Luke decided the connection was still not sufficiently integral and added Jesus, at table, referring to "this passover." John severed the link (restoring the original independence of the Last Supper), making the Supper an ordinary meal just before Passover. As usual, O'Reilly and Dugard have just chosen what they think makes for an exciting story, a kind of ancient police procedural or murder mystery.

THE HOLE IN HOLY COMMUNION

It is quite striking that *Killing Jesus* completely omits from the Last Supper the institution of the Eucharist, the sacrament of the Lord's Supper. In this our authors are following John, who replaces the ritual with what may be intended as a new sacrament, that of feet washing. But John does not completely banish the Eucharist. He has moved it back to the Galilean ministry in chapter 6, where one can find it wedged into the Bread of Life discourse. "I am the living bread that came down from heaven; if anyone eats of this bread, he will live forever; and the bread which I shall give for the life of the world is my flesh" (John 6:51). "Truly, truly, I say to you, unless you eat the flesh of the Son of man and drink his blood, you have no life in you; he who eats my flesh and drinks my blood has eternal life" (John 6:53, 54).

I think that the whole scene, together with the words of institution, is fictive, a combination of myth and liturgy. All this has no place in a historical reconstruction of the life of Jesus. No reader will be surprised at my verdict. But it would be astonishing if O'Reilly and Dugard, who evidence no sense of critical historiography, dropped the gospel account of the institution because they believe it didn't happen.

So what *do* O'Reilly and Dugard think happened at the Last Supper? Though summarized in surprisingly cursory fashion, as if to get it out of the way, our authors include the scene of Jesus washing the disciples' feet.

> Jesus begins the evening by humbling himself and washing each man's feet with water. This is a task normally reserved for slaves and servants, and certainly not for a venerated teacher of the faith. The disciples are touched by this show of servility and the humility it implies. Jesus knows them and their personalities so well and accepts them without judgment: Simon the zealot, with his passion for politics; the impulsive Peter; James and John, the boisterous "sons of thunder," as Jesus describes them; the intense and often gloomy Thomas; the upbeat Andrew; the downtrodden Philip; and the rest. Their time together has changed the lives of every man in the room. And as Jesus carefully and lovingly rinses the road dust from their feet, the depth of his affection is clear. (pp. 219–20)

This is almost unrecognizable when compared to John's text (13:1–17). The real thing ends with a commandment: "If I, then, your Lord and Teacher, have washed your feet, you also ought to wash one another's feet. For I have given you an example, that you also should do as I have done for you. . . . If you know these things, blessed are you if you do them" (John 13:14–15, 17). It is plausible that, as some have suggested, the feet washing is intended as a metaphor and that the real point is the same as Colossians 3:13b: "forgiving each other; as the Lord has forgiven you, you also must forgive." But I think Mennonites and others who practice feet washing as a sacrament (or church ordinance) are correct. The description of feet washing as an example and the specific injunction to wash one another's feet point to the story being a ceremonial etiology,[2] a story explaining, perhaps fictively and after the fact, a ritual.[3] But you'd never guess this from *Killing Jesus*.

O'Reilly and Dugard substitute for this a bizarre scene of sentimentality and touchy-feely schmaltz. Like Leo Buscaglia or Wayne Dyer, Jesus is just gushing. One feels embarrassed for Jesus; one fears he is making a bit of a fool of himself. Not the way this scene is played in the Gospel of John, mind you, but in *Killing Jesus*. There is nothing about either the moral or ritual significance of Jesus' action. Instead we read a groundless psychological thumbnail of several of the disciples. Peter is "impulsive"? Good old Pete? Is this because he professed his loyalty to Jesus but did not live up to it? Because John says he was the one who sought to defend his Master with violence in Gethsemane? To chalk these things up to being "impulsive" is a way of making the character into a Sunday school cartoon, a Disney version of the apostle. And "sons of thunder" characterizes James and John as hotheads? This is another psychologizing trivialization. The title "Boanerges," assigned them in Mark 3:17, is the tip of an archaic theological iceberg, a reference to Castor and Pollux, sons of the Thunderer, Zeus. Thomas' proverbial negativity is simply a result of the character's narrative function as the one who puts up the hurdle of skepticism for the miracle-working hero to leap.[4] "Simon the zealot, with his passion for politics" is a ludicrous domestication of a member of the revolutionary Zealot movement. O'Reilly and Dugard make Simon sound like a political junkie addicted to C-SPAN and *Hardball*. And "upbeat Andrew"? "Downtrodden Philip"? What the *hell*? *Killing Jesus* makes the apostles look like the Seven Dwarves.

What is the origin of the story of Jesus acting the menial role of a slave? I believe it is a prime example of how an originally mythic story of Jesus became progressively historicized, a process O'Reilly and Dugard are carrying further in their pseudo-historical *Killing Jesus*. We can still see the original on display in an ancient hymn quoted in Philippians 2:6–11.

> Who, though he was in the form of God
> did not count equality with God a thing to be grasped,[5]
> but emptied himself,
> taking the form of a servant,
> being born in the likeness of men.
> And being found in human form
> He humbled himself
> And became obedient unto death (verses 6–8)

The hymn is reminiscent of the labors of Hercules. Transforming this myth into narrative form, Mark decided to have Jesus say this about himself:[6] "Whoever would be first among you must be slave of all. For the Son of man also came not to be served but to serve, and to give his life a ransom for many" (Mark 10:44–45). Luke rewrote this saying and transferred it to the Last Supper: "Let the greatest among you become as the youngest, and the leader as one who serves. For which is the greater, one who sits at table, or one who serves? Is it not the one who sits at table? But I am among you as one who serves" (Luke 22:26–27). But Luke does not go so far as to depict Jesus playing waiter at their table. It is just a saying, just a metaphor. Luke uses the same imagery elsewhere:

> Let your loins be girded and your lamps burning, and be like men who are waiting for their master to come home from the marriage feast, so that they may open to him at once when he comes and knocks. Blessed are those servants whom the master finds awake when he comes; truly,

> I say to you, he will gird himself and have them sit at table, and he will come and serve them. (Luke 12:35–37)

John has taken the next step. Just as he had borrowed Luke's beggar named Lazarus and made him into Lazarus of Bethany, so now he makes Luke's magnanimous master into the Lord Jesus who literally girds himself with a towel, has his disciples recline at table, and washes their feet. O'Reilly and Dugard take it from there. But history it's not.

HOLD IT RIGHT THERE, ISCARIOT!

O'Reilly and Dugard try to preserve a historical character for John's Last Supper so they can mine it for their "history" of Jesus' execution. They shamelessly sidestep a major problem with taking John's account seriously. After Jesus drops the bombshell that one of those present would shortly hand him over to the authorities, the disciples all rush to demand, "Is it I?" Peter asks the Beloved Disciple to get Jesus to reveal the name, and Jesus pinpoints Judas by dipping his bread into the dish simultaneously with Judas. But the others remain oblivious. How? O'Reilly and Dugard "explain" that, amid the hubbub following Jesus' announcement, they didn't catch the exchange between Peter, the Beloved Disciple, and Jesus. But Peter did. Why on earth did he, even if not the others, rise to his feet and bar Judas' path? Of course, it is because the narrator cannot have Peter or anyone else get in the way of his advancing plot line. He simply neglects any narrative motive, and O'Reilly and Dugard cannot bail him out. It is much the same as an old *MADtv* skit in which the robot Terminator returns from the future to prevent the death of Jesus. At the Last Supper, when Jesus announces the imminent betrayal, the Terminator, seated alongside the disciples at the table, blasts Judas with an automatic assault rifle, whereupon Jesus resurrects him. The robot guns him down again, and Jesus restores his life again, then rebukes the Terminator, "Stop killing Judas!" Jesus tells him his saving destiny must go forward. That's pretty much what's going on in John.

CULT OF THE CORN KING

One always hears that the Last Supper marked Jesus' reinterpretation of Passover as a memorial of his own saving death, the transformation of the Jewish ritual into the Christian one. And that is probably not an inaccurate description as long as we are talking about how the gospel writers viewed it. But to ascribe this understanding to the historical Jesus is a big mistake.

Above, I mentioned ritual etiologies. This is one of them. Long ago, New Testament scholar Alfred Loisy pointed out what should have been obvious: the story of the institution of the Eucharist presupposes that the ritual is already being practiced, that readers are familiar with it, and that the story seeks to explain the elements of the ceremony. "This is my body" presupposes the familiar use of bread in the ritual and reveals the true or esoteric significance, perhaps to the newly baptized, now being admitted to the sacramental mystery for the first time. Likewise with "This is my blood." Loisy says,

> All this would be intelligible enough to a Christian reader familiar with a developed Eucharistic rite as practised in the group for which the Gospel was intended: but perfectly unintelligible on the occasion when the sayings are supposed to have been uttered. . . . These mystic sayings have no natural sense except as referring to an established Christian sacrament, and as explaining it.[7]

On the other hand, none of this makes any sense in a Jewish context, given all that we know about Judaism of the period—or of *any* period. To Jews, the notion of blood drinking had always been absolutely abhorrent. See Genesis 9:4: "You shall not eat flesh with its life, that is, its blood." Leviticus 7:26–27 says, "You shall eat no blood whatever, whether of fowl or of animal, in any of your dwellings; whoever eats any blood, that person shall be cut off from his people" (cf. also Lev. 17:10–14 and Deut. 12:16, 23). Even metaphorical blood drinking would have been unthinkable, like a religious use of child-molestation imagery. It is simply out of the question to imagine Jesus telling fellow

Jews to eat his flesh and drink his blood. Even John 6:52 ("How can this man give us his flesh to eat?") underestimates the grossness of the implied blasphemy.

So the body and blood rite cannot fit with any sort of Jewish worship. But we don't have to look very far to find an altogether natural context for it, where it must have originated: the Egyptian Osiris cult and the Greek mysteries of Dionysus. These were very ancient religions known for centuries to Jews, and not just Diaspora Jews but Palestinian Jews as well. Palestine had been part of the Egyptian empire as far back as the third millennium BCE. And Dionysus worship had been familiar to Jews as least as far back as the mid-second century attempt of the Seleucid king Antiochus IV Epiphanes to convert Jews to Hellenism, at which time many Jews joined in the rites of the wine god (2 Macc. 6:7–9). It was widely believed that the Jewish Jehovah and the Greek Dionysus were but different names for the same deity anyway, and the whole religion of Sabazios presupposed their identity.[8] The "blood" of Dionysus was, of course, wine. His "flesh" was grain, bread. The same was true of the grain god Osiris (whom Greeks also identified with their own Dionysus). The devotees of Osiris shared a sacred meal of bread and wine, sometimes bread and beer.

The words attributed to Jesus at the Last Supper obviously presuppose such symbolism and thus the same world of ideas. Jesus is speaking as the Corn King, who presides over the ritual consumption of his body and blood, which are grain and wine. The ritual script provided in the scene has nothing whatsoever to do with the ostensible theme of the Jewish Passover, the ancient exodus from Egypt, but everything to do with fertility celebrations. In that context, the whole makes plenty of sense. For our purposes here we need not delve into the larger questions of whether Christianity actually started out as a vegetation cult or merely assimilated the myths and rituals of one somewhere along the way. It is sufficient for us to peg this ritual formula as the product of such a context.

Loisy also points out how this sequence is not integral to its present setting in the Markan Last Supper scene. It seems to interrupt the theme of the surrounding verses.

> The natural sequence after "they all drank of it" is "I will drink of it no more," etc. This was the order in the basis-story: it spoke *only* of the bread that he would eat no more and of the wine that he would drink no more till they ate and drank together in the Kingdom of God. The institution of the mystic Supper ("this is my blood," etc.) is a highly distinct afterthought in the development of the Gospel catechesis.[9]

Why this vow? It meant that Jesus expected the apocalypse to dawn in a mere matter of days. Joachim Jeremias sums it up: "By a solemn vow of abstinence He forswears all feasts and wine for the future, so as to set before His disciples and impart to them His own complete certainty that the final consummation is near at hand."[10] It is strikingly ironic that, whereas the vow presupposes that ongoing history is about to be cut off, the words of institution presuppose just the opposite, since they seek to launch a new ritual to be performed in generations to follow. This only underlines the composite (and therefore fictional) nature of the Last Supper narrative.

Chapter Twelve

TRIAL AND ERROR

The gospel accounts of Jesus' trials before the Jewish Sanhedrin and Pontius Pilate swarm with difficulties, though to read the "History" by O'Reilly and Dugard, one would never suspect this. They have simply used the time-dishonored method of scissors-and-paste historians, that is, precritical pseudo-historians. They have merely chosen the bits from all the conflicting gospels that strike them as good raw material for their edifying novel.

COURT REPORTERS?

O'Reilly and Dugard follow the lead of the gospel writers in assuming the position of omniscient narrators. They know what they know because they are creating the story (with the help of Matthew, Mark, Luke, and John) as they go along. It does not seem to occur to them that, if they were really writing, as they claim, a genuine history of Jesus' trial, they would not be entitled to include anything for which they could not supply testimony. But they do. How on earth do they, like the evangelists, pretend to know what was said by Jesus, Caiaphas, and others, in closed-door sessions? "He will be questioned extensively, and what he says will be written for the ages" (pp. 224–25). Uh, by *whom*, pray tell? Peter and the Beloved Disciple only got as far as the high priest's courtyard. They could not have heard anything of what transpired inside. Could Nicodemus or Joseph of Arimathea, members of the Sanhedrin, have told the disciples what had happened, once things had died down?

This will not work, because there is no hint of any dissenting voices being raised at the trial, unlike in the earlier scene where Nicodemus sticks up for Jesus and receives a sharp rebuke (John 7:50–52). Mark 14:64 says quite clearly that "they all condemned him as deserving death." Nicodemus, too? Not if he was a fictional character, a "narrative-man," created by John to symbolize chicken-hearted would-be followers of Jesus in Yavneh-era Judaism (ca. 80–90 CE). What about Joseph of Arimathea? Mark never implies Joseph was a disciple. If he had been, then we could imagine him reporting to the disciples after the trial. But this is how Mark introduces him after the crucifixion: "Joseph of Arimathea, a respected member of the council, who was also himself looking for the kingdom of God [to dawn], took courage and went to Pilate and asked for the body of Jesus." This does not make him a follower of Jesus. Many or most Jews are said to be hoping for the swift arrival of the kingdom (Mark 12:28, 34; Luke 2:25, 38, 17:20, 19:11).

Nor does Joseph's desire to give the crucified Jesus a decent burial imply discipleship, since seeing to the burial of those dead who had no one to take care of it was a very important act of charitable piety in Judaism, as witness Tobit 1:16–19, 2:3–4, 7–8; Matt. 8:21. Matthew does not even hesitate to depict the villainous priests as being concerned for the burial of indigents (27:7). "Josephus the historian actually tells us that pious people undertook the task of burying crucified victims who otherwise would have been buried in a common grave for malefactors."[1] So Mark may well have pictured Joseph as having voted against Jesus and yet being concerned that the pathetic heretic receive a decent burial.

But Luke thought it better to "clarify" things and to enhance Joseph's reputation: "He was a member of the council, a good and righteous man, *who had not consented to their purpose and deed*, and he was looking for the kingdom of God" (Luke 23:50b–51). Still, Luke has forgotten to exempt Joseph from the Sanhedrin's villainy: "Then the whole company arose, and brought him before Pilate" (Luke 23:1).

Matthew goes even farther in sanitizing and sanctifying Joseph: he "was also a disciple of Jesus" (27:57b). And, as far as Matthew is concerned, Joseph was not even a member of the council. John 19:38 does not make Joseph a Sanhedrinist either, and now Joseph has become a clone of John's character Nicodemus: "Joseph of Arimathea . . . was a disciple of Jesus, but secretly, for fear of the Jews" (John 19:38). Nobody in here but us chickens.

Thus even if Joseph of Arimathea *had* been a member of the Sanhedrin and present for the trial, as in Mark and Luke, he would have had no connection to Jesus' disciples. If he was a disciple but not a member of the council, as in Matthew and John, he would not have been privy to their proceedings. There is absolutely no reason to nominate him as the source of information about Jesus' trial. And Nicodemus—did he even exist?

WHO'S THE LAW-BREAKER HERE?

Jewish and Christian critics have long raised red flags at various points in the Trial narrative. If one supposes, as Matthew, Mark, and Luke do, that Jesus' Last Supper was a Passover meal, then Jesus' trial before the Sanhedrin was also on Passover Eve, and that is patently absurd. These pious guardians of Torah orthodoxy left home, where the Torah required them to stay put, on Passover? "Why is this night different from all other nights?" "Sorry, son. Mommy's going to have to field that one. I gotta be somewhere. Later!" Of course, O'Reilly and Dugard figure Caiaphas—er, and *every single Jew on the council*—was an unscrupulous bastard who regarded "God's covenant with Abraham as just so much chin music."[2] Unless, of course, he could make a buck from it. But even if that were so, there are some things even a stinking hypocrite dare not do—like publicly flouting the holiest customs of one's people, the very traditions one's job is to uphold. "Pass me another slice of that lamb, will you, honey . . . *Good God!* Look out the window! Isn't that Lord Caiaphas? What the . . . ?"

O'Reilly and Dugard consider this a minor speed bump: "But the religious laws state that no trials can be held during Passover, and none can be held at night" (p. 207).

"Everything about Jesus's interrogation is illegal: it takes place at night, Jesus is asked to incriminate himself without a lawyer, and Annas has no authority to pass sentence" (p. 229). Well, so what? Let's get on with the story . . .

In the *Killing Jesus* gospel, as in traditional Christian storytelling (which is what *Killing Jesus* really is, despite O'Reilly's Jay Carney–like protestations), Jesus gets condemned for blasphemy. But even if somehow the New Testament writers had any information about what Jesus said at the trial, it does not come close to blasphemy.

"'I charge you under oath,' fumes Caiaphas, 'by the living God: tell us if you are the Christ, the Son of God'" (p. 232). This much of the "Is It Legal?" segment comes right out of Matthew 26:63, almost verbatim. But Jesus' reply is taken from Luke 22:67–69: "If I tell you, you will not believe me. And if I asked you,[3] you would not answer. But from now on, the Son of Man will be seated at the right hand of the mighty God" (p. 232). O'Reilly and Dugard clumsily paraphrase Luke's "right hand of the Power of God" to "right hand of the mighty God."

They go on to Luke 22:70, with an important modification: "Are you the Son of God?" the priests demand. "'Yes,' he tells them. 'It is as you say.'" Luke actually has him reply, "You say that I am." Matthew has the same equivocal, even evasive, reply. O'Reilly and Dugard have been listening to those Evangelical apologists again. They prefer Mark's reply: "I am" (Mark 14:62). So they try to get us to believe that the Matthew/Luke version is just an idiom that means the same thing. That is why O'Reilly and Dugard paraphrase Jesus' reply as "Yes. It is as you say." If you want to paraphrase it, surely it ought to be "If you say so."

I don't know why, if O'Reilly and Dugard preferred an unequivocal affirmation of Jesus' messianic identity, they didn't just go with Mark's "I am." But I'm glad they didn't since I don't think that is what Mark wrote. A few manuscripts read, "You say." This has to be the original text. It is certainly what Matthew and Luke were reading in their copies of Mark. There is no way either one of them would have found a ringing "I am" in Mark and changed it to the vague "You say that I am." It is much more natural to picture Matthew and Luke copying Mark's original "You say" and a subsequent scribe not liking what he read in Mark and changing it to "I am," making Jesus sound more decisive.[4]

Killing Jesus then switches over to Mark 14:62 but sneaks in an embellishment: "Then Jesus looks straight at Caiaphas: '*You* will see the Son of Man seated at the right hand of the Power, and coming with the clouds of heaven'" (p. 233). Caiaphas is furious, "for Jesus is implying nothing less than that Caiaphas is an enemy of God. 'He has spoken blasphemy,' the high priest tells the Sanhedrin'" (p. 233). Oh no; this is no good. First, the Greek for "You will see" is in the plural, not the singular, so Jesus cannot be speaking to Caiaphas in particular. But even if he had been, it is hard to see how this would make Caiaphas "an enemy of God." O'Reilly and Dugard are just having fun writing their novel again: more conflict, more mind reading, more nonsense.

Second, nothing Jesus says in this scene would have been considered blasphemy, much less worth the death penalty. It was not blasphemy (defaming God) for a man to claim he was the Messiah and to be wrong. About a century after the ostensible time of Jesus, Simon bar Kokhba believed himself to be the destined Messianic king and actually managed to achieve a brief window of independence from Rome. There is some reason to believe he managed to rebuild some version of the Jerusalem Temple.[5] The great Rabbi Akiba endorsed him. But before long, bar Kokhba was defeated. Akiba's colleagues rebuked him for backing the wrong horse, but this did not destroy his reputation as a holy scholar of Torah. Nor was bar Kokhba written off as a blasphemer. Instead, he was viewed as a fallen hero. His noble death may even have been the origin of the doctrine (attested as of the third century) of a preliminary "Messiah ben-Joseph," whose mission was to die in battle to atone for the sins of Israel that had blocked divine redemption. He would have prepared the way for the subsequent Messiah ben-David to vanquish the pagans.[6]

There is nothing in the words of Jesus to his interrogators to suggest he believed himself to be a divine incarnation. Even as a mortal man, the Messiah might be expected to sit at God's right hand, to be exalted to heaven, even as many believed Enoch, Moses, Elijah, and others had been. Remember, as O'Reilly and Dugard themselves point out, "Son of God" need have denoted no more than "Davidic king," and nothing Jesus says here goes beyond that.

Seeing the problem here, some scholars, like Ethelbert Stauffer,[7] have sought to vindicate the trial narrative by suggesting that Jesus' declaration (at least according to most manuscripts of Mark) "I am" was supposed to refer back to the "theophany formula" in Exodus 3:14, "I am that I am." But that is farfetched desperation. Caiaphas asks Jesus, "Are you the Christ?" Jesus answers, "I am." Doesn't that simply mean "Yes, I am the Christ"? It recalls the scene in *Monty Python's Life of Brian* when Brian finds there is no way to get his point across to his overenthusiastic fans.

> "I am not the Messiah, will you please listen! I am *not* the Messiah. D'you understand. *Honestly!*" [Someone in the crowd shouts out,] "Only the true Messiah denies his divinity." Brian: "What? Oh! (*in exasperation*) What sort of a chance does *that* give me? . . . All right! I *am* the Messiah!" The crowd: "He *is*! He *is* the Messiah!"[8]

On this theory we must imagine Jesus getting frustrated every time he answers a mundane question ("Who's in the mood for some ice cream?") with "I am," and then having to explain, time after time, that, no, he's not claiming to be Jehovah. It's almost inviting an Abbott and Costello "Who's on first?" routine.

THE BEAT GOES ON

While leading up to their favorite chapter, the one about the execution of Jesus by John Wilkes Booth and Lee Harvey Oswald, O'Reilly and Dugard continue to crucify not Jesus but the gospels. We find both the addition of details with no basis at all in any gospel text ("The beating [of Jesus by the guards] goes on for hours," p. 230), and the telepathic conjuring of the inner deliberations of characters, who have become just that, literary figments rather than historical personages. They also, as we should expect by now, include various dubious gospel anecdotes if they sound good. I am reminded of a scene in Isaac Bashevis Singer's novel *Satan in Goray*, in which a popular rabbi is supposed to be inspecting animals but doesn't really give them a second look.

> They said that since becoming the slaughterer of Goray he had never once found any beast to be unclean and unfit to be eaten—this in order to win the favor of the butchers. Whenever the question arose, he ruled the beast clean, and he had abandoned all the laws of purity. . . . "Hurry! It's clean! It's clean!"[9]

We read that, in accord with John 18:31, the Jewish authorities have no power to execute convicted criminals, which is why the priests approach Pontius Pilate to do their dirty work. Is this true? The evidence is not clear, but Alfred Loisy seems on the right track when he suggests that this restriction of their authority is another Johannine anachronism.[10] John's Gospel has the Sanhedrin excommunicating believers in Jesus already in his lifetime (John 9:22), even though John also has Jesus predict that such a synagogue expulsion program will occur *in the future*: "I have said all this to you to keep you from falling away. They will put you out of the synagogues. . . . But I have said these things to you, that when their hour comes you may remember that I told you of them" (John 16:1–2a, 4). The same would seem to be true of the powerlessness of the Sanhedrin. After the disastrous defeat by the Romans in 73 CE, the Sanhedrin was reconstituted as a strictly religious body with no jurisdiction, as before, over civil and criminal matters. This does imply that the Gospel of John is telling the story of Jesus as if it had happened in the postwar period. These anachronisms are a tool for bringing to bear the perspective of Jesus upon issues current in the evangelist's own day. This is another one of them.

Among the gospels, only Luke has Jesus appear on trial before both Pontius Pilate and Herod Antipas (Luke 23.6–12). Pilate, upon hearing that Jesus is a Galilean, attempts to fob Jesus' case off onto Herod Antipas, Tetrarch of Galilee. But this is nonsense. Pilate would not have been required, or even entitled, to extradite a Galilean who had committed a crime in Jerusalem, for example, threatening to demolish the Jerusalem Temple. Why did Luke double the trial? It must have been a creative, yet clumsy, attempt to harmonize two different but parallel Passion accounts, one that had Pilate hand Jesus over to execution, the other placing the blame on Herod. Luke could not bring himself to choose between them. This is the inevitable implication of the bizarre notion that Herod, to whom Pilate had delegated the case, declared Jesus not guilty—yet sent Jesus back to Pilate for *his* judgment. Antipas did not, please note, decline to hear the case. He heard it and exonerated Jesus (Luke 23:14–15)! So why did he send him back? And if he did, as per Luke, why didn't Pilate release him? It just doesn't work.

But O'Reilly and Dugard are fine with it. It is fine for them to speculate on what both Herod and Pilate must have been thinking, what political and public relations factors they weighed, and why they came to the decisions they did. But they present their speculations as fact, as if Pilate and Herod had left behind memoirs recording these thoughts. This is all sheer fiction, but it is presented as history. *Killing Jesus* is more like Lew Wallace's 1880 novel *Ben-Hur* than, say, D. F. Strauss's *The Life of Jesus Critically Examined* (1835). Why do they indulge in such imaginary mind reading? It is a desperate exercise in fundamentalist harmonization, in this case, trying to make it look even remotely plausible that a contemptuous Jew baiter like Pilate, as Philo and Josephus describe him, would lift a finger to get one more deluded Messiah off the hook. Even the evangelist Matthew knew something was amiss in Mark's portrayal of Pilate trying to free Jesus, so he added some narrative motivation by including the apocryphal touch of Mrs. Pilate having ominous nightmares about Jesus and sending a note to her hubby to steer clear of this case (Matt. 27:19). "You're a regular Pontius Pilate the minute you start!" (*Miracle on 34th Street*).[11] O'Reilly and Dugard are engaged in the same futile exercise, trying to save face for the story as history, which it isn't.

I have already mentioned the enormity of having Pilate cave under "pressure" from a crowd of nobodies in his courtyard who threaten to rat him out to Rome if he sets Jesus free. "Pilate's soft on sedition!" Afraid of their "clout," Pilate accedes to the mob's request that he release Barabbas instead, *a known killer of Romans in an insurrection!* Rome's not going to take a dim view of *that*? Come on, Bill. Get real, Martin.

Our authors unquestioningly repeat from the gospels the business about a Passover clemency custom. Each year, as a show of Roman magnanimity, the governor would supposedly release one prisoner of the crowd's choice (Mark 15:6). Not only is this inherently incredible;[12] there is no mention of any such practice in any ancient extra-biblical source. And thus, the entirety of the Barabbas story (and with it, the story of Pilate's advocating for Jesus' release) goes down the drain.

FOR AZAZEL

For a long time now, both Jewish-Christian ecumenists and historical critics have suspected that Jesus was simply arrested and executed by the Roman occupiers and put to death as a rebel, which he was. Jesus' revolution having failed, his sect reacted by becoming a quietistic community, praying for an apocalyptic deliverance from Rome but leaving it to God to do the job his own way and in his own time. Accordingly, the gospel writers, increasingly alienated from Judaism, were eager to reassure Rome that Christians presented no threat and thus deserved no persecution. So they wrote up a version of the story of Jesus that, while acknowledging that Jesus was executed as an anti-Roman seditionist, tried to explain it away. They shifted the blame to the Jews in order to exonerate the Romans. According to this new version, the Sanhedrin, furious at Jesus for outwitting and publicly embarrassing them, framed an innocent Jesus for sedition and tricked Pilate into taking the blame for Jesus' death. Poor Pilate! Bullied and manipulated into doing the Jews' dirty work!

We are in a position analogous to that with King Herod and the Slaughter of the Innocents: it was the *kind* of thing Herod would do, but there was no independent corroboration outside the Bible, and the story, besides being beset with inherent implausibilities, conformed a bit too closely to Josephus' Moses nativity. Same here: the Jewish Talmud (*Pes.* 57a) describes the priestly aristocrats as villains: "Woe to the house of Annas! Woe to their serpent's hiss! They are High Priests; their sons are keepers of the treasury; their sons-in-law are guardians of the Temple; and their servants beat the people with staves." So they do make believable villains in the story, but when we examine the gospel accounts of the trial, they have important strikes against them: the anachronism of the blasphemy charge, the lack of any way Christians could have known what was said at the trial, and the blooper of having the trial on Passover Eve. Add to that the potholes in the Pilate episodes, and it does begin to look like we are reading propaganda fiction, something distressingly close to *The Protocols of the Elders of Zion*. (This nineteenth-century fiction, concocted by the Czarist secret police, purported to "leak" the minutes of a secret cabal of Jewish leaders plotting to take over the world. It was intended to provoke persecution of Jews and worked pretty well.)

We can cite another historical analogy. In the eighteenth century, Jacob Frank was a libertine, nihilistic would-be Messiah who taught that everything the Torah had forbidden was now permitted, even commanded![13] His followers conducted secret orgies behind a pretense of conventional piety. Frank eventually led his cult to a pretended mass conversion to Catholicism. To demonstrate his new loyalty, he began to slander the Orthodox Jewish population and to incite pogroms against them! Of course, Mark never thought of going that far, and I don't mean to say he did. But I think you can see the similarities: switching sides and vilifying one's parent faith in order to secure one's position with the authorities.

ANOTHER JESUS

Killing Jesus briefly contrasts with Jesus the Nazarene another man named Jesus, Jesus ben-Ananias, of whom we read in Josephus. First, here is O'Reilly and Dugard's summary:

> Thirty-two years from now, a peasant named Jesus ben-Ananias will also predict the Temple's destruction. He will be declared a madman at first, but his life will be spared by order of the Roman governor—but only after he is flogged until his bones show. . . . When Jesus ben-Ananias continued for seven more years to proclaim loudly and publicly that the Temple would be destroyed, a Roman soldier permanently silenced him by catapulting a rock at his head. Four months later, the Romans destroyed the Temple as punishment for a Jewish revolt. (pp. 194–95)

"But the time of Jesus is different" (p. 195). But maybe *not* so different. Here is the Josephus text. I'm sure you will spot the striking parallels before I point them out.

> An incident more alarming still had occurred four years before the war at a time of exceptional peace and prosperity for the City. One Jeshua, son of Ananias, a very ordinary yokel, came to the feast at which every Jew is supposed to set up a tabernacle for God. As he stood in the temple he suddenly began to shout: "A voice from the east, a voice from the west, a voice from the four winds, a voice against Jerusalem and the Sanctuary, a voice against bridegrooms and brides, a voice against the whole people." Day and night he uttered this cry as he went through all the streets. Some of the more prominent citizens, very annoyed at these ominous words, laid hold of the fellow and beat him savagely. Without saying a word in his own defence or for the private information of his persecutors, he persisted in shouting the same warning as before. The Jewish authorities, rightly concluding that some supernatural force was responsible for the man's behaviour, took him before the Roman procurator. There, though scourged till his flesh hung in ribbons, he neither begged for mercy nor shed a tear, but lowering his voice to the most mournful of tones, answered every blow with "Woe to Jerusalem!" When Albinus—for that was the procurator's name—demanded to know who he was, where he came from and why he uttered such cries, he made no reply whatever to the questions but endlessly repeated his lament over the City, till Albinus decided he was a madman and released him. (*The Jewish War* VI, 302)[14]

Jesus ben-Ananias comes into Jerusalem for one of the great feasts, just as Jesus does periodically throughout the Gospel of John. Once there, he takes advantage of the huge, milling crowds to take his stand publicly and begin shouting prophecies, again, as the Johannine Jesus does: "On the last day of the feast [of Tabernacles, John 7:2], the great day, Jesus stood up and proclaimed, 'If any one thirst, let him come to me and drink,'" and so on. Jesus ben-Ananias warns of doom "against bridegrooms and brides," just as Jesus does in Luke 17:26–27: "As it was in the days of Noah, so will it be in the days of the Son of man. They ate, they drank, they married, they were given in marriage, until the day when Noah entered the ark, and the flood came and destroyed them all." Both Jesuses were beaten up for prophesying the destruction of the Jerusalem Temple: "And some began to spit on him, and to cover his face, and to strike him, saying to him, 'Prophesy!' And the guards received him with blows" (Mark 14:65). "Aha! You who would destroy the temple and build it in three days!" (Mark 15:29). Both endured their ordeals in stolid silence (Mark 14:61). Each was hauled before the Roman procurator, Pilate in one case, Albinus in the other, and flogged (Matt. 27:26). Each procurator asks his Jesus, "Where are you from?" (John 19:9) "But Jesus gave no answer," neither Jesus. Both men are, sooner or later, killed by Roman soldiers, and each expires with a mournful cry. And eventually, both Jesuses' doom-prophecies on Jerusalem and the Temple are amply fulfilled.

It is this sequence of close parallels that convinces Theodore J. Weeden that the New Testament evangelists used Josephus' account of the Passion of Jesus ben-Ananias as the basis for their stories of Jesus.[15] This has perhaps never occurred to scholars because of their insistence on the earliest feasible dates for the writing of the gospels,[16] and these are the apologists upon whom O'Reilly and Dugard are dependent. Burton L. Mack dismisses the conventional dating of Mark, the earliest gospel.

> Howard Clark Kee . . . does not include Mark's knowledge of the Jewish War as a consideration in determining [the gospel's] provenance. He leaves the impression that the power of the apocalyptic imagination could have created the Gospel of Mark even before the end of the Jewish War and the destruction of the temple. One detects a growing trend in recent scholar-

> ship to agree with this position. The pre-70 C.E. date is convenient, for it (1) supports traditional sensibilities . . . , (2) does not threaten the sense that some modicum of insight or truth may reside in the predictions [of Mark 13] after all, whether made by Jesus or Mark, and (3) keeps the earliest gospel pressed back as far toward the beginning as possible in the hope of closing the gap between Jesus and the stories about him.[17]

Accordingly, it is simply unthinkable for most scholars, much less axe-grinding apologists, to recognize it when they see the influence of the late first-century historian Josephus on the gospels, much less their actual use of Josephus. But it is there.[18] And it is here, in the Passion narratives.

Once again, the back-dating of the events surrounding Jesus ben-Ananias into the career of Jesus Christ is another example of the general gospel tendency to retroject the events of the Jewish War some forty years earlier. More Mack:

> Evidence in support of the seriousness of the times was given with the destruction of the temple. If that could be understood as an act of judgment by God upon an intransigent Israel, the seriousness of the Jewish rejection of Jesus and the kingdom could be imagined. Mark made the connection at the level of social history and its rationalizations. He projected them back upon the time of Jesus by creating a narrative setting of conflict and rejection for the teachings and activities of Jesus. Before Mark, the memories of Jesus had not been given, had not needed, such a setting.[19]

Have Bill O'Reilly and Martin Dugard provided a history of the trials, interrogations, and beatings suffered by Jesus at the hands of Annas and Caiaphas, Herod Antipas, and Pontius Pilate? These names belong to people who did live in the first century. Even Jesus was a historical figure, though it is not clear whether he lived contemporary with these gents or later in the time of Albinus. At any rate, fictional novels of the period abound with the names of famous figures of the day, but that does not anchor the adventures recorded there in the immovable ground of real history. And we must render the same verdict on the novel called *Killing Jesus*.

Chapter Thirteen

CROSS EXAMINED

FORD'S THEATRE, DEALEY PLAZA, AND GOLGOTHA

Finally O'Reilly and Dugard get to the payoff. One can only wonder whom they will "kill" next. My guess would be Dr. Martin Luther King Jr. We'll have to wait and see what the Holy Spirit tells them. Meanwhile, let's examine their inquest on the death of Jesus Christ.

The fictionalizing process continues unabated, as our "historians" feel entitled to deductively dump all their background research into the narrative. What *usually* happened at crucifixions *must* have happened in Jesus' particular case. So it *did* happen. So we learn how many whippersnappers flogged Jesus, something the gospels never bother telling us. Apparently able to gaze back through the millennia like Rudolf Steiner or Edgar Cayce, O'Reilly and Dugard assure us that Jesus "has cried out in pain during his scourging, but he has not vomited or had a seizure, as many do" (p. 243). But, according to their "method," we might have expected our authors to deduce that, if many *did* puke and seize up, then Jesus did, too. Of course, we know he didn't because he's our hero.

O'Reilly and Dugard are happy to retell "the old, old story" of Pilate's troops deriding Jesus as a clown-king. "Jesus does nothing as they drape that filthy purple cloak over his naked body, knowing it will soon stick to his wounds. The soldiers then make a false scepter from a reed and thrust it into Jesus's hands, again mocking his claim of being king" (pp. 243–44). But can we be so sure this happened? Granted, this part is found in the gospels; O'Reilly and Dugard didn't make this one up. But some of us think the story was first told about a different king of the Jews, and with a different set of mockers. Philo of Alexandria describes a bit of street theater by Alexandrian ruffians along the route of the visiting Herod Agrippa I (who also appears in Acts 12), returning through Egypt from Rome, where he had just been officially named king of Judea.

> There was a certain madman named Carabbas . . . , the sport of idle children and wanton youths; and they, driving the poor wretch as far as the public gymnasium, and setting him up there on high that he might be seen by everybody, flattened out a leaf of papyrus and put it on his head instead of a diadem, and clothed the rest of his body with a common door mat instead of a cloak, and instead of a sceptre they put in his hand a small stick of . . . papyrus . . . and when he had been adorned like a king, the young men bearing sticks on their shoulders stood on each side of him instead of spear bearers . . . , and then others came up, some as if to salute him, and others as though they wished to plead their causes before him. . . . Then from the multitude . . . there arose a . . . shout of men calling out "*Maris!*" And this is the name by which it is said that they call the kings among the Syrians; for they knew that Agrippa was by birth a Syrian, and also that he was possessed of a great district of Syria of which he was the sovereign. (*Flaccus*. VI, 36–39)[1]

So here is a man who is actually the king of the Jews being mocked by being depicted as a royal street bum. The main difference is that the Alexandrian hooligans dress up *another* man in order to show their disdain for the Jewish king, whereas the Romans dress up the *real* king, Jesus, as a clown. But the clincher is the name: *Carabbas*. Remind you of anyone? It is as if, in the transmission of the story, the clown-king has been split into two characters (a common phenomenon):[2] one the mock-king (who, however, in the gospels is also the real king) and the other the *surrogate* for the real king, who is executed in his place, Jesus dying on the cross intended for Barabbas.[3] I'd say this particular Jesus story, his mockery as King of the Jews, stopped being history even before O'Reilly and Dugard got to it.

Next we read of Jesus' coronation by the Roman toughs.

> In an atrocious display, they begin to cut a tall white shrub. *Rhamnus nabeca* features rigid elliptical leaves and small green flowers, but its most dominant characteristic is the inch-long curving thorns that sprout

> closely together to form a crown. When they are done, this wreath makes a perfect complement to the reed and the purple cloak All hail the king! (p. 244)

Let's assume for the moment that our authors have identified the right plant, and that it has thorns. It seems more likely, given what Caesar's crown actually looked like, that what the soldiers did was to bend the branch into a circle and fit it onto the back of Jesus' head, where a yarmulke would be or like the pope's white skullcap. The Roman crown was a tiara with spikes radiating out, like Lady Liberty's crown, only hers comes forward from behind her ears to enclose her forehead. The idea was a sort of halo, suggesting the dawning rays of the sun coming up over the horizon. This does not justify the crown of thorns pictured by millennia of maudlin pietism, which informs the narrative of *Killing Jesus* at this point.

> Jesus is too weak to protest when the crown of thorns is fitted onto his head, and the spikes pressed hard into his skin. . . . They brush up against the many nerves surrounding the skull almost immediately and then crash into bone. Blood pours down his face. (p. 244)

All Mark says is, "plaiting a crown of thorns, they put it on him" (Mark 15:17b). That's it. There is no hint that the "crown of thorns" was like some kind of rigid hairnet or helmet, a miniature iron maiden for Jesus' head. There is no suggestion in the text that Jesus was made to look like Pinhead in the *Hellraiser* movies, or that he was masked in flowing blood. This all comes from the gory devotionalism of medieval Catholicism.

But the text may not even mean to depict a crown of thorns at all. The same Greek word, ακανθινον, can just as easily denote "acanthus leaves." This would mean the soldiers mocked up a laurel wreath for Jesus. Sorry if it's not as bloody as you want it to be.

LA DOLCE VITA

Let's have a little Bible knowledge quiz. Which gospel is it that says Jesus shouldered his cross but, weakened as he was by his flogging and beating, staggered beneath the weight of it, and a bystander was yanked from the crowd to carry it the rest of the way for him? Matthew? Mark? Luke? John? All of them? The answer is *none* of them, unless you want to consider *Killing Jesus* a gospel, and maybe you should. The Synoptic Gospels directly conflict with John, and that is not some minor goof or a matter of variant traditions. The fact is that Matthew 27:32, Mark 15:21, and Luke 23:26 all show Jesus unable from square one to hoist that cross and carry it to Golgotha, as can well be imagined. John 19:17 has Jesus carry the cross *the whole way*, with no mention of anyone taking over for him anywhere along the way. Why this difference? It is pretty obvious to anyone not blinded by a desire to have all the gospels agree. The Synoptics quote Jesus as saying, "If any man would come after me, let him deny himself and *take up his cross and follow me*" (Mark 8:34 and parallels). John noticed what no one else had: that, given this saying, it wouldn't look too good if Jesus was not up to taking up *his* own cross! So he changed it. O'Reilly and Dugard, as they often do, follow Church tradition and split the difference. They are building on the sand of spurious harmonization. Building what? More sanguine grue: "Each stumble drives the thorns on his head deeper into his skull" (p. 247). Which gospel says that? Same answer.

"Jesus's vision has blurred" (p. 245). Odd thing: I can't find the word "blurred" in my concordance. Remember the old hymn "Were You There When They Crucified My Lord?"? Apparently, O'Reilly and Dugard were. As for me, when writing history, I'd prefer to stick with Jacob Neusner's rule of thumb: "What we cannot show, we do not know."[4]

NAIL SOME SENSE INTO THEM![5]

Quiz time again. Which gospel's crucifixion account says that Jesus got *nailed* to the cross? Same answer again! None of them. Sometimes people were just *tied* to the cross. It was not intended to be a particularly bloody death; the cross killed its victims through exposure and slow asphyxiation. It took days, or was supposed to. Where do we get the idea that Jesus was nailed to his cross? From one episode in one *resurrection* narrative. You know the one I mean: the story of Doubting Thomas in John 20:24–29. "Unless I see in his hands the print of the nails . . ." It sounds like an afterthought, and it is. This episode is a sequel to John 20:19–23.

> On the evening of that day, the first day of the week, the doors being shut where the disciples were, for fear of the Jews, Jesus came and stood among them and said to them, "Peace be with you." When he had said this, he showed them his hands and his side. Then the disciples were glad when they saw the Lord. Jesus said to them again, "Peace be with you. As the Father has sent me, even so I send you." And when he had said this, he breathed on them, and said to them, "Receive the Holy Spirit. If you forgive the sins of any, they are forgiven; if you retain the sins of any, they are retained."

This is the Johannine version of both Matthew's Great Commission (Matt. 28:18–20: "All authority in heaven and on earth has been given to me. Go therefore and make disciples of all nations, baptizing them in the name of the Father and of the Son and of the Holy Spirit, teaching them to observe all that I have commanded you") as well as the commission of church-legal authority to the disciples (Matt. 18:18: "Truly I say to you, whatever you bind on earth shall be bound in heaven, and whatever you loose on earth shall be loosed in heaven"). Clearly, in John 20:19–23 we are witnessing the equipping and commissioning of the eleven disciples (no Judas) for their subsequent ministry. It is assumed that they are all present for it. And then comes the Doubting Thomas episode, where we read that Tom was out at the time! This is a different story that does not presuppose the scene in

John 20:19–23. It only presupposes the general belief that the other ten had seen the risen Jesus, and not even a particular appearance. The Doubting Thomas story is just like this one told of the miracle worker Apollonius of Tyana.

> The young man in question . . . would on no account allow the immortality of the soul, and said, "I myself, gentlemen, have done nothing now for nine months but pray to Apollonius that he would reveal to me the truth about the soul; but he is so utterly dead that he will not appear to me in response to my entreaties, nor give me any reason to consider him immortal." Such were the young man's words on that occasion, but on the fifth day following, after discussing the same subject, he fell asleep where he was talking with them, and . . . on a sudden, like one possessed, he leaped up, still in a half sleep, streaming with perspiration, and cried out, "I believe thee." And when those who were present asked him what was the matter; "Do you not see," said he, "Apollonius the sage, how that he is present with us and is listening to our discussion, and is reciting wondrous verses about the soul?" "But where is he?" they asked, "For we cannot see him anywhere, although we would rather do so than possess all the blessings of mankind." And the youth replied: "It would seem that he is come to converse with myself alone concerning the tenets which I would not believe." (*Life of Apollonius of Tyana* 8:31)[6]

The purpose of both this story and that of Doubting Thomas is obviously to encourage latter-day readers to have faith even in the absence of sight. Sure, they weren't lucky enough to be there to see the living Savior himself, but really they aren't at a disadvantage. Someone just like them was vouchsafed sufficient assurance, and that ought to be good enough for you, too. "Last of all, as to one untimely born, he appeared also to me" (1 Cor. 15:8). "Without having seen him, you love him; though you do not now see him, you believe in him and rejoice with unutterable and exalted joy" (1 Pet. 1:8). Or at least that's the idea. Of course, the Doubting Thomas story really only pushes the problem back one step instead of solving it; now you have to envy the certainty specially made available to Thomas, because you weren't there for *that*, either, were you?

The evangelist John just did not notice the inconsistency between his two successive episodes. He was concerned only to make two different points. In 20:19–23 his goal was to reinforce the apostolic credentials of the disciples, *including Thomas*, while in 20:24 the point is to use Thomas as a stand-in for the reader who wishes he had been present for a resurrection appearance like that in 20:19–23. Each serves its purpose; the trouble is that they don't fit together very well. And for our purposes, that means the sole reference to Jesus having been nailed to a cross is a secondary addition to the story.

But someone who reads the text more carefully than O'Reilly and Dugard do might point out that John 20:19–23 already implies that Jesus had nail wounds in his hands: "He showed them his hands and his side" (verse 20a). Good point, but this, too, is secondary. The whole episode has been rewritten from its original appearance in Luke 24:36–43.

> And as they were saying this, Jesus himself appeared among them and said to them, "Peace to you." But they were startled and frightened, and supposed that they saw a spirit. And he said to them, "Why are you troubled, and why do questionings rise in your hearts? See my hands and my feet, that it is I myself; handle me, and see; for a spirit has not flesh and bones as you see that I have." And when he had said this, he showed them his hands and his feet. And while they still disbelieved for joy, and wondered, he said to them, "Have you anything here to eat?" They gave him a piece of broiled fish, and he took it and ate it before them.

Notice what has changed from Luke to John. For one thing, Luke lacks the imparting of the Holy Spirit. Perhaps John has taken Luke's reference to "a spirit" and rewritten it. At any rate, Luke has the Spirit imparted to the disciples forty days later, on Pentecost (Acts 2:1–4), so he's not going to include it here. For another, and this is really my point, in Luke Jesus shows his hands *and feet*, not his hands *and side*, as he does in John. Luke's purpose is to show Jesus as physically resurrected, with a substantial body. He is trying to refute a rival belief, present in 1 Corinthians 15:42–50 and 1 Peter 3:9, to the effect that Jesus experienced a purely spiritual resurrection.[7] John takes this for granted but rewrites the scene in order to refute a different belief, namely that Jesus did not really die on the cross but was taken down alive and rescued. The point of changing Luke's reference to Jesus' hands and *feet* to a mention of his hands and *side* is to accentuate Jesus' mortal wound from the spear thrust on the cross: "one of the soldiers pierced his side with a spear, and at once there came out blood and water" (John 19:34). But this, too, is secondary, as you can see from the way it fails to fit the immediate context. Let's back up.

> Since it was the day of Preparation [for the Passover], in order to prevent the bodies from remaining on the cross on the Sabbath (for that Sabbath was a high day), the Jews asked Pilate that their legs might be broken [to hasten death by asphyxiation], and that they might be taken away. So the soldiers came and broke the legs of the first, and of the other who had been crucified with him; but when they came to Jesus and saw that he was already dead, they did not break his legs. But one of the soldiers pierced his side with a spear, and at once there came out blood and water. (John 19:31–34)

Uh, wait a second here. In verse 33 the soldiers observed that Jesus was *already* dead and so did not break his legs. But in the very next verse they decide to *ascertain* that he's dead, which we were just told they already knew. Verses 34–35 are a secondary insertion, as are verses 36–37, "For these things took place that the scripture might be fulfilled, 'Not a bone of him shall be broken.' And again another scripture says, 'They shall look on him whom they have pierced.'"

We can see now that John has added both the spear thrust in 19:34–35 and the post-resurrection reference to it in 20:20. The reference to Jesus' hands is left over unchanged from Luke 24:39–40, where it did not denote nail wounds, only physical materiality, and therefore we cannot be sure John was implying a reference to nail wounds when he retained the Lukan mention of the hands. So was Jesus gruesomely staked to the cross like a vampire? No particular reason to think so, as long as we are trying to reconstruct the history of the matter and not just expanding the gospels, as they stand, into a novel.

CRUCIFIED ON A PSALM

Perhaps the most astonishing aspect of the oldest crucifixion account, Mark's, is that it is essentially just a transposition of Psalm 22. Think back to the list of "prophecies" that O'Reilly and Dugard claim were fulfilled by the life of Jesus. Two of them come from the Twenty-Second Psalm. Psalm 22:16 reads: "Yea, dogs are round about me; a company of evildoers encircle me; they have pierced my hands and feet." Aha, they cry: surely this is a prediction of the crucifixion—at least of somebody. Thousands of poor wretches were crucified at the hands of Phoenicians (who invented the bloody game) and Romans after them. But it isn't even clear that this psalm refers to any of them. Notice the context: this man's enemies are closing in on him in some unspecified manner, and the psalmist metaphorically calls them wild dogs who growl and snap at him. But there is not a hint of his being nailed to a cross. Wouldn't we have to infer that his hands and feet are getting bitten and wounded as he tries to bat and kick the bloodthirsty hounds away? At least animals are mentioned; crosses are not, and it seems far-fetched to read crucifixion into the scene—unless one is heaven-bent on *making* this a prophecy of Jesus. And this is exactly what O'Reilly and Dugard, following their childhood catechism instructors, are doing.

The other verse from the same psalm reads: "They divide my garments [in the psalm this is synecdoche for "possessions"] among them, and for my raiment they cast lots" (Ps. 22:18). The psalmist's enemies (or those of the client for whom he sings) have so thoroughly triumphed over him, or think they have, that they regard him as being as good as dead—so who gets what? "*He* ain't gonna be needing 'em anymore!" The whole form of the psalm as a "one size fits all" composition presupposes that the predicament is common enough. Think of poor Scrooge secretly watching the laundress, the undertaker, and the charwoman selling off his possessions after finding his corpse one morning. It is not some rare and astonishing thing that must one day transpire as an unprecedented event. That is just absurd, and whoever says otherwise lacks any historical or literary sense. That is a severe judgment, but it must be made.

O'Reilly and Dugard are thinking, as you know, of Mark's crucifixion scene, where it says the Roman soldiers threw dice to determine who would get Jesus' Ferrari, his iPhone, and his sunglasses. Of course Jesus was an itinerate mendicant who lacked even a piece of floor to lay his head on at night (Matt. 8:20) and would have had no possessions to divide.[8] So the application of Psalm 22:18 at this point is not even apt.

It is striking that Mark 15's crucifixion account parallels Psalm 22 at other points as well, not least of which is the cry of Jesus from the cross: "My God, my God, why have you forsaken me?" (Mark 15:34; Ps. 22:1). Also, when Mark 15:29 says Jesus' hecklers "wagged their heads" and hurled insults at him, this reflects Psalm 22:7–8: "All who see me mock at me, they make mouths at me, they wag their heads; 'He committed his cause to the Lord; let him deliver him, let him rescue him, for he delights in him.'") This is another one of those lament psalms, not a prophecy or prediction or prognostication in any way.

And this is the most interesting part: Mark never says that it *is*. There are a number of places in the gospels where an event in Jesus' life is said to be a fulfillment of Old Testament prophecy (Mark 1:2, 7:6, 14:27; Matt. 1:22–23, 2:5–6, 15, 17–18, 23, 3:3, 4:13–16, 12:17–21, 13:14–15, 13:35–36, 21:4), but, strikingly, none of the parallels to Psalm 22 in Mark's crucifixion account are said to be fulfillments of scripture. What this suggests is that Mark was not trying to draw attention to Psalm 22 but was using it as a template upon which to construct his story of the cross. He had neither any earlier version to draw upon nor any memories from anyone who may have seen the crucifixion. *Did anyone see it? Did it even happen?*

The other gospels appear to be stricter or looser rewrites of Mark's version. Where they add to it, most of the new material also seems to be derived from scripture, not memory. For instance, Matthew 27:43 adds more mockery from the priests, scribes, and elders: "He trusts in God; let God deliver him now, if he desires him; for he said, 'I am the Son of God.'" Matthew plainly derived these words from the Wisdom of Solomon 2:12–20 (which he obviously had to condense):

> But let us lie in wait for the righteous man, because he makes it hard for us, and opposes our works, and upbraids us for sins against the law, and accuses us of sins against our training. He professes to have knowledge of God, and calls himself the servant of the Lord. He became to us a living reproof of our thoughts. He is grievous for us even to behold because his life is unlike that of other men, and his ways are alien to us. He disdains us as base metal, and he avoids our ways as unclean. The final end of the righteous he calls happy, and he claims that God is his father. Let us see if his words are true, and let us see what will happen at the end of his life! For if the righteous man is God's son, he will uphold him, and he will rescue him from the grasp of his adversaries. With outrage and torture let us put him to the test, that we may see for ourselves his gentleness and prove his patience under injustice. Let us condemn him to a shameful death; for surely God shall intervene as this fellow said he would!

First Peter 2:21–23 speaks of the interrogation of Jesus, but everything he says is derived, again, from scripture, Isaiah 53:9, 12. What, no memory of the "event"? One wonders if even this crucial episode might have been derived, in whole or in part, from contemporary stories about other well-known figures, such as Cleomenes, a radical Spartan king who was deposed and exiled for his land-reform policies and was finally crucified (already dead, having killed himself in anticipation of arrest) by the Alexandrian authorities.

> And a few days afterwards those who were keeping watch on the body of Cleomenes where it hung, saw a serpent of great size coiling itself about the head and hiding away the face so that no ravening bird of prey could light upon it. In consequence of this, the king was seized with superstitious fear, and thus gave the women occasion for various rites of purification, since they felt that a man had been taken off who was of a superior nature and beloved of the gods. And the Alexandrians actually worshipped him, coming frequently to the spot and addressing Cleomenes as a hero and a child of the gods. (Plutarch, *Agis and Cleomenes*, XXXIX)[9]

Note the parallels with the gospels. A miraculous portent accompanies the crucifixion of the king. Here it is a snake protecting the face of Cleomenes from the ravages of carrion birds. Mark, of course, has the darkness at noon (15:33) plus the ripping of the Temple curtain (15:38), while Matthew 27:51–53 adds an earthquake for good measure. The onlookers, duly impressed, declare the dead man a son of God, as in Mark: "And when the centurion, who stood facing him, saw that he thus breathed his last, he said, 'Truly, this man was a son of God!'" (Mark 15:39).

DEAD END

Who anointed the body of Jesus with scented unguents? According to John, it was Jesus' secret admirers Joseph of Arimathea and Nicodemus, but in the Synoptics, it was Mary Magdalene and her associates who intended to do the job, though their discovery of the empty tomb made their plans moot. These accounts cannot be harmoniously combined, since in Mark we read that the women attentively observed Jesus' burial by Joseph (who, however, does nothing but deposit the corpse in the tomb), and they resolve to return the morning after the Sabbath to do the anointing themselves. Had Joseph, with his twin Nicodemus, anointed the body with the extravagant amount of unguent John says they brought (John 19:39–40), and the women watched the interment (which Mark says, not John), they surely would have seen that the anointing of the dead had been accomplished, obviating any need for their return. And, sure enough, in John, the women do return to the tomb but not to do the anointing. O'Reilly and Dugard try to harmonize the contradiction.[10] They tell us that their intra-narrative counterparts Nicodemus and Joseph did not have time, with the Sabbath beginning so soon, to anoint the body for burial, so all they could do was to pack it in a hundred pounds of spices to prevent the onset of decay-reek (p. 254). But, fellas, that *is* to anoint the body for burial. They pretend it isn't so they can have Mary Magdalene and the others arrive Sunday morning to *really* anoint the body (p. 259). Absurd.

O'Reilly and Dugard go back to the Akashic Records for another bucketful of fiction unhinted at in the historical sources:

> Pilate is relieved. Soon he will be on his way back to Caesarea, there once again to govern without the constant interference of the Temple priests. But Caiaphas will not go away. Wearing expensive robes and linen, he postures before Pilate, not knowing how the Roman governor will report back to Rome. Caiaphas has much at stake, and he is uneasy over Pilate's hand-washing display, which makes it clear that the governor is trying to distance himself from this proceeding. He will lose everything if Emperor Tiberius blames him for the death of Jesus. So Caiaphas stands firm, looking for any sign of approval from Pilate. But the Roman governor has had enough of this arrogant priest. Without a word, he stands and walks away. (p. 257)

We can imagine such a scene taking place, but that's all. And that's all O'Reilly and Dugard are doing: imagining. The problem is, they are shamelessly passing it, and so much else, off as history.

One of the wildest embellishments Matthew made to Mark is his posting of Roman guards at Jesus' tomb. This he did in order to co-opt and refute a contemporary rumor that, if Jesus' tomb was, as Christians say, found empty, it was because Jesus' followers absconded with his corpse in order to mount a resurrection hoax (Matt. 27:62–66). Matthew goes the detractors one better by saying, "Yeah? Well, did you know Pilate posted guards to *prevent* a stunt like that? And that Jesus rose anyway? Huh? Then why didn't they ever *say* anything about it? Um . . . , er, because those rotten high priests paid them to keep mum about it! Yeah, *that's* the ticket!" (Matt. 28:1–4). This is fiction pure and simple. You mean, if this happened, Mark, Luke, and John would somehow have neglected to mention it? Not a chance. The whole thing goes in the same X-file along with Matthew's moving star, his double demoniacs, and his "Night of the Living Dead" cameo in Matthew 27:52–53. O'Reilly and Dugard seem to understand that they cannot even maintain their pretense of impartial history writing if they include this episode, but they do borrow a detail from it. They have one single guard posted to prevent the mischievous theft of the body. When the women get to the tomb in the *Killing Jesus* version, not only the corpse of Jesus is gone but the Roman soldier is, too! Now what do you suppose could have happened to him?

PLAYING IT CUTE

To understand what O'Reilly and Dugard are really doing as they end their book, oh so impartially and objectively, we have to step back into the eighteenth century and look at the state of religious debate in those days. This was a time when many, even theologians, were much impressed with the Newtonian model of the universe. They viewed the cosmos as a gigantic mechanical system set in place by the Creator to purr along smoothly and efficiently on its own steam under the regime of natural laws. Many religious believers hailed this conception as proof that the world was the work of a Designer. But there was a pretty stiff price to pay. They could not consistently believe in miracles anymore. If God had planned everything adequately (and how could he not?), then it would be both blasphemous and superstitious to picture him suspending or violating the very laws of nature that he had put in place. This led to the Protestant Rationalist approach to the Bible.

Rationalist Protestants had inherited the old belief in the complete historical reliability of scripture, only they could no longer appeal to the traditional basis for it, divine inspiration. That, of course, would be a miracle, a divine intervention into the normal process of literary composition. They were not ready to go the whole way with the emerging Higher Criticism and admit that the Bible was filled with legend, myth, and contradictory accounts. So here's what they had to do. They posited (because it was the only thing they could think of) that the narratives of the Bible had been written by eyewitnesses. The accuracy of the stories was not guaranteed by divine inspiration (a matter of sheer faith anyway), but if the writers were on the scene, their reporting could be trusted. But the biblical "reporters" were ancient people, not modern. They had no knowledge of science. Therefore, when they beheld strange and astounding events, they could not surmise the actual causation involved, so, as men of their time, they jumped to the only conclusion available to them: a miracle had occurred. The Protestant Rationalists exercised considerable creativity in suggesting the "real" causal links that *must* have been in play.

This is where we get what has now become a joke, that Jesus did not walk on the waves but only knew where the stepping stones were.

David Friedrich Strauss delighted in exposing the strained, implausible, and downright incredible character of these explanations.[11] Strauss made a breakthrough when he suggested that the traditionally orthodox Protestants were right in insisting that the miracle stories made no sense without supernaturalism, but they were wrong in taking them as sober history. Instead, they were myths and legends. The story of the resurrection of Jesus must be understood as the story of a divine miracle of a dead man being restored to life, and therefore as a legend. The Rationalists were as little prepared to accept this as the orthodox were. What *did* the Rationalists make of the resurrection?

They believed that Jesus had not perished on the cross but had merely passed out. He was revived by his friends Joseph and Nicodemus (as well as whoever the "men" or angels at the tomb were, probably Essenes). The spices and unguents were really medicines. It was a question of how to connect the dots: Jesus was crucified and Jesus appeared alive a few days later. The Rationalists could not bring themselves to discount either "report." They could not erase either of the dots. So how to connect them? Not by a miracle; there weren't any miracles. So the connection must be that Jesus did not die between point A and point B. Nor was he resurrected. He cheated death and appeared still alive.

If Strauss battled both the Rationalists and the orthodox, they did not neglect to battle one another. The orthodox argued against the Rationalists' contrived explanations of what the orthodox still believed were miracles. If they could knock down all the silly rationalizations proposed by their opponents, then, by default, the traditional miraculous explanation would be vindicated. They were wrong, of course; they were committing the fallacy known as Affirming the Consequent: Even if you do debunk my explanation, that doesn't mean yours is automatically correct. There may be yet a third alternative that neither of us has thought of or that we both find unpalatable (such as Strauss's).

It is seldom noticed how, in all of today's debates on the resurrection of Jesus, like the one between William Lane Craig and John Dominic Crossan, recommended by O'Reilly and Dugard (p. 279), the conservative apologists continue to argue as if their opponents were the old Rationalist Protestants. The apologists tacitly take for granted that all the gospel scenes leading up to the empty tomb are accurate reporting. Who would deny that Joseph of Arimathea requested, then buried, the body of Jesus, that the women visited the tomb and found it empty, and that the disciples experienced visitations from the risen Jesus? We're all agreed on that, right? Then how best to connect the dots? Apologists proceed to (try to) knock down all possible non-supernatural explanations: the Wrong Tomb Theory, the Hallucination Theory, the Swoon Theory, the Stolen Body Theory, and so on. What's left? Why, Jesus must have risen miraculously from the dead!

Not surprisingly, no one seems to have read Strauss.[12] It does not occur to apologists, as it never did to the Rationalists, that the gospel Passion narratives are designed to prepare the way for the miraculous resurrection. They are not open-ended, a bald-faced collection of facts, as O'Reilly and Dugard seem to think. They are like the cocked wheel on the supermarket cart, subtly steering you in the "right" direction. The Passion narratives are following the trajectory of a particular plot. The trials, the beatings, the spitting and mocking, are all part of the darkness before the dawn of the resurrection. No wonder the reader who takes them literally finds himself ineluctably drawn to a particular conclusion, just like the reader of a detective novel does. And that is pretty much what *Killing Jesus* is. When you get to the final sentence, "To this day the body of Jesus of Nazareth has never been found" (p. 259), you get the message. And it is a religious message, not a historical one.

* * *

There is no chapter in *Killing Jesus* recounting the resurrection, though none is really needed, given what I have just said. Let me suggest that, if O'Reilly and Dugard had elected to cover the resurrection in the same moment-by-moment pseudo-documentary style they employed in the preceding chapters, the result would be comical, just as the contrived miracle-explanations of the old-time Rationalists are. It would rightly look fully as preposterous as it would had they decided to include the moving of the Wise Men's star from Jerusalem to Bethlehem, and for the same reason. To make my point, I have supplied what O'Reilly and Dugard omitted: a chapter on the resurrection.

The Missing Chapter

RAISING JESUS

The alarm goes off precisely on schedule, awakening the Nazarene from his three-day nap. The rude sound of "clock-crow" helps shock his sluggish blood back into circulation. For that he is grateful. He sits up, swings his tingling legs off the rock shelf and onto the cold stone floor. The impact does not reopen the cruel wounds in his nail-pierced feet. The holes in his extremities have already begun to heal over. He hopes they do not heal *too* fast, because he has that appointment with Doubting Thomas later in the day.

There will be no time to relax; he has so many resurrection appearances scheduled, but he doesn't mind. After three days of being dead, he can use a little activity.

Jesus begins to grow impatient. Where is that angel? He is overdue, and it is getting pretty chilly inside the tomb. He guesses Gabriel has been intercepted by Satan or one of his bat-winged henchmen. Still, they shouldn't be able to give him much trouble. They never have before.

And, sure enough, there's the knock. Must be tough on the knuckles. If an angel can even feel pain.

The rapping on the stone is immediately followed by the rasping and grinding of the huge millstone as Gabriel shoulders it aside. Jesus' enemies thought to confine him here forever. Too bad, Jesus thinks, that they aren't here to see this. He'd love to see their faces.

Gabriel helps him out into the dawning sunlight, careful not to let Jesus bruise his feet on any stones. They exchange polite chitchat. Gabriel tells him the emperor has told his propaganda minister, Carnius, to put the word about that Jesus' followers have stolen his body as part of a hoax. The Nazarene chuckles at this; does anyone believe a thing that man says anymore?

Jesus waves a quick good-bye as the angel spreads his shining wings and launches skyward. Jesus wishes he had wings, too, because he desperately wants to be out of here and on his way to Galilee and, simultaneously, to Jerusalem, before those dizzy dames get here. How tired he is of the claustrophobic attentions of Mary Magdalene, Mary of Bethany, Mary the wife of Clopas, and Mary the sister-in-law of Mary the mother of Mary, and the rest. A guy needs a break sometimes, and three days was not enough of one.

He clocks out and nods to the young man dressed in a white sheet who shows up to take the next shift. Isn't he an Essene or something?

Jesus has no sooner rounded the corner of a boulder when he hears the incessant yakking of the girls, fumbling with their Avon baskets of various ointments and perfumes they had planned to smear on his lifeless body. He knows it's just an excuse to get their hands all over him at last. Their clucking gossip is suddenly cut off as they see the young man, who is trying to keep the morning breezes from blowing his sheet up over his crotch. "When is somebody going to invent some underwear?" the fellow thinks.

The last thing Jesus hears as he tries to increase the distance between himself and his disappointed fans is something about telling Peter and the rest to go meet him in Galilee. No address. Good hunting, fellas. And Jesus realizes he'd better get a move on if he's going to get there ahead of them.

But it's not going to be that easy, it turns out, because here come the women, Mary, Mary, Mary, and Mary. They must have picked up his scent. He rolls his eyes skyward as they drop to the ground and start clasping his knees. His joints are still stiff, so their embrace hurts. What, are they trying to tackle him?

"Good to see you, too, ladies. You know, I'd like to stay and do a few parables, but I have to get to Galilee before lunch. You be sure to tell Peter and the others to meet me there, okay?" And with that, he manages to pull himself free and get underway again. But he has a sneaking suspicion that Peter's not going to be getting any messages today. The girls are more than likely headed for the Magdalene's beauty parlor.

The sun is rising higher and higher in the azure sky, making Jesus sweat as his bare feet slap the well-worn road north. So many have traveled it, to and from Jerusalem three times a year for the feasts, that the surface has become hard-packed. Almost like the brick pavement of the Appian Way, which Caesar had built long ago using unionized stonemasons and burly legionnaries who were supposed to be on furlough but were called back for the occasion. Even now, Tiberius, fresh out of his favorite orgy chamber, is probably urinating on the surface of that very road. And he's no doubt thinking to himself, "I'd rather screw Herod's pig than Herod's son." You know those Romans. They've all watched that movie *Caligula* too many times.

Jesus reflects on the fact that Tiberius must have been named for the River Tiber in Rome and that things have come full circle since there's now a body of water named after him, the Lake of Tiberias, otherwise known as the Sea of Galilee, though it's not really a sea, more of a lake, but the peasants of Galilee like to make everything sound grander than it is. That's why Jesus, when he was a boy, was so surprised the first time his parents took him swimming there, because he expected it to be a lot bigger. But it was Mary and Joseph's turn to be surprised when young Jesus built a scale-model sandcastle in the precise image of Herod's Temple.

These are the exact thoughts that occupy Jesus as he makes the long trek. He never tells anyone this, but we can be pretty sure this is what he is thinking about.

That is, until he overtakes a pair of glum-looking men who must have set out even earlier than he did. Probably weren't waylaid by a bunch of admiring groupies. As he gets closer, Jesus knows he's seen them somewhere before. And then it hits him. These are a couple of his disciples named, let's see, Cleophas and Ralph. He met them backstage a couple of times when they asked him to autograph their livestock.

Jesus claps Cleophas on the shoulder and says a hearty "Shalom," but the man only mumbles something in reply. Ralph says nothing at all and barely manages to suppress a sob.

"What's the trouble, fellows? Was Pita Hut closed for breakfast or something?" Jesus thinks it a good joke, since Cleophas is wearing a checkered burnoose that looks a lot like one of the tablecloths from Pita Hut. But nobody laughs.

Cleophas wipes a tear away with the corner of the tablecloth, then says, "What, are you the only visitor to Jerusalem unaware of what happened there during the festival?"

"I guess I am. Fill me in?" Jesus is eager to hear what they think happened. He knows he may not recognize it, given the way every report he hears about himself is so wildly distorted overnight.

"We hoped Jesus of Nazareth might be the promised liberator of Israel, but I guess we kind of jumped the gun. First there was that big anointing scandal. Then he got arrested and crucified. And then this weird rumor started spreading like wildfire through the nail salons. Some of our women claimed they found his tomb empty, and a young man or an angel or maybe two men, or possibly two angels, or was it Jesus himself who met them? Or come to think of it, maybe it was John the Baptist or Moses or Aaron, or Mahalalel or one of the kangaroos Noah had on the ark. Or was it . . ."

"I get the picture already," Jesus assures them. "Hey, Dumb and Dumber. Were you guys absent the day they explained that the Messiah had to suffer a whole lot, let's say, at least six whole hours, which, come to think of it, I guess isn't all *that* bad when you compare it to . . . , uh, where was I? Oh yea and verily. He had to suffer all that stuff before he could enter into his glory. *Comprende?*" And with that he proceeds to pluck a long list of scripture verses out of context and claim they predicted these things.

Finally, Cleophas, hoping to change the subject, says, "Hey, behold! There's another Pita Hut, and this one's open for business! After that lecture, I bet you wanna wet your whistle, huh?"

"Sure, why not?"

Soon they are busily munching, and Jesus excuses himself to hit the bathroom. He doesn't come back. He has slipped out the back way, because he's due on some mountain in Galilee, and he's about to be late. And he hates good-byes, especially when he's eager to get away.

And Ralph says to Cleophas, "Didn't our hearts burn with reflux as he twisted the scriptures on the road?" So after they leave the tip, they get up and start retracing their steps for Jerusalem, not on purpose, though. They turn the wrong way out of the parking lot and keep going until things start to look a little too familiar.

Jesus just makes it to the tallest mountain of Galilee. He is tired from all his power-walking and decides to take the ski lift to the top. The disciples are already there, waiting for they know not what. They are plenty surprised to see him, you bet. As he prepares to address them, Jesus realizes he doesn't really have much to say and wonders why he didn't just phone it in. But he's here now, so . . .

"All power in heaven and on earth has been given to me, and I thought about using it to end war and to put a stop to disease and famine, that sort of thing. But then I thought, no, it would do more good to start a new religion. So I am sending you out to all the nations to spread the word and baptize new members, forgetting everything I said and substituting some abstract theology instead, doesn't much matter *what*, since nobody's ever going to be able to understand it anyway. And don't forget to take offerings. Look at the time, will you? I'd like to tell you that I shall be with you, even unto the consummation of the age. But the fact is I've got to run. Good luck to you."

As Jesus heads for the lift again, one of the disciples, possibly Judas not Iscariot, or was it Andrew not Goliath, or Bartholomew of the hundred hats, asks him, "Lord, if you want us to spread the gospel throughout the earth, how about creating some modern transportation? An airplane maybe? A scooter?"

"Sorry, no time," Jesus replies.

For the risen Jesus is a truly busy man having a busy day. He begins the long trek back to Jerusalem. Once there, he locates the Upper Room where he had so recently hosted his Last Supper (well, *next* to last, unless you count the stop at Pita Hut as the Last Lunch). He pops into the room so quickly those inside think he has appeared out of thin air. He's pretty good at that and used to take his parents by surprise in their bedroom when he was a mischievous lad.

The faces are familiar: it's the twelve disciples minus that rat bastard Judas.

"Hey, didn't I just leave you guys?"

The disciples gasp with shock, unable at first to believe their Master has returned to them alive.

"Uh, how short a memory do you guys *have*? Didn't we just play this scene up in Galilee? Remember? The mountain? Well, more like a hill, really . . .

"I guess you must not remember this, either? I'm sending you eleven out to forgive sins, but if you want to retain them, I guess that's up to you. Selling indulgences might not be a bad idea, either. . . . Say, I didn't have much of a lunch . . . got anything here to eat?"

"Just Communion wafers. I know it's not much," answers Peter, hastily wiping chocolate from around his mouth.

"What are you doing with *those*? I mean, I forgot to institute the Sacrament in this version. Look, I gotta have something more substantial. I'm going to find a supermarket, not Piggly Wiggly, though, and grab a can of kosher tuna. Back in a few."

Jesus is not gone five minutes before Thomas enters the room carrying a stack of pizza boxes. No pepperoni or pork sausage, you can count on that. The others joyously exclaim, "We have seen the Lord!"

"Yeah, right," Thomas says. "I remember one day when it was raining, Matthew climbed up on the roof and yelled through that gap in the thatch that he was Jehovah and told me to start building an ark. I still don't know what to do with all those animals I collected."

"No, this is for real!" Simon Zelotes insists.

Thomas shakes his head. He got stuck going all the way to Rome to pick up the pizzas because he lost a bet. Not twice in a single day. "Sorry, guys, but unless I see him with my own eyes and put my finger into his nail prints and stick my hand into his side wound, I'm not buying it. Well, I guess seeing him might be enough. The rest of it sounds kind of disgusting . . ."

At this point Jesus returns. "Tom? You just getting here? I was sure I saw you a little while ago, with the rest of them. I'd have waited till you got back . . ."

"No, Lord," Thomas reassures his Master. "Remember, I'm a twin. You were seeing my brother Mort." At this Mort gives a sheepish wave.

But Jesus has to be on his way again. Miles to go before he ascends. Back up to Galilee. He thinks to himself: "This sure could have been better organized." Once out of the Holy City, he heads for familiar stomping grounds, the shores of the Sea of Galilee, getting there a bit late because the signs had been changed to read "This way to the Lake of Tiberias," and he'd forgotten they were the same thing.

Despite Jesus' fast pace this first day back in the land of the living, time seems to be dragging by, because the Nazarene sees by the position of the sun that somehow it's still early morning. And out a little way from shore he spots a boat with a few fishermen toiling away, wearily dropping empty nets back into the water.

"Ho there, lads! Any luck?"

"Not a minnow," one of them shouts back. "Don't rub it in."

"I think your luck's about to change," Jesus replies. And at once a huge variety of sea creatures—barracudas, flounders, porpoises, octopi, sharks, sperm whales, and coelacanths—explode from the churning waters and flop into the boat, smashing and sinking it. One or two of the less important disciples, like Lebbaeus and Thaddeus, who occur only in a few manuscripts, are swiftly gobbled up by the sharks, but the rest of them manage to hang on to broken boards from the prow of the boat and swim ashore. The disciple whom Jesus loved says to the disciple whom Jesus only liked okay, "It is the Lord!"

When they reach the shore and find Jesus unwrapping some fish sandwiches he has picked up at the nearby McDothan's, they are speechless with astonishment.

Jesus cannot hide his irritation. "How many times do we have to go through this? It's me, Jesus, and, yes, I am risen from the dead. Get used to it."

And when they have finished their breakfast and put away the left-over packets of tartar sauce, Jesus picks a flower and says to Peter, "Simon, do you love me more than these clowns?" When Peter answers, "Sure, Lord; you know damn well I love you," Jesus plucks one petal and drops it to the ground. Then he repeats the question, "Simon, do you love me?" And Peter, wondering what he's getting at, and why he's calling him Simon instead of Peter, says with a note of impatience, "I told you, Lord, I love you. Don't make me say it again. The guys are looking at me kinda funny, if you know what I mean." But Jesus asks him the third time, his fingers ready to pluck another petal, "Simon, how about it, are you sure you love me?" Looking sheepishly around at the others, who are now openly snickering, Peter replies, "Yes, yeah, sure, 'I love you,' okay?" And Jesus says to him, "Then go start a group called Promise-Keepers and print up embarrassing bumper stickers that say 'Real Men Love Jesus.'"

And Peter, red-faced, turns and notices the disciple whom Jesus loved following them, perhaps becoming a little jealous, and Peter asks, "Lord, what about *him*?" And Jesus rebukes him, saying, "If it is my will that he start a Christian dating service, what is that to you? You follow me."

Peter then asks, "Where, Lord?"

And Jesus replies, "Back to Jerusalem, of course. That's where the launch pad is, stupid."

A few hours later, back on the Mount of Olives, Jesus begins the countdown and bids farewell to the disciples, who are, frankly, by now just as happy to see him go, though they don't tell him that, but we know what they were thinking nonetheless.

Jesus begins to feel that rising elevator sensation and notices that his feet are no longer touching the ground, which he welcomes, as his feet ache from all that walking. The ground falls away farther and farther beneath him, and the figures of his disciples shrink until they appear to be no larger than the clay sparrows he made and brought to life that time when he was a kid.

As Jesus rises ever higher, he can see the setting sun's light turning the golden pinnacle of the Temple bright as a beacon. As he rises still higher, he can see his parents' house in Nazareth.

From his lofty perch he can now see for the first time that the walls of a rock garden in Capernaum spell out "Antipas sucks."

The atmosphere is getting increasingly rarified, and Jesus wonders if he will be able to breathe soon or even need to.

There are no more birds swerving aside to avoid him.

The Nazarene passes through the blue haze of the sky as if penetrating the top of a circus tent. It is not long before he is marveling at the incredible brightness of the stars unsheathed by the vanished atmosphere. The moon comes into view, and Jesus is startled at the sight of all the craters marring its surface. He knew it had looked kind of splotchy, but he's always thought those spots were oceans. Guess not.

After a while Jesus begins to black out. He knows what it feels like to die and briefly wonders if he is dying again. But when he awakens he will be told that God had placed him in suspended animation for the long, long journey, for the distance from Earth to heaven is much vaster than he had been led to believe.

Space was very cold, though not unendurable. But now he feels the comforting warmth of the Divine Presence. He looks down to see golden cobbles beneath his feet, which no longer show any signs of violation by a Roman spike.

A crowd gathers around him, seemingly from out of nowhere. All wear robes made of cloth of platinum, glistening with celestial fire as the nimbus of their halos reflects from the shimmering folds. And they are wearing blue-and-white paper name tags. One says "Hello, my name is Adam," another "Noah," a third "Jonah." He is surprised at the foreign sound of some of the names, as well as the exotic features of their bearers: "Gautama," "Socrates," "Aesop."

Like long-lost relatives they embrace him, shake hands, pat him on the back, until the crowd spontaneously parts like the Red Sea did before Moses (who is also there). And the multitude opens like a curtain to reveal to Jesus the mighty form of his Heavenly Father.

Jehovah is an old deity. In days past he has fought Chaos dragons; mandated genocide; commanded the construction, then the destruction, of temples as the whim took him; exiled his people, then rescued them.

And now he has had the busiest of days, with a couple of hurricanes to whip up, a plague to start in China, and several wars to escalate. He kept an eye on a supernova and jump-started a quasar. He decided not to allow life to evolve on Mars. Too much trouble here on earth, so why bother with another risky investment? But the biggest chore was the prayers—all those prayers! As soon as you get through them all, there are always more waiting. But now the Prodigal is home, and the Almighty can put all his headaches on the shelf for the moment.

And Jehovah says to the Nazarene, his woolly-bearded face beaming, "I'm delighted to see you again, my boy. Don't you recognize me? Well, I'm sure it'll start coming back to you. Hey, I could sure use your help answering some of these prayers."

Appendix One

WHEN WERE THE GOSPELS WRITTEN?

If we want to know anything about the dates of the gospels, we are going to have to say good-bye to the rumors circulating among Christian bishops in the second century and look instead at the internal evidence. What can we deduce from what these four texts actually say?

The Gospel of Mark is usually dated at around 70 CE. Some even place it as early as 40 CE. As far as I, your humble correspondent, am concerned, this is wishful thinking pure and simple, motivated by nothing other than apologetics. Those who prefer these dates are just trying to shrink the distance in time between Jesus and the gospels, as if that would make them historically accurate. Even the commonly held notion of a process of oral tradition connecting the historical Jesus to the written gospels may be principally an apologetical device aimed at dragging the gospels' contents back to a historical Jesus. The alternative is to recognize the largely literary, that is, fictive, character of the gospels.

The most important indicator of Mark's date of writing is the way(s) he deals with the delay of the Parousia, the second advent of Jesus. Mark presupposes the same crisis that actuated John 21:20–23 and 2 Peter 3:3–4, the death of the first generation of the disciples. Mark contains what appears to be an earlier document, which Timothée Colani dubbed "the Little Apocalypse"[1] (Mark chap. 13), just as the Book of Revelation appears to have assimilated an earlier apocalypse, the "little scroll" into Revelation chapter 11. The Little Apocalypse is usually thought to date from around 70 CE, as it is thought to reflect the events of the fall of Jerusalem. But Hermann Detering has shown that the Little Apocalypse more likely refers to the Roman recapture of Jerusalem at the end of the bar-Kokhba revolt in 136 CE.[2] While it is possible that, as Colani thought, this document was subsequently interpolated into Mark, it seems far more likely that it is earlier because other passages in Mark seem to presuppose it. If this is true, then obviously, Mark gets catapulted into the second century, not very long before Irenaeus mentions it.

The Little Apocalypse sets a deadline for the imminent end of the world: "I tell you truly, this generation shall not pass away before these things come to pass" (Mark 13:30). But nothing happened. That generation passed into history, and history went on. This was quite the embarrassment, just as it was to the authors of John chapter 21 and 2 Peter chapter 3 (not the actual apostle Peter, as the complex Greek and many other considerations demonstrate). The backpedaling commenced. The first strategy, when some few oldsters remained, was to restrict the scope of this promise, so that now it was only "some standing here" who "will not taste death until they see the kingdom of God coming with power" (Mark 9:1). But then it became too late for that: the whole generation passed away ("the fathers fell asleep" as 2 Peter 3:3 puts it).

Next, someone went back and added to the text of Mark 13 a condition for the Parousia coming: world evangelization (Mark 13:10). Presumably, if Christians failed to accomplish this assignment, the Parousia could be delayed. And so it happened. But eventually, some decided that the evangelistic penetration of the Roman Empire was sufficient to satisfy that condition (Col. 1:6).

So next Jesus was made to disavow the very knowledge he professed to reveal in Mark 13:30. As soon as Jesus has given the deadline of the contemporary generation, he is made to correct himself: "But of that day or that hour no one knows, not even the angels in heaven, nor the Son, but only the Father" (and note the late, theological sound of "the Son").

And then someone sought to defuse the embarrassment of the Mark

9:1 promise that at least "some" of that "greatest generation" would endure to the end. The passage was too well-known to simply omit, so it was reinterpreted, making it seem to refer to something *else* that *did* transpire back in that generation. How about the Transfiguration? But if the prediction referred to something that happened back then, there is a new problem: why didn't *everybody*, at least all of the disciples, see it? Well, Jesus must have chosen an inner circle of just three disciples to see it, for some reason excluding the other nine. So "some" of those standing there with Jesus in 9:1, but not all, saw the "predicted" Transfiguration, as if this were a plausible fulfillment of a prediction of the coming of the kingdom of God. It is, as harmonizations usually are, very strained.

For people to come to recognize there is a problem with the Parousia being long overdue means they have been waiting and hoping so long that they can no longer tell themselves it still might happen on schedule. Therefore, the rewrites and reinterpretations we have charted in Mark function like tree rings, each one marking a delay of many years. There is no way such a document can have been written by 70 CE, even if Detering is wrong about the 136 date for the Little Apocalypse.

Matthew has used Mark, so scholars tend to allow a decade between Mark and Matthew. But we may have to allow more time than this simply because of evidence of stratification not only in the new portions of Matthew but also even in those rewritten from Mark (or from Q). Matthew based the Sermon on the Mount on the Q sermon from which Luke's Sermon on the Plain also derives. Within the Sermon on the Mount, Matthew has grouped sayings topically. For example, the section about the piety of the hypocrites (6:1–18) falls neatly into segments about almsgiving, prayer, and fasting. They look balanced and symmetrical, but suddenly we find that someone has interrupted the flow, adding into the prayer section the Lord's Prayer and a comment about forgiveness (vv. 9–15). This is a sign of another layer being added to an earlier draft of Matthew. Likewise, Matthew based his mission charge on Mark 6:8–11, but he added his "not-so-great commission," restricting evangelism only to Jews and excluding Samaritans and Gentiles, in 10:5. But someone has superseded this, adding the Great Commission in chapter 28.

And, as Arlo J. Nau shows, the treatment of Peter in Matthew's Gospel presupposes at least two stages on the path between Mark and our canonical Matthew.[3] Mark had been pretty hard on the twelve disciples, apparently reflecting that evangelist's distaste for the Christian faction that made them their figureheads. Jesus is forever rebuking their stupid remarks and their inability to understand him. In Matthew we find a pronounced attempt to rehabilitate them and to mitigate Jesus' disapproval. This, obviously, is because the Matthean church community, unlike Mark, venerated the Twelve. Peter in particular is praised and honored. But alongside these edits we notice attempts to take Peter back down a peg. Jesus congratulates Peter on his confession of faith at Caesarea Philippi, but then calls him "Satan" (restoring Mark's "Get thee behind me, Satan," which the first Matthean redactor had probably chopped because it made Peter look so bad). Jesus gives Peter the "keys" of *halakhic* authority (Matt. 16:19) but then redistributes them to the Twelve as a whole (18:18). Peter joins Jesus walking on the water (14:28–29), like Robin with Batman, but then he sinks (14:30–31). And so on. This means that we have to allow some years between the publication of Mark's Gospel and the first round of "Matthean" rewriting and expansion, which still did not give us our present Matthew, and then more years before a second "Matthean" editor reworked the whole thing. There must, then, be a longer interval between Mark and our canonical version of Matthew than most would like to think. Again, we can read the tree rings.

Matthew swarms with legendary embellishments. Think of all the seismic activity on Easter weekend, earthquakes somehow missed not only by the Weather Channel but by all three other gospels as well. Then there is the enormity of the mass wave of resurrections coincident with the crucifixion of Jesus. "The earth shook, and the rocks were split; the tombs also were opened, and many bodies of the saints who had fallen asleep were raised, and coming out of the tombs after his resurrection they went into the holy city and appeared to many" (Matt. 27:51a–53). Even apologists won't defend that one.

Matthew was not satisfied with Mark's empty tomb story, in which the women discover the tomb already open with a young man dressed in white waiting for them. So he changed it, leaving the tomb closed until the women arrive, then having a glowing angel swoop down from heaven and roll the stone away. Not too shabby. And then there is the business, reflected in no other gospel, about the Sanhedrin prevailing upon Pilate to post armed guards at the tomb. This sort of legendary embellishment does not exactly inspire confidence, and it implies a later stage than we find in Mark, even at *his* latest.

Luke's Gospel is not mentioned until Irenaeus includes it among the four gospels he is willing to accept in ca. 180 CE. Justin Martyr (150?) may refer to the Book of Acts (the sequel to Luke), but we are not sure because there is only a single phrase common to both. Scholars have proposed three different approximate dates for the Gospel of Luke. Adolf Harnack believed it was written, along with the Book of Acts, by or around 60 CE, before the traditional date of Paul's execution.[4] Harnack decided that there was no other way to explain the lack of any mention in Acts of Paul's death, or at least of the outcome of his trial, unless we suppose that Luke wrote during the period of Paul's house arrest in Rome. If Luke knew Paul had been martyred, can we imagine that he would not have made much of it?

Though conservative apologists like W. Ward Gasque[5] now delight in invoking Harnack in favor of an early date so they may argue for the historical accuracy of Luke and Acts, Harnack himself admitted that Acts was untrustworthy and simply fabulous at many points, that Luke was habitually inaccurate, and that early dating was by no means incompatible with any of these phenomena. Unlike his latter-day fans, Harnack was no apologist for biblical inerrancy.

Harnack accepted the theory of Luke's dependence upon Mark, and he knew his early dating had to take that into account: Mark and Q must have been early, too. This, however, brought up another problem, in that most scholars regard Luke as having taken the Markan "abomination of desolation" prophecy (Mark 13:14ff.) and historicized it in light of the actual events of 70 CE (Luke 21:20, cf. 19:43). Luke seems to have taken the trouble to re-narrate the apocalypse in terms of a literal description. What was Harnack's answer to this? He said that both Mark and Luke were written before the Roman siege, and that Mark's "abomination of desolation" passage was a genuine before-the-fact prediction. Luke, Harnack said, could see that Mark's version of the prophecy denoted a Roman conquest and simply reworded the prediction in terms of typical Roman tactics. This seems to me a harmonization, an attempt to get out of a tight spot. There are, however, more serious objections to dating Luke-Acts before the death of Paul.

Is Luke ignorant of the martyr death of Paul? Most scholars today do not think so. Note that, at the end of Acts, Luke refers to Paul's two-year imprisonment as a thing completed, a rounded-off episode. "The imprisonment lasted two years." And *then* what happened? It is indeed puzzling that he does not tell us, but it also seems that he is assuming *something* else happened, in other words, the story went on. It may be that he intended to continue the story in a third volume of narrative that would have depicted an acquittal and further travels, and finally the death of Paul; or perhaps Paul's death and the ministry of Aristarchus, Barnabas, and so on. On the other hand, it may be that the fact of Paul's death was so well-known that it would have been superfluous to state it. "This is how he came to his famous death. You know the rest." As if a biography of Lincoln ended with: "And thus he entered Ford's Theatre for the 2:15 p.m. performance, the same one attended by John Wilkes Booth."

It may be that Luke, sensitive to the disapproval of the Romans in a politically charged climate, where Christians were viewed as subversive and liable to persecution, wanted to gloss over the execution of Paul by Rome. He certainly evidences an apologetic sensitivity elsewhere in both the gospel and Acts.

In any case, Luke has Paul predict his martyrdom in pretty explicit terms in Acts 20:25 (verse 22 notwithstanding). "You shall see my face no more"—a prediction he could make only if he knew he would be dead. In fact, the passage as a whole, the farewell speech to the Ephesian elders, is an easily recognizable "Last Testament" piece, a common device to put "famous last words" into the mouth of a famous man (as in Plato's *Crito*, *The Testaments of the Twelve Patriarchs*, of Abraham, Moses, Job, and others). Specifically, the "prediction" of Gnostic heretics emerging later to forage among the churches of Asia Minor seems to be a much later, post-Pauline way of dissociating Paul from the floodtide of "heresy" that overtook the area by the second century. Luke seeks here to absolve Paul of the blame of it, contrary to the heretics themselves who claimed him as their patron saint.[6]

Luke draws a large-scale series of parallels between the Passion of Jesus and that of Paul. Both undertake itinerant preaching journeys, culminating in a last, long journey to Jerusalem, where each is arrested in connection with a disturbance in the Temple. Each is acquitted by a Herodian monarch as well as by Roman procurators. Each makes, as we have seen, Passion predictions. Is it likely that Luke wrote this in ignorance of what finally happened to Paul?

The majority of current scholars gravitate to a date of 80–90 CE. I think this is simply an attempt to push Luke as far back as possible while admitting that neither Mark nor Luke were written before the death of Paul (62 CE) or the fall of Jerusalem (70 CE), and this in order to keep it within the possible lifetime of a companion of Paul, which is what tradition made Luke.

The Tübingen critics[7] of the nineteenth century, which include Franz Overbeck, F. C. Baur, and Edward Zeller,[8] dated Luke-Acts in the second century, 100–130 CE. More recently Walter Schmithals, Helmut Koester, John C. O'Neill,[9] and Richard I. Pervo[10] have maintained the second-century date.

Ferdinand Christian Baur placed Luke-Acts late on the historical timeline because of its "catholicizing" tendency. That is, he showed how there was a conflict in early Christianity between nationalist Torah-observant Jewish Christianity on the one hand, and more open, Torah-free Hellenistic/Gentile Christianity on the other. The first was led by James, Peter, and the Twelve, while the latter was led by Paul, the Seven Deacons, Apollos, Priscilla, Aquila, and others. Baur showed how most of the New Testament documents could be placed on either side of this great divide. On the Jewish side were Matthew, James, and Revelation. On the Gentile side were the four authentic Pauline Epistles, Hebrews, John, the Johannine Epistles, and Mark.

Later there arose the catholicizing tendency, that is, the tendency to reconcile the two parties. The pseudonymous 1 and 2 Peter either give Pauline thought under Peter's name or have Peter speak favorably of Paul while denigrating those who quote Paul against the memory of Peter. Interpolations into the Pauline Epistles, as well as pseudonymous epistles attributed to Paul, make him friendlier to Judaism and the Law. Acts attempts to bring together the Petrine and Pauline factions by a series of clever moves. First, Peter and Paul are paralleled, each raising someone from the dead (Acts 9:36–40, 20:9–12), each healing a paralytic (3:1–8, 14:8–10), each healing by extraordinary, magical means (5:15, 19:11–12), each besting a sorcerer (8:18–23, 13:6–11), each miraculously escaping prison (12:6–10, 16:25–26). If one praises God for the work of Peter, then one can scarcely deny God was at work in Paul, too (and vice versa).

Second, Luke makes Peter a universalizing preacher to the Gentiles, as witness the Cornelius story (Acts 10–11) and especially the speech of Peter in Acts 15, which echoes that of Paul in Galatians 2, aimed at Peter! At the same time, he makes Paul still an observant Jew, claiming still to be a Pharisee (23:6), piously taking vows and paying for those of others (21:20–24), attending Jerusalem worship on holy days. He makes it clear that there is no truth to the prevalent "rumors" that Paul had abandoned legal observance (Acts 21:24).

Having vindicated Paul as a true and divinely chosen preacher of the gospel, and this conspicuously in the teeth of Jewish Christian opponents, Luke seems to deny him the dignity of the apostolate itself, redefining the office in an anachronistic fashion that would have excluded even the Twelve (Acts 1:21–22)! Paul is subordinated to the Twelve as their dutiful servant. He makes a beeline to report to them after his conversion, in direct contradiction to Galatians 1:15–19. He does nothing without their approval and preaches of *their* witness to the risen Christ (13:30–31), not his own. In short, Luke has Petrinized Paul and Paulinized Peter, so as to bring their respective factions closer together. All this bespeaks a time well after Paul himself.

Hans Conzelmann also argued for a date for Luke-Acts significantly after Paul and presupposing the passage of sufficient time to make it apparent that history had entered a new era. I think his observations imply a second-century date for Luke-Acts, though he did not place Luke-Acts quite so late. The apocalyptic enthusiasm of the earliest Christians was premature; the world would keep on going, and a new era of salvation history had commenced. And this is why Luke wrote Acts: The story of salvation was not yet over. Jesus was the decisive "center" of it but not the culmination of it. Conzelmann says that Luke rewrote the story of Jesus to "de-eschatologize" it and to make it fit into an ongoing world in which the Church had more of a role than merely awaiting the end.[11]

Conzelmann envisioned Luke's salvation history as consisting of three great eras. The first was that of Israel. In Luke it would be represented by the first two chapters of the gospel with Zechariah, Elizabeth, Miriam (Mary), Simeon, and Anna as quintessential Old Testament characters (actually modeled on characters in the stories of the infancy of Samuel: Simeon = Eli, Elizabeth = Hannah, etc.)[12]

The second period was that of Jesus. It forms the middle of time, the strategic pivotal zone of history. It brings to an end the time of Israel and commences that of the Church. John the Baptist is the pivotal figure, marking the shift of the eons (Luke 16:16) from the time when the Law is preached to the time when the kingdom of God is preached. Within the period of Jesus there is a further breakdown: in the center of it lies the public ministry of Jesus, when the full blaze of heavenly light dispels the shadows. Wherever Jesus goes, evil flees, like the Canaanites before the advancing Israelites. This Conzelmann called the "Satan-free" period. It begins with Jesus warding off Satan by successfully withstanding his temptations. At the end of this story Luke says Satan "departed from him until an opportune time (*kairos*)" (Luke 4:13). That time comes at the betrayal story when, as in John, Luke says that Satan entered into Judas Iscariot to engineer Jesus' betrayal. Between these two events we see either an editorial elimination of Satan's activity or a continual banishing of his forces from the field.

In the first case, notice that Luke has omitted the rebuke of Jesus to Peter, "Get behind me, Satan!" from Mark's scene of Peter's confession. Why? The period must have been Satan-free! In the second case, note that Jesus rides roughshod over the forces of evil, witnessing Satan falling precipitously (Luke 10:18–19) from his position of power in one of the lower heavens ("the powers of the heavens shall be shaken" Luke 21:26b) and freeing those oppressed by the devil (Luke 13:16; Acts 10:38) apparently without resistance. Some see these two motifs as contradictory: how can the period of the ministry be free of the machinations of Satan and yet be the time of unceasing battle between Jesus and Satan? But I think they misunderstand the idea that Satan seems completely unable to reinforce his vanquished troops. Where is he?

Once the Satan-free period is over (and Jesus knows it is over as of the Last Supper) he warns the disciples that it will no longer be so easy as it has been up to this point. Whereas they could travel preaching the gospel unmolested thus far, now they had best carry weapons to protect themselves (22:35–36). It is only now that we learn of Satan's demand to thresh the Twelve like wheat (22:31). If Conzelmann is right about this, we can detect for the first time the perspective, much like our own, of a distinctly later period, one from which the time of Jesus already looks something like a never-never-land. It is unlike the mundane and difficult time in which we live, but a pristine "once upon a time" of origins. It is, from the standpoint of the reader and the writer, long over. We are now in the third period, that of the Church, when the gospel is to be preached and tribulation is to be endured. This is not a work of the apostolic age, it seems to me.

Conzelmann's Luke also tends to push the eschatological fulfillment off into the future. At first this is not obvious, since he retains the passage from the Markan apocalypse in which we are told that this generation will not pass before all these things are fulfilled (Luke 21:32 matches Mark 13:30). But we dare not ignore the many subtle changes Luke makes in his sources elsewhere. In Luke's version of the Little Apocalypse, the false prophets announce not only that "I am he," but also that "The time is at hand!" (21:8, cf. 2 Thess. 2:1–3). Now the events Jesus predicts lead up only to the historical destruction of the Jerusalem Temple by Roman troops (21:20), not to the very end of all things, as Mark 13:10 had expected.

The fall of Jerusalem will usher in a new period, "the times of the Gentiles," an era of Gentile dominion over Israel, as in the visions of Daniel 7. Thus there is a distancing buffer between the events of 70 CE and the end, and Luke sees himself standing right in the middle.

At the story of Peter's confession, Jesus predicts that some there will see the kingdom of God coming, but not " in power" as Mark had it (cf. Luke 9:27 and Mark 9:1). He wants to avoid the embarrassment that the Twelve all died and there was still no second coming (cf. 2 Peter 3:4; John 21:23). At the Trial scene Jesus no longer tells his contemporaries that *they will see* the Son of man seated at the right hand of Power (as in Mark 14:62, "you will see"), but rather simply that from now on he will be seated there (Luke 22:69). He wants to avoid the embarrassment that the Sanhedrin members are dead and that the coming of the Son of man and the kingdom of God has not transpired.

Luke introduces the *three impatient questions*. In Luke 17:20–21 Jesus is asked about signs whereby the arrival of the kingdom may be counted down. His answer is that there will be no such anticipation. It is not the kind of thing that even *could* come that way, since it is an inner spiritual reality.

In Luke 19:11ff., Luke has very heavily redacted the parable of the Talents (which survives in something more like its original Q form in Matthew 25:14ff.) in order to make the point that, before the kingdom comes, the Son of man is going to have to go *very far away* (i.e., heaven—cf. Acts 1:10–11) and thus be absent a long time before he can return as king.

In Acts 1:6–7ff., even after forty days of "inside teaching" from the risen Christ himself, the Twelve are still so dense that they expect an immediate theocratic denouement. He rebukes them as he did so often in the days of his ministry. The artificiality of the scene is plain to see. How bad a teacher could Jesus have been? How damn stupid can the disciples have been? Hence it is redactional. The point is to urge readers not to trouble themselves about matters of eschatology but to get busy spreading the gospel.

Then there is Luke's replacement of horizontal with vertical eschatology. Luke alone among the gospel writers speaks of people going to heaven or hell as soon as they die. The parable of Lazarus and the Rich Man (17:19–31) and the thief on the cross story (23:43) both have such a picture. Also see Luke 20:38b, where Luke adds the idea of present immortality, "for all live unto him," just as in 4 Maccabees 7:19 ("to God they do not die, as our patriarchs Abraham, Isaac, and Jacob died not, but live to God"). Earlier Christians thought of attaining the end-times kingdom or not. One thinks of going up to heaven only when the prospect of an imminent end has faded (1 Thess. 4:13–14; 2 Cor. 5:1–4; Phil. 1:23).

The attempt of Luke to point up the innocence of Jesus and Paul at every opportunity surely leans in the direction of a later date. Luke wants to find an accord between Church and Empire. All in all, we get a view very much like that of the late first-, early second-century Pastoral Epistles (1 and 2 Timothy and Titus).

Charles H. Talbert, though again without actually holding to a second-century date, showed how Luke shares the agenda and the views of the second-century Apologists Irenaeus, Justin Martyr, and Tertullian.[13] These men faced the challenge of "heresies" (competing forms of Christianity), which they sought to refute by claiming an exclusive copyright on the "apostolic tradition." The Apologists relied heavily, in their polemics against the Gnostics, on the idea of "apostolic succession" of bishops. That is, the twelve apostles had been the apprentices of the Son of God. They alone saw the whole of his ministry and thus were in no danger of taking things he said out of context as, for example, Irenaeus accused the Valentinians of doing. In the Pseudo-

Clementines Peter takes Simon Magus to task precisely over this issue: how can the Magus hope to have a correct understanding of Christ and his teachings derived, as he claims, from occasional visions of him? If he were really taught by Christ, he ought to agree with Peter, who saw and heard everything the Messiah did and said.

Luke seems already to be setting up the twelve apostles as a college of guarantors of the orthodox tradition of Jesus. As Talbert notes, Luke makes explicit in Acts 1:21–22 that he views as apostles only those who have seen and thus can verify all the events of the Jesus story as they are preached elsewhere in Acts, namely the baptism on through the ascension. The artificiality of this is evident from the simple fact that the Twelve cannot all have been present at these events even on Luke's own showing! But he does make the effort, as Talbert shows, to have the disciples miss nothing, at least as of the point when they join Jesus. For instance, while they are away on their preaching tour there is nothing recorded of Jesus—otherwise the witnesses could not attest it. Jesus would have been a tree falling in the forest with no one there to hear the sound.[14]

Günther Klein has gone one step further and argued that, whereas we hear from Paul about "the Twelve" and "the apostles," and from Mark and Matthew about "the disciples," the notion of a group of "the twelve apostles" is a Lukan creation to restrict the office of apostle, originally much wider, to the narrow confines of the Twelve.[15] The one reference to the twelve apostles in Mark (3:14, occurring in only some manuscripts) would make sense as a harmonizing interpolation. In Mark 6:30 and Matthew 10:2, the term "apostles" seems to be used in a non-technical sense ("The ones sent out returned"; "the names of the twelve sent out are these"), since *apostoloi* means "sent ones."

Note that Luke has every step of the fledgling Church carefully overseen by the vigilant eye of the Twelve, who stay magically untouched in Jerusalem even when the whole Church is otherwise scattered by persecution (Acts 8:1): They authenticate the conversion of the Samaritans, the ordination of the Seven, the conversion of Cornelius, the ministry of Paul. In the same way, the Apologists held that it was the bishops of the Catholic congregations who were appointed by the apostles to continue their work, teaching what they themselves had been taught, as it were, from the horse's mouth. Luke has Paul tell the Ephesian elders that he taught them everything he knew (Acts 20:20—against Gnostic claims that he had taught the advanced stuff only to the illuminati, as he pointedly says that he *did* in 1 Corinthians 2:6–7). In Acts 20:28 Paul even calls them "bishops," though translations hide it (cf. 2 Tim. 2:2).

Tertullian denied the right of "heretics" even to quote scripture in their own defense (much as Justin did Jews), claiming that the scripture was meaningless unless interpreted in accordance with the tradition of the apostles. And what was that? Well, whatever the current Catholic interpretation happened to be. Even so, Luke is careful to have the Twelve appear as recipients of the risen Christ's own scriptural interpretation (Luke 24:25, 43–44), which, however, Luke refrains from giving in any detail—writing himself a blank check.

Tertullian fought against the Gnostic idea of a spiritually resurrected Christ, as opposed to a physically resurrected one. Is it any accident that Luke has the same concern, as opposed to the presumably earlier view of 1 Corinthians 15:49–50 and 1 Peter 3:18?

J. C. O'Neill argued that Acts belongs in the second century because its theology has the most in common with the writings of that time (again, including the Apologists).[16] The view that Jews have forfeited their claim on God and have been shunted aside is surely impossible before the second century. Had it become clear earlier than this that Jews in toto had completely rejected the Christian message? Hardly. Yet in Acts, not only is this a fait accompli, but (as Jack T. Sanders also shows[17]) Luke seems to view the Jews of the Diaspora, the only ones he knows as historical entities (as opposed to the Sunday school lesson Jews of Jerusalem) as horned caricatures who oppose the gospel out of base envy—a motivation retrojected from a later period in which Christianity has begun to overwhelm Judaism in numbers, surely too late for the lifetime of Paul or one of his companions.

The theology of the supersession of the Temple seen in Stephen's speech (Acts chapter 7) is borrowed from post–70 CE Hellenistic

Judaism, where, as we see in Justin's *Dialogue with Trypho* and the *Sibylline Oracles*, Jews had begun to make virtue of necessity and to spiritualize Temple worship.

The Apostolic Decree (Acts 15), proclaiming that Jewish Christians have every right to observe the ancestral Law of Moses, and the stress on James securing Paul's public endorsement of the idea, seem to reflect a later period attested in Justin Martyr, where Jewish Christians were on the defensive against their more numerous Gentile Christian brethren, many of whom deemed them heretical for keeping the law at all. Justin himself allowed their right to do so if they did not try to get Gentiles to keep it. This dispute seems to provide the natural context for Acts 21:20–25, making Luke a contemporary of Justin. Had these questions really been decided back in the days of Peter and Paul, why would Christians still be debating them some eighty years later?

Similarly, the Decree as set forth in Acts 15 seeks to provide (long after the fact) apostolic legitimization for the cultic provisions attested in second-century sources, but not earlier for the most part. Minucius Felix, the Pseudo-Clementines, Biblis (quoted in Eusebius), the Syriac *Apology of Aristides*, and Tertullian all mention that Christians do not consume the blood of animals or the meat of strangled animals. Revelation and a late section of 1 Corinthians (10:14–22) ban eating meat offered to idols. Matthew forbids consanguineous marriages (*porneia*) to Gentile converts, forbidden in Acts 15:20 at about the same time. The strange thing about this is that in none of these documents is the prohibition traced back to the Apostolic Decree of Jerusalem, which, if genuine, must have been treasured as the first ecumenical conciliar decision in the Church. Conversely, when Paul's epistles deal with the issues, they never mention the Decree, which would seemingly have been an authoritative way of dealing with the questions. It looks like Luke has simply collected these various second-century Christian mores and retrojected them into the Golden Age of the apostles to give them added weight.

The titles of Jesus in Acts are those used of him in the second century, particularly "Servant of God" (Acts 3:13, 4:27). Despite the desperate desire of Joachim Jeremias[18] and others to trace this back to an imaginary "Suffering Servant of Yahweh" theology of the earliest Church, there is no evidence that such a specter ever existed. But the title does occur in later documents like the *Didache*, 1 Clement, and the *Martyrdom of Polycarp*. It is late Christology, not early.

Likewise, the natural theology of Acts chapter 17, the Areopagus Speech, reflects that of the second-century Apologists, who sought to make common ground with their pagan audience, for example, Justin Martyr's theory that Socrates and Plato should be viewed as "Christians before Christ" inspired by the divine Logos.

Many scholars have detected striking parallels between Acts and the ancient Hellenistic novels.[19] These were popular picaresque fictions produced for several centuries, reaching the height of popularity in the second century CE. They were most often romances but also sometimes chronicled the travels and miracles of teachers like Apollonius of Tyana. Rosa Söder notes five features shared by the novels and the Apocryphal Acts of the second century (more on these in a moment).[20] They are also shared with the canonical Acts. First, they feature *travel* (cf. the apostolic journeys of Peter and Paul). Second come tales of miracles and oddities. The apostles do numerous miracles, some quite fanciful, like Peter's healing shadow, Paul's healing hankies, Peter striking Ananias and Sapphira dead with a word. Third is the depiction of fabulous and exotic peoples (like the bull-sacrificing pagans of Lycaonia, Acts 14:8–19; the superstitious natives of Malta, 28:1–6; and the philosophical dilettantes of Athens in Acts chap. 17). Fourth, the novels have some sort of religious propaganda function. Fifth, they feature chaste eroticism between separated lovers who resist all temptations during their separation. (I believe such a narrative underlies the mentions of Joanna and the female entourage of Jesus in Luke).[21]

Rosa Söder adds five more important traits less often found in the Apocryphal Acts but common to the novels—and the canonical Acts. First, the sale of the hero into slavery (like the imprisonments of Paul, Peter, Silas, Acts 12:6, 16:26, 21:33, 26:29). Second, persecution. Third, crowd scenes (e.g., in Ephesus, the Artemis riot in Acts chap.

19:23–41). Fourth, divine help in time of great need, and fifth, oracles, dreams, and divine commands.[22]

If the heyday of the novel genre was the second century, it also seems the best period to locate Luke-Acts. It was also the heyday of the various Apocryphal Acts of the Apostles, novelistic fantasies about the missionary exploits of the apostles Paul, Peter, John, Andrew, Matthias, and Thomas. As many scholars note, the similarities between the ancient novels and the Apocryphal Acts imply that the latter represent a Christian adaptation of the former. There are, however, two prominent features of the Apocryphal Acts that are either *not* shared with the novels or else are significantly reworked from the novel genre. The first is that an apostle (the star of the particular Acts) in effect takes the place of Christ, becoming virtually a second Christ, preaching, healing, traveling, even repeating Jesus' martyrdom in significant respects. The line between them is quite thin. In every major Acts, Christ sooner or later appears to someone in the physical guise of the apostle, so it goes both ways. Secondly, the Apocryphal Acts employ stories apparently borrowed from female storytellers in the communities of "widows"—consecrated, charismatic, celibate women. These stories depict the conversion of young noblewomen or matrons to encratism (the "good news" of celibacy as a requirement for baptism).[23] Upon chancing to hear the preaching of the starring apostle, the woman dumps her husband or fiancé, then becomes an inseparable follower of her preacher, infuriating her "ex," who uses his connections with the pagan governor to have the apostle arrested, even martyred. Luke-Acts has both features, though in the case of the second, it has broken up the story (of Joanna) and redistributed the fragments elsewhere. The core is Luke 8:1–3.

Also, the canonical Book of Acts shares with the Pseudo-Clementines and the Acts of Peter the legend of the miracle-contest between Simon Peter and Simon Magus. As Gerd Lüdemann has pointed out, the appearance in Acts 8:22 of the rare word *epinoia* must be a reference to the doctrine of the Simonian sect, attested in patristic and heresiological writers (i.e., later writers), to the effect that Simon's consort Helen, a former prostitute, was the incarnation of the Epinoia, the archetypal First Thought.[24] I believe that Luke's Acts was not necessarily the first in the genre, though it is quite likely the earliest one we have. Luke's innovation was not to continue the story after Jesus by writing an Acts, but rather to write both a gospel and an Acts, both already established genres. This makes a second-century date more likely.

Finally, Luke seems to have a lot in common with our friend Papias, bishop of Hierapolis in Asia Minor, who wrote about 140–150. Luke and Papias are strikingly similar at five points. Both mention extant written gospels, but both prefer their own research, derived from those who heard the first apostles, something both Papias and Luke came on the scene too late to do. Both mention the prophesying daughters of Philip. Papias is said to actually have met them. Both know the grotesque legend of the ghastly death of Judas by swelling up and exploding. Both wrote their own "gospels." Papias' was called *An Exposition of the Oracles of our Lord*, which Eusebius said contained "certain strange parables" of an apocalyptic nature. Significantly, Papias does not mention Luke's Gospel in his discussion of previous gospels, presumably because it did not yet exist. I suggest he and Luke were contemporaries, both men of antiquarian tastes and the same interests.

The Gospel of John must be the very latest of the canonical gospels, stemming from the middle of the second century, as implied by the fact that its author made use of the other gospels. It is now customary for scholars to pooh-pooh a second-century date due to that assigned the earliest surviving papyrus fragment of it, P52 (the John Rylands Papyrus), namely ca. 125–175 CE. Supposedly, the handwriting is typical of that period. But that dating is arbitrary and circular. There are too few samples of relevant penmanship from the period for comparison, and some scholars have recently rejected any certainty about the date of P52.[25] So, as usual, we must get along on the basis of internal evidence.

C. H. Dodd[26] has amply demonstrated close Johannine affinities with the Hermetic literature, a variety of Egyptian, non-Christian Gnosticism. Rudolf Bultmann[27] has made the Gnostic and Mandaean character of many passages equally clear. True, as Raymond E. Brown maintained, John has similarities to the sectarian Judaism of the Dead Sea Scrolls. Brown thought these similarities were adequate as an excuse to rule out Gnosticism and to interpret John safely within the Jewish tradition.[28] But not so fast! Bultmann was surely correct in understanding the religion of the Scrolls as a kind of Gnosticizing Judaism. There also looks to be a significant dose of Marcionite theology in John's Gospel. Would all these influences make it necessary for us to imagine one single author influenced by all these doctrines? While that would be by no means implausible, given the fantastic syncretism of the Hellenistic environment, the text of John abounds in contradictions suggesting a composite text that has been edited and adapted by several Johannine factions and splinter groups.

Second, there is the matter of the *sources* underlying John. I regard Bultmann's theory as still the best. He posited that the fourth evangelist employed a Synoptic-style narrative of numbered miracles of Jesus, the so-called Signs Source.[29] Second, John employed a Gnostic-Mandaean Revelation Discourse Source, monologues of the heavenly revealer, probably originally John the Baptist but subsequently changed to Jesus. Third, the evangelist incorporated a Passion narrative (though he may instead have reworked Mark's). At several points, it looks like John is correcting the Synoptics, though Dodd made a good case that John did not know the other gospels but just used some of the same or similar fragments of oral traditions.[30]

Third, there is the *narrative discontinuity* in the gospel. Bultmann and others take this to imply that, very early, the text was accidentally disassembled, then clumsily put back together, like 2 Corinthians.[31] As an alternative, Brown and others have divided the present text into successive stages of expansion.[32] Such a process would also explain the inconsistencies. But that still leaves us wondering why there was apparently so little effort taken to smooth out the result. As it is, we see Jesus suddenly placed in a location we just saw him leave, or appearing someplace new with no notice of his having gone there, and so on. So it makes the best sense, as far as I am concerned, to stick with Bultmann.

He showed that much of the editing must have been the work of an "Ecclesiastical Redactor," whom David Trobisch very plausibly identifies as Polycarp, second-century bishop of Smyrna.[33] His self-appointed task was to "sanitize" an original text that he and others deemed heretical, too Gnostic-sounding, though hardly without spiritual merit. Even after he retooled it, however, the book still smacked of Gnosticism,[34] and some thought it was the work of the Gnostic Cerinthus.

The community from which the Gospel of John emerged had fragmented (see 1 John 2:18–19), especially over Christological doctrines, some holding that Jesus Christ had appeared on Earth in a body of real, material flesh and blood, while others claimed it was merely the *likeness* of sinful flesh. Both groups used the same gospel, but each scribe began to "correct" his sect's copy, to bring it into line with his group's theology. Polycarp (or whoever the Ecclesiastical Redactor was) must have gathered copies representing both (or more?) versions of John and combined them as best he could, with the result that our gospel points in various directions, sometimes swinging back and forth from one sentence to another. Finally, someone has added chapter 21 onto the end of the book, which had already seemed to conclude with 20:30–31.

But who wrote it? That is a difficult question to answer, because in a sense it is the wrong question. Who shall we name as "the" author of Matthew, with its conflicting stages of writing and rewriting? Which redactor or corrector or interpolator of the fourth gospel is to be considered "John"? In any case, the apostle John, son of Zebedee, had nothing to do with it. Granted, John 19:34–35 claims to rest on the testimony of an eyewitness to the crucifixion, but, as we have seen, the passage contradicts its context and also seems to protest too much. John 21:24 ascribes the previous twenty chapters to some one of the original disciples, but chapter 21 is a later addition to the gospel. This means that this writer's claim that chapters 1–20 are the work of an eyewitness disciple is no different from or more reliable than Irenaeus vouching for the apostolic authorship of Matthew, and is equally as dubious.

One must also distinguish the *author* from the *narrator* of the gospel. Perhaps, like the authors of many gospels that did not make it into the official canon, the author of John had nothing to do with any historical Jesus but created a fictive narrator who *is* supposed to be one of the Twelve. There is no reason to exempt the fourth evangelist from using the same device as others who ascribed their work to Matthias, Thomas, Clement, Peter, and so on.

Appendix Two

DO ANCIENT HISTORIANS MENTION JESUS?

Like all Christian apologists, Bill O'Reilly and Martin Dugard boast that Jesus Christ is not merely a creature of the New Testament but is also well attested by non-Christian historians of the period.

> The Roman historians Pliny the Younger, Cornelius Tacitus, and Suetonius all mention Jesus in their writings. The secular Greek-speaking historians Thallus and Phlegon, the satirist Lucian of Samosata, and the eminent Jewish historian Flavius Josephus also mention Jesus. (p. 262)

But these mentions of Jesus are of no help in authenticating the historical existence of Jesus. You might as well point out that there are entries on Jesus in modern encyclopedias, too, but this proves nothing either. The constant appeal to these scant passages reveals something very significant about the whole approach of apologists. They cite these ancient snippets like fundamentalists citing scriptural proof-texts, without any attempt to scrutinize the worth of the sources they cite. I propose to exercise such scrutiny here. And, to get ahead of the game, we will find that even if these passages are all authentic products of the individuals to whom they are ascribed, none would be of any help because they are simply too late. Sure, they are closer to the events (if there *were* any events) than we are, but that is not close enough.

Or, perhaps to put it more accurately, they are not as far away from the events as we are. But you know the saying: "A miss is as good as a mile." What we would need from someone like Josephus or Tacitus is front-line reporting. And they are all too late for that. These writers are valued as ostensibly objective sources of information since their authors cannot be suspected of Christian bias. But that also means that, as outsiders, they must have been dependent upon reports of what Christians were preaching and teaching in their day. It would be altogether different if any of these writers had quoted some letter from the first third of the first century CE, in which, say, some traveler chanced to write home to his wife and mentioned having heard the famous Nazarene Jesus preach or having seen him cast out a demon. But this is what none of them do. As of now, we possess no such testimony. Who knows? Maybe someday some archaeologist will discover such evidence, and that would shake things up pretty well. But for now, we don't have anything.

FLAVE-A-FLAVIUS

But we do have Josephus. In our copies of Josephus (penned many centuries after he composed his histories) we find a famous and much-disputed passage called the *Testimonium Flavianum.*

> Now there was about this time Jesus, a wise man, if it be lawful to call him a man, for he was a doer of wonderful works, a teacher of such men as receive the truth with pleasure. He drew over to him both many of the Jews, and many of the Gentiles. He was the Christ; and when Pilate, at the suggestion of the principal men amongst us, had condemned him to the cross, those that loved him at the first did not forsake him, for he appeared to them alive again the third day, as the divine prophets had foretold these and ten thousand other wonderful things concerning him; and the tribe of Christians, so named from him, are not extinct to this day. (*Antiquities of the Jews* 18.3.3)

Josephus was, of course, no Christian, but a Jew who sucked up to the Romans after abandoning his position as a leader of Jewish forces in the war with Rome. He not only predicted that the general Vespasian would ascend to the Imperial throne, he pretty much ordained him as the Messiah of Israel. Is it likely he would have written this passage, awarding the crown to a rival Messiah, Jesus? And if he had, wouldn't that mean Josephus was a Christian? But he wasn't. There is simply no way he could have written this passage. And he didn't. Origen of Alexandria in the mid-third century, had a much earlier copy of Josephus' *Antiquities of the Jews* than any that survives to our day, and Origen commented that Josephus "did not accept Jesus as Christ" (*Commentary on Matthew* 10.17). So it is plain that in his day the text did not contain our Josephus text about Jesus. Some have suggested, however, that Origen must have read *something* about Jesus in Josephus, perhaps omitted from our copies. Josephus must have made some negative comment about Jesus, right? Sure, he might have, for all we know, but remember, Josephus had proclaimed the Gentile Vespasian as the Christ. Seems to me that's all Origen would have to know to say that Josephus hadn't considered Jesus for the job.

Shlomo Pines[1] pointed out that there is another version of this passage, in Arabic, found in Agapius' *Book of the Title* by a tenth-century Melkite bishop of Hierapolis. It is a bit shorter.

> Similarly Josephus, the Hebrew. For he says in the treatises that he has written on the governance (?) of the Jews: "At this time there was a wise man who was called Jesus. His conduct was good, and (he) was known to be virtuous. And many people from the Jews and other nations became his disciples. Pilate condemned him to be crucified and die. But those who had become his disciples did not abandon his discipleship. They reported that he had appeared to them three days after the crucifixion, and that he was alive; accordingly he was perhaps the Messiah, concerning whom the prophets have recounted wonders."

Apologists like to claim this shorter version as an excuse to theorize that Josephus had written some version of the famous text, but without those elements that would make him look like a Christian.[2] Perhaps the Arabic version, they argue, represents something closer to what Josephus originally wrote. Nice try. It doesn't sufficiently mitigate the main difficulty. Even if Josephus wrote "only" that Jesus *might* have been the Messiah, this would be dangerous, implying that maybe he had been a little hasty in giving the honor to Vespasian. Besides, Agapius' version is not an earlier version of the *Testimonium Flavianum* but a later one, just an abridgment of the longer, familiar version. Notice that the conclusion refers to wonders predicted for the Messiah; mustn't that imply some earlier reference to Jesus doing miracles? There is such a reference in the familiar Greek version, but not in this one.

Many of us think the entire passage is a fabrication by the fourth-century Church historian Eusebius. He is the first to "quote" it. It beggars credulity to think that, if the text were actually original to Josephus, no Christian until Eusebius should ever have mentioned it.

A closely related approach is to say, Agapius or no Agapius, that Josephus might have written a less Christian-sounding version, and that, instead of creating the *Testimonium* out of whole cloth, later Christian scribes might have just added a few Christian elements, like Jesus being the Christ. I'm afraid that's not going to fly, either, and for one simple reason: even the hypothetical version proposed by apologists still contains the final note that "the tribe of Christians, named from him, is not extinct to this day." But if the apologists are right, there has been no reference to Jesus as "the Christ," so how could Josephus have said the "Christians" were named for not "Christ" but "Jesus"?

There is a hilarious irony here. Apologists cannot abide the occasional suggestion of critics that this or that passage in the New Testament might have been an interpolation dating from that tunnel period between the original writing and our first extant copies. How convenient! You cannot allow that a passage might have crept into the text if you can't produce any manuscripts that lack it—even though we have no manuscripts at all, one way or another, from the relevant period.[3] But when it comes to Josephus, hey, anything goes! If the *Testimonium* as it stands cannot be authentic, then let's pretend it doesn't, er, *didn't* contain the problem portions. They would really prefer to claim the whole juicy Jesus passage *as is*, for apologetics. But no one will fall for that.

THE CART BEFORE THE HORSE

Then again, the whole matter looks rather different once we consider the possibility that the gospels are later than Josephus and cobbled major portions of the Jesus story together *from Josephus*. We have already seen how striking parallels with Josephus' Moses nativity suggest that Matthew appropriated it as the template for Jesus' birth story. There is even more reason to believe that the Markan Passion narrative is based on Josephus' account of the interrogation and flogging of the Jerusalem prophet Jesus ben-Ananias.[4] And this is very significant, for it means the most important portion of the very first gospel's Jesus story is derived not from something like the *Testimonium Flavianum* but from a passage about *a different Jesus*. In short, it is nonsense to suggest that Josephus referred to the Christian Jesus if that very character was a subsequent creation partly based on Josephus' tales of Jesus ben-Ananias, Simon bar-Giora, and so on.

ANOTHER JOSEPH

Much speculation surrounds the figure of Joseph of Arimathea. Of course, the traditional view is that this Joseph was a historical figure. Subsequent to the gospels, legend made him Jesus' uncle. The risen Jesus appeared to him in the prison cell where Joseph had been cast because of his association with the crucified criminal Jesus. He gave his uncle the chalice he had used at the Last Supper and told him to take it to Europe. Eventually, Joseph reached Brittany (which he never would have done if he'd had any idea what writers like Dan Brown would make of his visit there!) and then crossed the channel to deposit the relic at Glastonbury, where he died, leaving behind a souvenir shop for tourists.

Dennis R. MacDonald makes him a legend on the other end of his biography, too.[5] MacDonald thinks Joseph of Arimathea began as a Christianization of the Homeric character King Priam. Just as Priam dared to visit the camp of his enemies to beg for the return of the corpse of his son, Hector, from the Greek Achilles, who had slain him, so did his Christian counterpart Joseph entreat Pontius Pilate to let him take charge of Jesus for proper burial. The theory is quite plausible. But there is another good one to consider.

Suppose Joseph of Arimathea turned out to be a fictionalized version of Josephus the historian? His Romanized name was Flavius Josephus because of his association with the Flavian dynasty, but his Hebrew name was Joseph bar-Matthias. Does that have a familiar ring? Hmm: "Joseph b*ar-Matthias*"? "Joseph *of* Arimathea"? Suspiciously close, you might say. But maybe that's just a curiosity, no more than a coincidence? Could be. But consider this passage from Josephus' autobiography, depicting a scene near the end of the Jewish War, when Josephus was palling around with his new friend, Titus, the Roman commander.

> I saw many captives crucified, and remembered three of them as my former acquaintances. I was very sorry at this in my mind, and went with tears in my eyes to Titus, and told him of them; so he immediately commanded them to be taken down, and to have the greatest care taken of them, in order to their recovery; yet two of them died under the physician's hands, while the third recovered.[6]

This may be the origin of the gospel episode in which Joseph asks a Roman official for the body of one of three crucified men, leaving the others to chance. We usually don't think to ask why he didn't seek a decent burial for all three men, only for Jesus. Remember, Mark gives no hint that Joseph had any allegiance to Jesus to make him want to see to his burial. He was, for all we are told, simply a pious man engaged in an act of charity: burying crucified criminals since no one else would. So why only Jesus? But it does make sense as a rewrite of this episode from the life of Joseph bar-Matthias. Josephus *did* obtain the release of all three crucifixion victims, still alive at the time, but, just as in Mark, Jesus was the only one to return to life, so in the *Life of Josephus*, only one of the three, once taken down, survives. It makes a lot of sense. And obviously, if we accept this explanation, we have even more reason to think that Josephus was prior to the gospels and served as a source for them.

NEXT OF KIN

There is a second passage in Josephus' *Antiquities* (20:9:1) in which he describes the death of a certain James, saintly brother of a certain Jesus, considered the Anointed. Apologists insist that, even if you are mean enough to take the *Testimonium Flavianum* from them, this one, by the skin of its teeth, still is enough to allow them to say, as O'Reilly and Dugard do, that Jesus is a historically attested figure. But is it?

> And now Caesar, upon hearing of the death of Festus, sent Albinus into Judea, as procurator. But the king deprived Joseph of the high priesthood, and bestowed the succession to that dignity on the son of Ananus, who was also himself called Ananus. Now the report goes that this eldest Ananus proved a most fortunate man; for he had five sons who had all performed the office of a high priest to God, and who had himself enjoyed that dignity a long time formerly, which had never happened to any other of our high priests. But this younger Ananus, who, as we have told you already, took the high priesthood, was a bold man in his temper, and very insolent; he was also of the sect of the Sadducees, who are very rigid in judging offenders, above all the rest of the Jews, as we have already observed; when, therefore, Ananus was of this disposition, he thought he had now a proper opportunity [to exercise his authority]. Festus was now dead, and Albinus was but upon the road; so he assembled the Sanhedrin of judges, and brought before them the brother of Jesus, who was called Christ, whose name was James, and some others [or, some of his companions]; and when he had formed an accusation against them as breakers of the law, he delivered them to be stoned: but as for those who seemed the most equitable of the citizens, and such as were the most uneasy at the breach of the laws, they disliked what was done; they also sent to the king [Agrippa], desiring him to send to Ananus that he should act so no more, for that what he had already done was not to be justified; nay, some of them went also to meet Albinus, as he was upon his journey from Alexandria, and informed him that it

> was not lawful for Ananus to assemble a Sanhedrin without his consent. Whereupon Albinus complied with what they said, and wrote in anger to Ananus, and threatened that he would bring him to punishment for what he had done; on which king Agrippa took the high priesthood from him, when he had ruled but three months, and made Jesus, the son of Damneus, high priest.

But it is quite likely that Josephus intended no reference to James the Just, the "brother of the Lord" or to the Christian Jesus. It makes a lot more sense if the ambushed James was supposed to be James, son of Damneus, the brother of Jesus, son of Damneus. These men do figure in the immediate context. The story is that Ananus arranged to have a rival for the priesthood eliminated on trumped-up charges but did not get away with it. Once his shenanigans became known, he was booted from his position, and the brother of the murdered James was awarded the office Ananus had sought to usurp. So the slain James was avenged at least insofar as his surviving brother, Jesus, received the office James would have had. The reference we now read to "Jesus called Christ" might originally have read (or denoted) "Jesus, called/considered high priest." In both Daniel 9:26 and in the Dead Sea Scrolls, "an anointed one" means "a high priest." Nothing about Jesus Christ and James the Just after all.

BAPTIST PREACHER

Josephus discusses John the Baptist as a figure of the recent past. But the passage (*Antiquities* 18.5.2) looks a bit suspicious. First, the writer seems surprisingly eager to rebut a sacramental interpretation of John's baptism: he

> commanded the Jews to exercise virtue, both as to righteousness toward one another, and piety towards God, and so to come to baptism; for that the washing would be acceptable to him, if they made use of it, not in order to the remission of some sins, but for the purification of the body; supposing still that the soul was thoroughly purified beforehand by righteousness.

Why would Josephus care about such niceties any more than Gallio did (Acts 18:14–15)? It sounds like sectarian theological hair-splitting that would fit more naturally among John the Baptist sectarians or early Christians. Maybe these latter-day Baptists had started to debate the nature of baptism and came to rationalize it, just like modern Christian Baptists do. They decided that baptism is not in and of itself a salvific act. It should not be viewed as some sort of magic but instead denotes a change of mind and heart that is what really saves. Or it may have been an interpolation into Josephus by someone trying to correct Mark, interpreting what he said about a "baptism for the forgiveness of sins" in a non-sacramental sense.

Another reason for regarding the passage as an interpolation is the presence of a redactional seam, a clue that a copyist has stitched in new material. Often you can tell this from similar opening and closing sentences. The copyist had to reproduce the peg from which the continuation of the original narrative depended. The passage just quoted begins with "Now, some of the Jews thought that the destruction of Herod's army came from God, and that very justly as a punishment of what he did against John." This looks like the interpolator's paraphrase of the closing words of the passage: "Now, the Jews had an opinion that the destruction of this army was sent as a punishment upon Herod, as a mark of God's displeasure against him." This last would have been the original, speaking of Herod's general impiety, while the other would have been the paraphrase that introduces John the Baptist by name, blaming Antipas' defeat on the Tetrarch's ill-treatment of John. So perhaps Josephus did not mention John after all.

ACTS OF JOSEPHUS

Our concern in this book is the gospels, not Acts, but it is worth looking at a few instances where Acts, too, seems to have used Josephus as a source, the point being to show that Josephus is not some independent corroboration of the New Testament but is rather the basis for some of it. We are used to the idea that we can no longer appeal to Matthew and Mark as independent sources of information about Jesus, their frequent agreements as "multiple attestations" of the same facts. Why not? Because Matthew is *based* on Mark. And so it is with the New Testament and Josephus.

Josephus discusses three of the numerous anti-Roman hooligans, prophets, and would-be Messiahs active in the decades preceding the war with Rome. He gives special attention to Theudas the Magician, an unnamed Egyptian, and Judas of Galilee. Acts mentions just these three as well, and it looks like he was working from Josephus, though, not having a copy at hand to double-check, he made a goof or two. For instance, Josephus mentions Theudas, active in the 40s CE, and then, in a flashback, he refers to Judas of Galilee, who led the revolt against the Roman taxation census of 6 CE. In Acts 5:36–37, Luke has Gamaliel give a brief history lesson:

> Before these days, Theudas arose, making himself out to be somebody, and a number of men, about four hundred, joined him. But he was slain, and all who followed him were dispersed and came to nothing. After him, Judas the Galilean arose in the days of the census and drew away some of the people after him; he also perished, and all who followed him were scattered.

Oops! Theudas' exploits were yet in the future when this scene was transpiring. He did not precede Judas, as Luke would have it, but came on the scene decades later. That's quite a goof! What happened? The answer is simple: Luke vaguely recalled the order in which Josephus had discussed the two rebels and assumed this was the historical order in which they had appeared. An innocent mistake.

Luke also mentions Josephus' Egyptian: "Are you not the Egyptian, then, who recently stirred up a revolt and led the four thousand men of the Assassins [*sicarii*] out into the wilderness?" (Acts 21:38). In one account (*Antiquities* 20.171) Josephus numbers the Egyptian's troops at four hundred, while in another (*Wars of the Jews* 2.261–263) he gives a figure of some thirty thousand. Luke may have confused the two, giving the Egyptian four thousand. Do you suppose it is merely a coincidence that Acts mentions the same three, and *only* the same three troublemakers, when there were plenty more active in the period to choose from?

> If Luke did not know Josephus, we are faced with an astonishing number of coincidences: he links Judas and the census as a watershed event, connects Judas and Theudas, connects the Egyptian with the *sicarii*, connects the Egyptian with the desert, and selects these three figures out of all the anonymous guerillas and impostors of the period.[7]

Robert Eisenman discerns yet other places where Acts seems to depend upon Josephus.[8] The visit of Simon Peter to the Roman officer Cornelius at Caesarea (Acts 10–11) looks like a parody of Josephus' story of one Simon, a pious synagogue leader in Jerusalem.[9] This man wanted Herod Agrippa I barred from Temple worship because of his alleged unclean Gentile ways. But Agrippa invited him to inspect his Caesarea home, where he found nothing amiss, and then Agrippa sent him away laden with presents. In Luke's hands, Josephus' Agrippa becomes the Gentile Cornelius. Luke borrowed the name Cornelius from elsewhere in Josephus, where Cornelius is the name of two different Roman soldiers. And Luke keeps the location of the story at Caesarea. Luke also retains the theme of conflict between Herod Agrippa I and Simon (now Simon Peter) but transfers it to Acts 12.

Luke's fascinating character Simon Magus (Acts 8:9–10) seems to be identical with a magician named Simon whom Josephus says helped Bernice convince her sister Drusilla to cast aside her husband, King Azizus of Emesa. Azizus had gotten circumcised to marry her, but now she proceeded to take up with the uncircumcised Felix instead. Acts mentions several of these people, including Bernice (Acts 25:13), Felix and Drusilla (Acts 24:24), and Simon.

Where did Luke get the idea for the Agabus prophecy of a severe famine to transpire in Claudius' reign (Acts 11:27–28), of Paul's mission from Antioch to bring famine relief to Jerusalem (Acts 11:29–30), and for the previous episode of Philip and the Ethiopian treasurer (Acts 8:26–40)? Again, very likely from Josephus. It all stems from Josephus' story of Helena, Queen of Adiabene. This was a realm adjacent to (or overlapping with) Edessa. Helena and her son, Prince Izates, converted to Judaism, though initially the prince refused circumcision on the advice of a Jewish teacher who reassured him that spiritual worship was more important than getting circumcised. The queen agreed, pointing out that Izates' subjects might take offense if he accepted such alien customs. But before long, a stricter teacher from Jerusalem, named Eliezer, came to visit Prince Izates, only to find him pondering over Genesis 17:9–14, in which God institutes the Abrahamic covenant of circumcision. Eliezer asked if Izates understood the implications of what he read. Then why did he not see how important it was to be circumcised? The prince agreed and got circumcised. Helena and Izates, enthusiastic converts to the faith of Israel, resolved to dispatch agents to Egypt and Cyrene to buy grain during the Claudius famine and to distribute it among the poor in Jerusalem.

These events appear in Acts as follows. Eisenman identifies Paul as the first Jewish teacher who tells Izates he does not need to receive circumcision if he has faith. Paul must be one of Helena's agents bringing famine relief to Jerusalem, which he is said to do "from Antioch" (that is, Edessa, one of several cities called Antioch) in Acts 11.[10]

We rejoin Helena's story back in chapter 8, with Philip taking the role of Eliezer. He accosts the financial officer of a foreign queen. He is returning home from worshipping in Jerusalem, through Egypt by way of Gaza. This is of course the Ethiopian eunuch. Luke has transformed Queen Helena of Adiabene into Candace the queen of Ethiopia. Reverting to an Old Testament prototype, Luke makes Helena, a convert to Judaism, into a New Testament version of the Queen of Sheba, who journeyed to Jerusalem to hear the wisdom of Solomon. In fact, there weren't any Ethiopian queens at this time. So the queen in question must have been a fictional version of another, Helena of Adiabene.[11]

When Philip asks the Ethiopian if he understands what he is reading, Luke has borrowed it from the story of Izates and Eliezer. In both, the question "Do you understand what you are reading?" leads to a ritual conversion. In Acts, the text is Isaiah 53, and the ritual is baptism. In Josephus, the text is Genesis 17, and the ritual is circumcision. The circumcision element survives (as a crude parody recalling Galatians 5:12) in the Ethiopian having been fully castrated. Even the location of the Acts episode comes from the Helena story, as the Ethiopian is traveling into Egypt via Gaza, as Helena's agents must have done in order to buy the grain. Luke's version cannot have been the original for the simple reason that a eunuch could not have gone to Jerusalem to worship since eunuchs were barred from the Temple.

TACIT AGREEMENT

Cornelius Tacitus (*Annals* 15:44), writing about 125 CE, asserts that Nero blamed the Roman Christians for torching the city. He was scapegoating them in order to divert suspicion from himself. In case his readers were unacquainted with Christianity, Tacitus explains they were a sect founded by one "Christus" or "Chrestus" (both versions appear in this or that manuscript).

> They got their name from Christ [Christus or Chrestus], who was executed by sentence of the procurator Pontius Pilate in the reign of Tiberius. That checked the pernicious superstition for a short time, but it broke out afresh—not only in Judaea, where the plague first arose, but in Rome itself, where all the horrible and shameful things in the world collect and find a home.[12]

Some have suspected this, like the *Testimonium Flavianum*, to be a Christian interpolation. It *is* odd that no Christian writers quote this material for two centuries. It would have been of great interest had it been available, so maybe it wasn't. Maybe it hadn't been written yet. For me, it's a toss-up. But the point is moot, since, as in the case of Josephus, even if the text is authentic and original, it does not constitute proof of a historical Jesus. It merely reflects what Christians were saying in the early second century. The same must be said about the second-century humorist Lucian of Samosata: Both were way too late to know any more about a historical Jesus than we do.

GAIUS OF THE GESTAPO

Gaius Plinius Secundus (Pliny the Younger), ca. 112 CE, reports that Christians in Bithynia, where he was the governor, "sang hymns to Christ as to a god." This tells us nothing about any historical Jesus, only about Christian worship. To invoke Pliny the Younger as an attestation of Jesus, as O'Reilly and Dugard do, is as futile as it would be to appeal to the bulletin of one's local Presbyterian church. They worship Christ as a god, too. No help there, I'm afraid.

> So far this has been my procedure when people were charged before me with being Christians. I have asked the accused themselves if they were Christians; if they said 'Yes,' I asked them a second and third time, warning them of the penalty; if they persisted I ordered them to be led off to execution. . . . But they maintained that their fault or error amounted to nothing more than this: they were in the habit of meeting on a certain fixed day before sunrise and reciting an antiphonal hymn to Christ as to God, and binding themselves with an oath—not to commit any crime, but to abstain from all acts of theft, robbery and adultery, from breaches of faith, from repudiating a trust when called upon to honor it. . . . Nor has this contagious superstition spread through the cities only, but also through the villages and the countryside. But I think it can be checked and put right. At any rate, the temples, which had been wellnigh abandoned, are beginning to be frequented again; and the customary services, which had been neglected for a long time, are beginning to be resumed; fodder for the sacrificial animals, too, is beginning to find a sale again, for hitherto it was difficult to find anyone to buy it. (Gaius Plinius Secundus, *Epistles* x.96).[13]

I hate to say this, but I suspect this one is a Christian interpolation, too. Not as certainly as the bogus Josephus passage, but more nearly certain than the Tacitus text being secondary. Here's why. We are to believe that this letter of Pliny to the Emperor Trajan seeks advice on how severely to persecute the growing numbers of Christians, even though Pliny admits they are really innocent of any wrongdoing. This doesn't make him wonder if they should perhaps cool it with the executions, though. I'm already smelling a rat here. This sounds to me like a Christian trying to create the impression that even Christians' persecutors believe them to be innocent. It sounds like the whitewashing of Pilate in the gospels. The goal is to make pagans think twice about joining that lynch mob. And I'm not blaming them! We've got the same awful stuff going on all over the world today. I'm for anything that might stop it.

Another thing that sets my alarms off is the impression the text gives that pagans persecute Christians for purely mercenary reasons. Everybody and his brother are converting to that darn religion, and it's ruining the economy! The sacrificial animals and their kibble are going begging because there are so few pagan worshippers anymore! The temples of Zeus and Apollo are in danger of closing! It is exactly the same sort of anachronistic nonsense we read in Acts 19:23–27, where the local idol mongers union calls for Paul to be rubbed out because he is converting so many suckers that the worship of Artemis will go begging. The makers of souvenirs will lose their livelihood. I don't believe it, and that would mean the letter is a fake.

O'Reilly and Dugard refer to Pliny as "the historian Pliny." He was no historian, and neither are they. Pliny was a Roman governor and an epistolarian, a self-important man of letters. But not a historian. This is no minor goof on the part of the authors of *Killing Jesus*. It means they had never heard of Pliny and had no idea who he was. They just picked his name out of a list of supposed witnesses to Jesus and assumed he was another historian like Josephus and Tacitus.

A BOY NAMED SUE

It shows how desperate apologists for the faith have become when they start calling the gossipy second-century biographer Suetonius to the stand. All he has to say on the subject (that is, if it *is* on the subject) is that Claudius "expelled the Jews from Rome, on account of the riots in which they were constantly indulging, at the instigation of Chrestus" (Suetonius, *The Twelve Caesars*. *Claudius* 25.4).[14] *This* is a reference to Jesus Christ? You've got to be kidding.

What does it even mean to *say* that Suetonius makes mention of the Christian Jesus, when he doesn't get the name right, when he locates him on the wrong continent, fifteen years too late, and in a totally alien context? Robert E. van Voorst, like many, thinks there is a garbled reference to Jesus here:

> Suetonius's statement indicates how vague and incorrect knowledge of the origins of Christianity could be, both in the first and early second century. Similar sounds and spelling led him, like others, to misread *Christus* as *Chrestus*. Continued public unrest over this Christ [as preached by missionaries] had led Claudius to . . . send the trouble-makers packing. From this initial misunderstanding came the idea that this Chrestus was actually present in Rome as an instigator in the 40s.[15]

But even this attempt to untangle the passage presupposes that it is tangled in the first place. "Hm, he must be talking about Jesus but he got it all wrong. It was Jewish Christian *preaching* of Jesus that caused the unrest." But it only seems tangled if you are hell-bent on making it a statement about Jesus. Why not assume it is accurate as it stands, and that Suetonius simply referred to a local troublemaker with the common name "Chrestus"?

THAT'S "*TH*ALLUS!"

Julius Africanus says that Thallus, a mid-first-century historian, explained the supernatural darkness at the crucifixion as a mere eclipse. Africanus thinks he was wrong. Apologists gloat over this as a very early pagan testimony to the gospel events. But hold on. Africanus does not actually quote any passage in which Thallus mentions Jesus or the crucifixion. It is just as likely that Africanus just found some reference in Thallus to an eclipse at what Africanus took for the date of Jesus' death, and he simply assumed Thallus was making reference to the Jesus story. Africanus could be sure the Good Friday darkness was not a natural eclipse because Passover occurs during the full moon, and an eclipse requires a new moon, plus the fact that eclipses don't last three hours! But these facts equally imply that Thallus was not talking about the Good Friday darkness. If he knew the gospel story, how could he have thought the darkness was an eclipse? In any case, Eusebius tells us that Thallus recorded no event after the 167th Olympiad, or 112–109 BCE. Julius Africanus, then, must have been mistaken.

HERE TODAY, PHLEGON TOMORROW

Like O'Reilly and Dugard, the veteran apologist J. N. D. Anderson was glad he could add the second-century writer Phlegon of Tralles to the list of pagan witnesses to Jesus. "Origen . . . states that Phlegon (a freedman of the Emperor Hadrian who was born about AD 80) mentioned that the founder of Christianity had made certain predictions that had proved true."[16] Alas, this is yet another case of desperate Dumpster-diving. For one thing, if Phlegon did say this, it need mean no more than that he had read Mark 13. For another, no such statement appears in what is left of Phlegon's writings.[17] For a third, Phlegon was no historian at all but was rather a "paradoxographer," a kind of second-century Charles Fort, a collector of weird reports and tabloid anomalies. He did compile prophetic oracles by the Sybil and other ancients, but he was also big on hermaphrodites, on gods and mortals who spontaneously changed their gender and genitals, people with fantastic life spans, and so on. This is bad company for Jesus to be in even if Phlegon did mention him in some writing now lost. Among the freak phenomena Phlegon compiled were several stories of individuals who had died, then came back to life a few days later.

A historical Jesus may well have existed and yet managed not to receive "press coverage" in the ancient world. But apologists obviously feel a bit insecure at the prospect of there being no ancient mentions of Jesus outside of Christian circles. This is why they try to create the impression, as O'Reilly and Dugard do, that Jesus was well known and widely attested to. O'Reilly frequently reads viewer mail whose authors are commenting not on some news or political issues he has discussed on the air but on *Killing Jesus*. It is sheer promotionalism. And in answer to one "pinhead" who challenged the very existence of Jesus as a historical figure, O'Reilly contemptuously dismissed the viewer's comment, replying that Jesus was documented by Greek and Roman—and even *Muslim* historians. The fact that O'Reilly thinks Muslim discussions about Jesus would prove anything shows just how clueless he is about history. Islam began over six centuries after Christianity did. A Muslim writer mentioning him is, again, no different from the *Encyclopedia Britannica* mentioning him.

Here again, it is glaringly obvious that O'Reilly and Dugard are practitioners of precritical "scissors and paste" historiography. They are like a whale, cruising through the ocean, mouth open to glean any plankton in its path. There is no attempt to evaluate materials from the past. Anything is as good as anything else, "all the news that fits, we print." Bill O'Reilly is quite skilled at distinguishing facts from spin, propaganda, and empty bloviation when it comes to political matters. This is one reason I like him so much. But he appears to be utterly incapable of separating fact from fiction when religion and history are on the table. In this matter he should be taken no more seriously than actor Sean Penn pontificating on foreign policy.

NOTES

INTRODUCTION: JESUS IN THE NO-SPIN ZONE

1. Carl Sandburg, *Abraham Lincoln: The Prairie Years and The War Years* (New York: Mariner Books/Houghton Mifflin Harcourt, 2002); C. A. Tripp and Jean Baker, *The Intimate World of Abraham Lincoln* (New York: Free Press, 2005).

2. Michael Baigent, Richard Leigh, and Henry Lincoln, *Holy Blood, Holy Grail* (New York: Dell, 1982, 1983).

3. David Mamet, *The Secret Knowledge: On the Dismantling of American Culture* (New York: Sentinel/Penguin, 2011), chap. 7, "Choice," pp. 38–49.

CHAPTER 1. HISTORICAL BACKGROUND OR HISTORICAL BALLAST?

1. R. G. Collingwood, *The Idea of History* (New York: Oxford University Books/Galaxy Books, 1957), p. 240: "If we filled up the narrative of Caesar's doings with fanciful details such as the names of the persons he met on the way, and what he said to them, the construction would be arbitrary: it would in fact be the kind of construction which is done by an historical novelist."

2. G. R. S. Mead, *Did Jesus Live 100 B.C.? An Enquiry into the Talmud Jesus Stories, the Toldoth Jeschu, and Some Curious Statements of Epiphanius—Being a Contribution to the Study of Christian Origins* (New Hyde Park, New York: University Books, 1968).

3. Robert M. Grant, *Irenaeus of Lyons (The Early Church Fathers)* (New York: Routledge, 1997), p. 33.

4. Throughout this book you will notice certain minor inconsistencies in the placement of apostrophes, the form of possessives, capitalization, even the spelling of names. I do not presume to tamper with the usages in quoted material. They reflect yesterday's conventions and different transliterations of foreign and ancient names. But I feel sure you will not be confused.

5. William E. Phipps, *Was Jesus Married? The Distortion of Sexuality in the Christian Tradition* (New York: Harper & Row, 1970).

6. Even the familiar notion, taken for granted in *Killing Jesus*, that Jesus

was a carpenter is historically tenuous. As Géza Vermes points out in *Jesus the Jew: A Historian's Reading of the Gospels* (London: Fontana/Collins, 1976), "carpenter," in the context of synagogue preaching, was a metaphor denoting "skilled exegete," as in the widely known proverb: "This is something that no carpenter, son of carpenters, can explain" or "There is no carpenter, nor a carpenter's son, to explain it" (pp. 21–22).

7. T. M. Luhrmann, *When God Talks Back: Understanding the American Evangelical Relationship with God* (New York: Vintage Books, 2012), chap. 6, "Teach Us to Pray," pp. 157–88.

8. Raymond E. Brown, *The Birth of the Messiah: A Commentary on the Infancy Narratives of Matthew and Luke* (Garden City, NY: Doubleday, 1977), pp. 114–15. It looks to me as if Matthew simply used Josephus directly.

9. Ibid., p. 174.

10. Martin Dibelius, *From Tradition to Gospel*, trans. Bertram Lee Woolf (New York: Scribner's, n.d.), pp. 108–109.

11. David Friedrich Strauss, *The Life of Jesus Critically Examined*, trans. George Eliot (Mary Ann Evans), Lives of Jesus Series (1835; repr., Philadelphia: Fortress Press, 1972), p. 513.

12. Rene Salm, *The Myth of Nazareth: The Invented Town of Jesus* (Cranford, NJ: American Atheist Press, 2008), shows that not one of the artifacts often claimed to attest to a Nazareth village in the ostensible time of Jesus can be shown to come from that period. So much for O'Reilly's pat assurance that archaeology has increased our confidence in gospel accuracy. And then there is the problem of there being no archaeological evidence of Jesus-era synagogues in Galilee, though the gospels have Jesus visiting them constantly.

13. Collingwood, *Idea of History*, pp. 234–38ff.

14. Similarly, one still reads in the footnotes in some Bibles that refer to variant textual readings: "Some authorities [i.e., manuscripts] have so-and-so.").

15. I. Howard Marshall, *Eschatology and the Parables* (Leicester, UK: Theological Students Fellowship, n.d.), p. 5.

16. Bart D. Ehrman, *Forgery and Counterforgery: The Use of Literary Deceit in Early Christian Polemics* (New York: Oxford University Press, 2013).

17. Collingwood, *Idea of History*, p. 260.

18. Ferdinand Christian Baur, *Paul the Apostle of Jesus Christ: His Life and Works, His Epistles and Teachings*, trans. Edward Zeller and A. Menzies (1873–1875; repr., Peabody, MA: Hendrickson Publishers, 2003), vol. 1, p. 214 and often throughout.

19. Eusebius, *The History of the Church*, trans. G. A. Williamson (New York: Penguin Books, 1965), p. 152.

20. Ibid.

21. David Friedrich Strauss, *The Life of Jesus for the People.* (London: Williams & Norgate, 1879), vol. 2, p. 76.

22. G. A. Wells, *Did Jesus Exist?* (Elek/Pemberton, 1975), p. 19.

23. "Synoptic" means that they share much the same viewpoint as compared with John.

24. Adolf Harnack, *What Is Christianity?* trans. Thomas Bailey Saunders (New York: Harper & Row Torchbooks/Cloister Library, 1957), p. 144.

25. Albert Schweitzer, *The Quest of the Historical Jesus: A Critical Study of Its Progress from Reimarus to Wrede*, trans. W. Montgomery (New York: Macmillan, 1961), pp. 85–87.

26. See my critiques of Craig, "By This Time He Stinketh: William Lane Craig's Attempts to Exhume Jesus," in *The Empty Tomb: Jesus Beyond the Grave*, ed. Robert M. Price and Jeffery Jay Lowder (Amherst, New York: Prometheus Books, 2005), pp. 411–31; Robert M. Price, *Jesus Is Dead* (Cranford, NJ: American Atheist Press, 2007), chap. 15, "William Lane Craig's 'Contemporary Scholarship and the Historical Evidence for the Resurrection of Jesus Christ,'" pp. 195–213.

27. See my critique of Moreland in Robert M. Price, *The Case against the Case for Christ: A New Testament Scholar Refutes the Reverend Lee Strobel* (Cranford, NJ: American Atheist Press, 2010), chap. 14, "The Circumcision Evidence: Is a Supernatural Resurrection the Best Explanation for Folks no Longer Trimming Their Sons' Foreskins?" pp. 251–54.

28. Dibelius, *From Tradition to Gospel*, pp. 108–109.

29. Niels Peter Lemche, *The Israelites in History and Tradition* (Library of Ancient Israel) (Louisville: Westminster John Knox Press, 1998), p. 154.

CHAPTER 2. BIRD MAN OF NAZARETH

1. Maurice Casey, *Is John's Gospel True?* (New York: Routledge, 1996).

2. This is an odd way of putting it; the "known world" usually means the extent of the world as then known to ancient geographers, as when we say, "Alexander conquered the known world." Surely the authors mean the same sort of thing as in the REM song "It's the End of the World as We Know It"?

3. Albert Schweitzer, *The Mystery of the Kingdom of God: The Secret of Jesus' Messiahship and Passion*, trans. Walter Lowrie (1914; repr., New York: Schocken Books, 1964), pp. 151–54, for example, "He never pointed to the coming Messiah, but to the expected Forerunner. So is to be explained the proclamation about 'him that is to come after him' (Mk 1:7, 8)."

4. The very early heretic Cerinthus taught that the Christ Spirit entered into Jesus at the Jordan and used him as his human host and channeler until the crucifixion.

5. See Appendix One for the dates of the gospels.

6. Robert Eisler, *The Messiah Jesus and John the Baptist: According to Flavius Josephus' Recently Rediscovered "Capture of Jerusalem" and other Jewish and Christian Sources*, trans. Alexander Haggerty Krappe (New York: Dial Press, 1931), p. 265.

7. Ibid., pp. 265–66.

8. Ibid., pp. 266–67.

9. Raymond E. Brown, "John the Baptist in the Gospel of John," in *New Testament Essays*, ed. Raymond E. Brown (Garden City, NY: Doubleday Image, 1968), pp. 179–81.

CHAPTER 3. HOW NOT TO BEHAVE IN CHURCH

1. J. Ramsey Michaels, *John: A Good News Commentary* (San Francisco: Harper & Row, 1984), pp. 32–33. See also Rudolf Bultmann, *The Gospel of John: A Commentary*, trans. G. R. Beasley-Murray, R. W. N. Hoare, J. K. Riches (Philadelphia: Westminster Press, 1975), p. 644.

2. Here we are already hearing the kind of exchange the Synoptics place at the trial (Mark 14:61–62; Matt. 26:63–64; Luke 22:67–70).

3. See Van A. Harvey, *The Historian and the Believer: Christian Faith and the Morality of Historical Knowledge* (New York: Macmillan, 1969), p. 88.

4. Raymond E. Brown, "Roles of Women in the Fourth Gospel," *Theological Studies* vol. 3, no. 4 (December 1975): 695.

5. The frame of the story says this was the first of Jesus' miracles, but it is obvious Mary is shown to be all too familiar with her son's superpowers. This inconsistency is a dead giveaway that the story has been borrowed from a different context, that of the Infancy Gospel tradition.

6. My grandfather, Welby Price, used to twit my teetotaling Southern Baptist grandmother with this story.

7. Brad H. Young, *Jesus the Jewish Theologian* (Grand Rapids, MI: Baker Academic Press, 1993); Ann Spangler and Lois Tverberg, *Sitting at the Feet of Rabbi Jesus: How the Jewishness of Jesus Can Transform Your Faith* (Grand Rapids, MI: Zondervan, 2009); Bruce Chilton, *Rabbi Jesus: An Intimate Biography* (New York: Doubleday, 2000).

8. Hyam Maccoby, *Jesus the Pharisee* (London: SCM Press, 2003); Harvey Falk, *Jesus the Pharisee: A New Look at the Jewishness of Jesus* (New York: Paulist

Press, 1985); Géza Vermes, *The Religion of Jesus the Jew* (Minneapolis: Augsburg Fortress Publishers, 1993); Amy-Jill Levine, *The Misunderstood Jew: The Church and the Scandal of the Jewish Jesus* (San Francisco: HarperOne, 2007); David Flusser, *The Sage from Galilee: Rediscovering Jesus' Genius* (Grand Rapids, MI: Eerdmans, 2007); Nehemia Gordon, *The Hebrew Yeshua vs. the Greek Jesus* (Arlington, VA: Hilkiah Press, 2005).

9. Albert Schweitzer, *The Quest of the Historical Jesus: A Critical Study of Its Progress from Reimarus to Wrede*, trans. W. Montgomery (New York: Macmillan, 1961), p. 206, might as well have been talking about O'Reilly and Dugard when he said this about nineteenth-century Jesus biographer Daniel Schenkel: "Schenkel is able to give these explanations because he knows the most secret thoughts of Jesus and is therefore no longer bound to the text."

10. Käte Hamburger, *The Logic of Literature*, trans. Marilynn J. Rose (Bloomington and Indianapolis: Indiana University Press, 2nd rev. ed., 1993), pp. 112–13: "Even those historical novels which adhere to historical truth just as exactly as an actual historical document does, nevertheless transform the historical person into a non-historical, fictive figure, transferring him out of a possible system of reality into a system of fiction. For the system of fiction is defined by the figure's not being presented as object, but as subject, portrayed in his I-originarity . . . it is the process of fictionalizing which renders non-historical all ever so historical raw material in a novel."

11. Tzvetan Todorov, *The Poetics of Prose*, trans. Richard Howard (Ithaca, NY: Cornell University Press, 1977), chap. 5, "Narrative-Men," pp. 66–79.

12. M. de Jonge, "Nicodemus and Jesus," *Bulletin of the John Rylands Library* 53 (1971): 337–59.

13. J. Louis Martyn, *History and Theology in the Fourth Gospel* (New York: Harper & Row, 1968).

14. Richard Francis Weymouth, trans., *The New Testament in Modern Speech: An Idiomatic Translation into Everyday English from the Text of "The Resultant Greek Testament"* (London: James Clarke, 1909), p. 246.

15. Hugh J. Schonfield, trans., *The Authentic New Testament*, A Mentor Religious Classic (New York: New American Library, 1958), p. 393.

16. Edgar J. Goodspeed, trans., *The New Testament: An American Translation* (Chicago: University of Chicago Press, 1939), p. 87.

17. William Barclay, trans., *The New Testament, Volume 1, The Gospels and the Acts of the Apostles* (London: Collins, 1968), p. 265.

18. Rudolf Bultmann, *The History of the Synoptic Tradition*, trans. John Marsh (New York: Harper & Row, 1972), pp. 31–32.

19. Graham Chapman, John Cleese, Terry Gilliam, Eric Idle, Terry Jones,

and Michael Palin, *Monty Python's Life of Brian (of Nazareth)* (New York: Ace Books, 1979), p. 109.

20. Even though there is no evidence of any settlement having been up there on the mountainside. Rene Salm, *The Myth of Nazareth: The Invented Town of Jesus* (Cranford, NJ: American Atheist Press, 2008), pp. 202, 217–18.

CHAPTER 4. FISHERMEN, PROSTITUTES, AND PHARISEES

1. Morton Smith, *Jesus the Magician* (New York: Harper & Row, 1978), p. 10: "Mark has no introduction to these stories; he wants the reader to believe that Jesus had never seen these men before. Their immediate responses to his unexpected and unexplained summons are miracles that testify to his supernatural power."

2. "He comes to us as One unknown, without a name, as of old, by the lakeside, He came to those men who knew Him not. He speaks to us the same word: 'Follow thou me.' and sets us to the tasks which He has to fulfill for our time." Albert Schweitzer, *The Quest of the Historical Jesus: A Critical Study of Its Progress from Reimarus to Wrede*, trans. W. Montgomery (1906; repr., New York: Macmillan, 1961), p. 403.

3. Mark, Luke's source, placed the incident of Jesus healing Simon's mother (afflicted with Epstein-Barr?) only after Jesus has called him to be a disciple. The impression Luke gives, of Jesus already being acquainted with Peter, seems to be the result of a goof, placing Mark's episodes in a different order.

4. See Robert M. Price, *The Incredible Shrinking Son of Man: How Reliable Is the Gospel Tradition?* (Amherst, NY: Prometheus Books, 2003), p. 158.

5. This connection stems from the topical arrangement of originally self-contained units in Mark. Mark chapter 2 stacks up various controversy stories in which Jesus outwits his detractors. The first one, that of the dispute over Jesus forgiving the sins of the paralytic (Mark 2:1–12), takes place in Peter's Capernaum home. The next one, about Jesus notoriously associating with tax collectors (Mark 2:13–17), takes place by the Lake of Galilee, but no town is named, nor is any location specified in the following controversy stories. This redactional accident is the sole basis for locating Matthew in Capernaum.

6. Graham Chapman, John Cleese, Terry Gilliam, Eric Idle, Terry Jones, and Michael Palin, *Monty Python's Life of Brian (of Nazareth)* (New York: Ace Books, 1979), p. 14.

7. "If you'd come today you would have reached a whole nation. Israel in

4 B.C. had no mass communication," *Jesus Christ Superstar*, "Superstar," lyrics by Tim Rice, 1969.

8. Joachim Jeremias, *The Sermon on the Mount*, trans. Norman Perrin. Facet Books Biblical Series 2 (Philadelphia: Fortress Press, 1963), chap. 2, "The Origins of the Sermon on the Mount," pp. 13–18.

9. Jack T. Sanders, *The Jews in Luke-Acts* (Philadelphia: Fortress Press, 1987), pp. 104–105, explains the accusation that the Pharisees loaded heavy burdens onto the backs of the faithful, which they themselves did not lift a finger to move (Luke 11:46). It is aimed not at anyone in Jesus' milieu but rather at Christian Pharisees in the early Church who tried to impose Torah observance on Gentile converts (Acts 15:5).

10. See W. D. Davies, *Introduction to Pharisaism*. Facet Books Biblical Series 16 (Philadelphia: Fortress Press, 1967).

11. E. P. Sanders, *Jesus and Judaism* (Philadelphia: Fortress Press, 1985), p. 40.

12. Charles Cutler Torrey, *Our Translated Gospels: Some of the Evidence* (New York: Harper & Brothers, 1936), p. 93, proposed that "leper" is a mistranslation from an underlying Aramaic version that designated Simon as "the jar merchant," which may make a little more sense of the passage.

13. John Lightfoot, *A Commentary on the New Testament from the Talmud and Hebraica*, Vol. 2: Matthew and Mark (1658; repr., Grand Rapids, MI: Baker Book House, 1979), on Matt. 27:56.

14. David Friedrich Strauss, *The Life of Jesus Critically Examined*, trans. George Eliot (Mary Ann Evans), Lives of Jesus Series (1835; repr., Philadelphia: Fortress Press, 1972), p. 222.

15. Traditionally, the rich man is read as turning down Jesus' challenge, but this is a misreading. "He went away sorrowful; for he had great possessions" (Mark 10:22). But Jesus *told* him to "*go*, sell what you have, and give to the poor." How do we know that's not what he's leaving in order to *do*? He went away sorrowful? That doesn't mean he's sorry he asked and is going to seek out some other guru who will give him an answer more to his liking. After all, Jesus comments on the man's departure, saying, "How hard it will be for those who have riches to enter the kingdom of God!" (Mark 10:23). That doesn't have to mean the man is not going to do it. His sorrow reflects the difficulty of the step he is perhaps now resolved to undertake.

CHAPTER 5. THE AMAZING JESUS

1. Albert Schweitzer, *The Quest of the Historical Jesus: A Critical Study of Its Progress from Reimarus to Wrede*, trans. W. Montgomery (1906; repr., New York: Macmillan, 1961), p. 150.

2. The Holy Infant of Prague is an avatar of Jesus in the form of a baby, dressed in a diaphanous gown and wearing a crown. This has got to be one of the creepiest and most grotesque forms of Catholic devotion, the adoration of Jesus as somehow still an infant. It reminds me of the joke where a tour guide in Paris points out a glass case containing three skulls, ranging from small to large. The guide announces that this is what remains of Napoleon. Someone in the crowd asks which one is Napoleon. The answer is: *all* of them. One is the skull of Napoleon as a child, the next when he was a young man, the third as an adult.

3. Burton L. Mack, *A Myth of Innocence: Mark and Christian Origins* (Philadelphia: Fortress Press, 1988), p. 42.

4. Much in the spirit, one might add, of the control freak Obama Administration today.

5. Mack, *Myth of Innocence*, p. 45.

6. Andrew J. Overman, *Matthew's Gospel and Formative Judaism: The Social World of the Matthean Community* (Minneapolis: Fortress Press, 1990), pp. 44–48, admits that "we have no evidence that the term 'rabbi' refers to an official office and function by the end of the first century," (p. 4) but goes on to argue that the gospels apply the term to Jesus as an informal honorific. But I think his reasoning is circular, simply taking for granted that the gospel stories are reliable history. Proper historical method would be to establish the date of the gospels in accordance with known external data.

7. Gerd Theissen, *The Miracle Stories of the Early Christian Tradition*, trans. Francis McDonagh (Philadelphia: Fortress Press, 1983), p. 171.

8. Mark C. Goodacre, "Fatigue in the Synoptics," *New Testament Studies* 44 (1998): 45.

9. Collingwood, *Idea of History*, p. 260.

10. Oscar Cullmann, *Jesus and the Revolutionaries*, trans. Gareth Putnam (New York: Harper & Row, 1970), p. 9.

11. The name "Zealot" was coined for these militants only in the lead-up to the Jewish War, but Josephus the historian traces the movement back to Judas the Galilean, who led the revolt against Roman taxation in 6 CE. He makes Judas the Galilean the founder of "the Fourth Philosophy," which in his day was called the Zealots. See Reza Aslan, *Zealot: The Life and Times of Jesus of Nazareth* (New York: Random House, 2013), p. 41.

12. S. G. F. Brandon, *The Fall of Jerusalem and the Christian Church: A Study of the Effects of the Jewish Overthrow of A.D. 70 on Christianity* (London: SPCK, 1951), pp. 104–105; S. G. F. Brandon, *Jesus and the Zealots: A Study of the Political Factor in Primitive Christianity* (New York: Scribner's, 1966), pp. 243–45; Cullmann, *Jesus and the Revolutionaries*, pp. 8–9.

13. Cullmann, *Jesus and the Revolutionaries*, p. 63.

14. Robert Eisler, *The Messiah Jesus and John the Baptist*, trans. Alexander Haggerty Krappe (New York: Dial Press, 1931), p. 252.

15. Mack, *Myth of Innocence*, p. 167.

16. Bertil Gärtner, *Iscariot*, trans. Victor I. Gruhn, Facet Books, Biblical Series, 29 (Philadelphia: Fortress Press, 1971), p. 7.

CHAPTER 6. THEOLOGY HIDDEN IN PLAIN SIGHT

1. I can't resist pointing out that Robert W. Funk and the Jesus Seminar were ceaselessly accused of being publicity hounds, when in fact they were simply trying to communicate the closely guarded findings of mainstream New Testament criticism to a public languishing in the doldrums of pulpit ignorance. Yes, that's seeking publicity, but only in the sense of letting one's light shine, exactly equivalent to the motives of scholars like Robert Eisenman, who managed to leak the long-shuttered Dead Sea Scrolls to the public.

2. Rudolf Bultmann, *Theology of the New Testament*, trans. Kendrick Grobel, Scribner Studies in Contemporary Theology (New York: Scribner's, 1951), p. 27.

3. Raymond E. Brown, *The Birth of the Messiah: A Commentary on the Infancy Narratives in Matthew and Luke* (Garden City, NY: Doubleday, 1977), pp. 29–31. The Spirit is not mentioned in the Transfiguration story, but in Jewish thinking, the Spirit was pretty much equivalent to the Shekinah glory cloud, which is featured in the story. Gershom Scholem, *Major Trends in Jewish Mysticism*, trans. George Lichtheim (New York: Schocken Books, 1973), p. 111.

4. William Wrede, *The Messianic Secret*, trans. J. C. G. Greig. Library of Theological Translations (Cambridge: James Clarke, 1971).

5. David Friedrich Strauss, *The Life of Jesus Critically Examined*, trans. George Eliot (Mary Ann Evans), Lives of Jesus Series (1835; repr., Philadelphia: Fortress Press, 1972), pp. 491–92.

6. Philostratus, *The Life of Apollonius of Tyana*, vol. 1, trans. F. C. Conybeare, Loeb Classical Library 16 (Cambridge, MA: Harvard University Press, 1912), pp. 457, 459.

7. Lucius Apuleius, *The Works of Apuleius Comprising the Metamorphosis, or*

Golden Ass, The God of Socrates, The Florida and His Defence, or A Discourse on Magic. A New Translation (Anon.) (London: George Bell and Sons, 1910), pp. 401–402.

8. Lucius Apuleius, *The Golden Ass*, trans. William Adlington, rev. Harry C. Schnur (New York: Collier Books, 1962), p. 241.

9. B. P. Reardon, ed., *Collected Ancient Greek Novels* (Berkeley: University of California Press, 1989), pp. 753–54. Gerald N. Sandy, trans., *The Story of Apollonius King of Tyre*.

10. Strauss, *Life of Jesus*, p. 495.

11. Though, like Lazarus, he had survived it. *The Son of Frankenstein*, directed by Rowland V. Lee (1939, Universal Pictures).

12. Strauss, *Life of Jesus*, p. 479.

13. Ibid., p. 484.

14. Graham Chapman, John Cleese, Terry Gilliam, Eric Idle, Terry Jones, and Michael Palin, *Monty Python's Life of Brian (of Nazareth)* (New York: Ace Books, 1979), p. 37.

15. Hermann Gunkel, *An Introduction to the Psalms. The Genres of the Religious Lyric of Israel*, trans. James D. Nogalski, Mercer Library of Biblical Studies (Macon, GA: Mercer University Press, 1998), chap. 6, "Individual Complaint Songs," pp. 121–98; Sigmund Mowinkel, *The Psalms in Israel's Worship*, trans. D. R. Ap-Thomas (Nashville: Abingdon Press, 1962), pp. 79–80.

16. Mowinkel, *Psalms in Israel's Worship*, pp. 46–78; Gunkel, *Introduction to the Psalms*, chap. 5, "Royal Psalms," pp. 99–120; J. H. Eaton, *Kingship and the Psalms*, Studies in Biblical Theology Second Series 32 (London: SCM Press, 1976), chap, 4, sec. 2, "The Enemies of God as Personal Enemies of the King," pp. 137–41.

17. Krister Stendahl, *The School of St. Matthew and Its Use of the Old Testament* (Philadelphia: Fortress Press, 1968); Richard Longenecker, *Biblical Exegesis in the Apostolic Period* (Grand Rapids, MI: Eerdmans, 1975), chap. 1, "Jewish Hermeneutics in the First Century," pp. 19–50.

18. This confusion has led to many writers claiming that Matthew was writing to convince fellow Jews that Jesus was indeed the Messiah. No, his "fulfillment" verses were for in-house consumption.

19. Gershom Scholem, *On the Kabbalah and Its Symbolism*, trans. Ralph Manheim (New York: Schocken Books, 1969), pp. 5–86.

CHAPTER 7. LIAR, PINHEAD, OR LORD

1. Albert Schweitzer, *The Quest of the Historical Jesus: A Critical Study of Its Progress from Reimarus to Wrede*, trans. W. Montgomery (1906; repr., New York: Macmillan, 1961), p. 29, describes the eighteenth-century life of Jesus by Johann Jacob Hess in words that exactly apply to *Killing Jesus*: "His Life of Jesus still keeps largely to the lines of a paraphrase of the Gospels; indeed, he calls it a paraphrasing history. It is based upon a harmonizing combination of the four Gospels. The matter of the Synoptic narratives is . . . fitted more or less arbitrarily into the intervals between the Passovers in the fourth Gospel."

2. H. P. Lovecraft, "Notes on Writing Weird Fiction," in *Miscellaneous Writings*, ed. S. T. Joshi (Sauk City, WI: Arkham House, 1995), pp. 113–16.

3. Schweitzer, *Quest of the Historical Jesus*, p. 220.

4. Jonathan Culler, *Structuralist Poetics: Structuralism, Linguistics, and the Study of Literature* (Ithaca, NY: Cornell University Press, 1975), pp. 137, 141.

5. Robert M. Fowler, *Let the Reader Understand: Reader-Response Criticism and the Gospel of Mark* (Minneapolis: Fortress Press, 1991), p. 21: "In these and other episodes the characters on the stage with Jesus demonstrate no grasp of the action taking place before their eyes. . . . [F]requently the characters on the stage show no signs of uptake. Only the audience witnessing the drama are in the position to grasp what is happening on the stage; only among the audience is uptake occurring. . . . [T]he three crystal-clear predictions of Jesus' death ([Mark] 8:31; 9:31; 10:32–34) secure no uptake within the story; if they have any function at all in the narrative, they function to alert the reader to what lies ahead. . . . [V]ast portions of the Gospel function for the reader *alone*."

6. Henry J. Cadbury, *The Making of Luke-Acts* (London: SPCK Press, 1961), pp. 123–26.

7. Jason BeDuhn, *Truth in Translation: Accuracy and Bias in English Translations of the New Testament* (New York: University Press of America, 2003), pp. 103–106, shows that the grammar dictates this translation, not "Before Abraham was, I am," as if to have Jesus apply to himself the self-revelation of Yahweh in Exodus 3:14. But it certainly depicts him as claiming his own preexistence.

8. In my *Pre-Nicene New Testament*, I translate John 8:42 as "I came forth from the Godhead and have appeared."

9. Some of the manuscripts lack "and the life," which I think actually makes the statement even more powerful.

10. David Friedrich Strauss, *The Life of Jesus for the People* (London: Williams & Norgate, 1879), vol. 1, pp. 272–73.

11. C. S. Lewis, *Mere Christianity* (1943; repr., New York: Macmillan, 1960), pp. 55–56.

12. Albert Schweitzer, *The Psychiatric Study of Jesus: Exposition and Criticism*, trans. Charles R. Joy (Boston: Beacon Press, 1948), pp. 60–64.

13. *Miracle on 34th Street*, directed by George Seaton (1947, Twentieth Century Fox Film Corporation).

14. Donald G. Dawe, *The Form of a Servant: A Historical Analysis of the Kenotic Motif* (Philadelphia: Westminster Press, 1963).

15. Adolf Harnack, *What Is Christianity?* trans. Thomas Bailey Saunders (New York: Harper & Row Torchbooks/Cloister Library, 1957) p. 144. Italics in original.

CHAPTER 8. TEMPLE TANTRUM

1. The cure is as bad as the disease, since the extravagant promise of Jesus has spawned endless rationalizations and disappointments.

2. F. F. Bruce, *The New Testament Documents: Are They Reliable?* (Grand Rapids. MI: Eerdmans, 1960), p. 74: "The whole incident was an acted parable."

3. Was Isaiah claiming to be God, too? If O'Reilly and Dugard's church had taught them that he was, we can be sure they would take the verse to imply *that*, too.

4. D. E. Nineham, *Saint Mark*, Pelican New Testament Commentaries (Baltimore: Penguin Books, 1969), p. 302.

5. Ibid., p. 304.

6. Ibid., p. 301.

7. S. G. F. Brandon, *The Fall of Jerusalem and the Christian Church: A Study of the Effects of the Jewish Overthrow of A.D. 70 on Christianity* (London: SPCK, 1951), pp. 103–105.

8. Ibid., p. 109.

9. Ibid., pp. 192–94.

10. Warmed over today by Reza Aslan, *Zealot: The Life and Times of Jesus of Nazareth* (New York: Random House, 2013), without acknowledgment.

11. Morton Smith, *Jesus the Magician* (New York: Harper & Row, 1978), p. 39.

12. Burton L. Mack, *A Myth of Innocence: Mark and Christian Origins* (Philadelphia: Fortress Press, 1988), p. 292. Nor is he the only one (see Nineham, *Saint Mark*, pp. 300–301). Some think the whole thing may be a fleshing out of Malachi 3:1–3: "Behold, I send my messenger to prepare the way before me, and the Lord whom you seek will suddenly come to his temple; the messenger of the

covenant in whom you delight, behold, he is coming, says the Lord of hosts. But who can endure the day of his coming, and who can stand when he appears? For he is like a refiner's fire and like fuller's soap; he will sit as a refiner and purifier of silver, and he will purify the sons of Levi and refine them like gold and silver, till they present right offerings to the Lord."

13. Nineham, *Saint Mark*, p. 301.

14. Another example would be the aftermath of the Transfiguration, where the disciples ask Jesus, "Why do the scribes say that first Elijah must come?" Jesus replies that he has, albeit figuratively, in the form of John the Baptist (Mark 9:13, cf. Matt. 17:13). But why are they asking this question, which implies that it is a problem that Elijah has *not* appeared? They have just seen Elijah in person atop the Mount of Transfiguration. What Mark must have done is to group together two alternative Christian attempts to explain how Jesus could have been the Messiah if the prophet Elijah had not returned, as expected, to herald him. Some pointed to the Baptizer as a figurative fulfillment of the prophecy. That must not have convinced too many people, so others said, "Oh, but he *did* come. But he appeared to a total of four people up on top of a mountain. Too bad you weren't there, I guess." Oblivious of the implications, Mark blithely included both, side by side. David Friedrich Strauss, *The Life of Jesus Critically Examined*, trans. George Eliot (Mary Ann Evans), Lives of Jesus Series (1835; repr., Philadelphia: Fortress Press, 1972), pp. 542–43.

15. S. G. F. Brandon, *Jesus and the Zealots: A Study of the Political Factor in Primitive Christianity* (New York: Charles Scribner's Sons, 1967).

16. Eusebius, *The History of the Church*, trans. G. A. Williamson (New York: Penguin Books, 1965), p. 268.

CHAPTER 9. MESSIAHS AND MATCHSTICK MEN

1. Also dubbed "*chreias*" (Vernon K. Robbins and others, e.g., Burton L. Mack, *A Myth of Innocence: Mark and Christian Origins* [Philadelphia: Fortress Press, 1988], p. 161), "apophthegms" (Rudolf Bultmann, *The History of the Synoptic Tradition*, trans. John Marsh [New York: Harper & Row, 1968], p. 11) and "paradigms" (Martin Dibelius, *From Tradition to Gospel*, trans. Bertram Lee Woolf [New York: Scribner's, n.d.], pp. 37ff.; Vincent Taylor, *The Formation of the Gospel Tradition: Eight Lectures* (London: Macmillan, 1957), pp. 63ff., called them "pronouncement stories."

2. Mack, *Myth of Innocence*, p. 176.

3. Bultmann, *History of the Synoptic Tradition*, pp. 26, 41.

4. Jack T. Sanders, *The Jews in Luke-Acts* (Philadelphia: Fortress Press, 1987), pp. 94–97, 111.

5. Morton Smith, *Jesus the Magician* (New York: Harper & Row, 1978), p. 170: "They are told to display his cleverness in escaping traps."

6. Mack, *Myth of Innocence*, p. 176.

7. Ibid., p. 203: "The pronouncement stories in the Gospel of Mark do not record debates Jesus had with the Pharisees. . . . They record the way people wanted to imagine the conflict and its resolution in retrospect. . . . They are fictions because they violate the basic ground rules of human discourse and dialogue. . . . No rationale is given for his authority to make these definitive pronouncements. The Pharisees are merely literary foils. Jesus' answers seem cogent only to Christian readers. If the scenes were actual records, Jesus' opponents would never have walked away with their tails between their legs as Mark portrays them."

8. Richard Longenecker, *Biblical Exegesis in the Apostolic Period* (Grand Rapids, MI: Eerdmans, 1975), p. 34.

9. Solomon Schechter, *Some Aspects of Rabbinic Theology* (New York: Macmillan 1910), p. 152.

10. Morna D. Hooker, *The Son of Man in Mark: A Study of the "Son of Man" and Its Use in St Mark's Gospel* (Montreal: McGill University Press, 1967), pp. 97–98.

11. Joachim Jeremias, *New Testament Theology. Volume I: Jesus Proclamation of the Kingdom of God*, trans. John Bowden (London: SCM Press, 1971), pp. 111, 140.

12. Schechter, *Some Aspects of Rabbinic Theology*, pp. 111, 140.

13. *Halakhah* is the word for the study of the Torah and how its provisions are to be observed as applied to day-to-day specifics.

14. Schechter, *Some Aspects of Rabbinic Theology*, p. 210.

15. Martin Dibelius, *The Message of Jesus Christ*, trans. Frederick C. Grant, International Library of Christian Knowledge (New York: Scribner's, 1939), pp. 152, 158, 161, 163–64.

16. R. Joseph Hoffmann, *Marcion: On the Restitution of Christianity: An Essay on the Development of Radical Paulinist Theology in the Second Century*, AAR Academy Series 46 (Chico, CA: Scholars Press, 1984).

17. If the placement seems odd, beginning with the final verse of one chapter and continuing through the beginning of the next, keep in mind that chapter and verse divisions were not original to the Bible but were introduced many hundreds of years later to make it easier to look up passages.

18. Their view of the Sadducees as Hellenized Modernists, even if incorrect, is by no means stupid. The Mishnah refers to the Sadducees as "Epicureans," but this seems to be a polemical reinterpretation, turning the tables on Sadducees so as to make them, not their rivals the Pharisees, appear the heretical innovators.

19. Washington Gladden, *Present Day Theology* (Columbus, OH: McClelland & Company, 1918), pp. 211–17.

20. T. W. Manson, *The Servant Messiah: A Study of the Public Ministry of Jesus* (Cambridge: Cambridge University Press, 1953), pp. 15–16.

21. Ibid., pp. 18–19. After embracing the nickname (or being unable to get rid of it), they redefined it as if derived from *Perushim*, "Separated Ones," or Puritans. Such redefinition of names was quite common in the Old Testament (Hermann Gunkel, *The Legends of Genesis: The Biblical Saga and History*, trans. W. H. Carruth [New York: Schocken Books, 1964], pp. 27–30.

22. For instance, Geddes MacGregor, *Reincarnation in Christianity: A New Vision of the Role of Rebirth in Christian Thought* (Wheaton, IL: Quest Books/Theosophical Publishing House, 1978).

23. Smith, *Jesus the Magician*, p. 170.

CHAPTER 10. THE IMP ACT SEGMENT

1. Tzvetan Todorov, *The Poetics of Prose*, trans. Richard Howard (Ithaca, NY: Cornell University Press, 1977), chap. 5, "Narrative-Men," pp. 66–79.

2. Frank Kermode, *The Genesis of Secrecy: On the Interpretation of Narrative*, Charles Eliot Norton Lectures, 1977–1978 (Cambridge, MA: Harvard University Press, 1979), pp. 84–86.

3. Hyam Maccoby, *Judas Iscariot and the Myth of Jewish Evil* (New York: Free Press/Macmillan, 1992).

4. Joseph Gaer, *The Legend of the Wandering Jew* (New York: Mentor Books/New American Library, 1961).

5. Ibid., p. 50.

6. That is, "If it seems a fair wage."

7. Kermode, *Genesis of Secrecy*, p. 86.

8. Ibid., p. 87.

9. Hyam Maccoby, *The Sacred Executioner: Human Sacrifice and the Legacy of Human Guilt* (New York: Thames & Hudson, 1982), p. 130.

10. C. S. Lewis, *The Screwtape Letters and Screwtape Proposes a Toast* (New York: Macmillan, 1970), p. 8.

11. The screenwriter for the nifty movie *Constantine* made the same sort of elementary blunder by referring to the sixteen "acts" in 1 Corinthians. Apparently some ignoramus thought references like "1 Corinthians 7:1" denoted act and scene, not chapter and verse.

CHAPTER 11. CHECK, PLEASE

1. Annie Jaubert, *The Date of the Last Supper: The Biblical Calendar and Christian Liturgy*, trans. Isaac Rafferty (Staten Island, NY: Alba House, 1965), pp. 95–102.

2. Hermann Gunkel, *The Legends of Genesis: The Biblical Saga and History*, trans. W. H. Carruth (New York: Schocken Books, 1964), pp. 30–34.

3. I should imagine Roman Catholics would detect in the story the origin of the sacrament of penance, but Raymond E. Brown, ed., *New Testament Essays* (Garden City, NY: Doubleday Image, 1968), chap. 4, "The Johannine Sacramentary," pp. 79–107, in his survey of Catholic thinking on the subject, does not mention such a view of the passage.

4. Gerd Theissen, *The Miracle Stories of the Early Christian Tradition*, trans. Francis McDonagh (Philadelphia: Fortress Press, 1983), p. 56.

5. "Grasped" might with equal justification be understood to mean "usurped" (a contrast with Lucifer or Adam) or "retained" (contrasting with his willingness to abase himself via the Incarnation). For the debate on this point, see Ralph P. Martin, *Carmen Christi: Philippians ii.5–11 in Recent Interpretation and in the Setting of Early Christian Worship*, Society for New Testament Studies Monograph Series 4 (Cambridge: Cambridge University Press, 1967), pp. 134–64.

6. That is just the process Strauss discerned behind the various "I am" statements of Jesus in John's Gospel: making Jesus apply to himself the predicates of Jesus in Christian devotion.

7. Alfred Loisy, *The Birth of the Christian Religion*, trans. L. P. Jacks (London: George Allen & Unwin, 1948), p. 249.

8. W. O. E. Oesterley, "The Cult of Sabazios," in *The Labyrinth: Further Studies in the Relation between Myth and Ritual in the Ancient World*, ed. S. H. Hooke (London: SPCK, 1935), pp. 113–58.

9. Alfred Loisy, *The Origins of the New Testament*, trans. L. P. Jacks (London: George Allen & Unwin, 1950), p. 101. He calls it "editorial artifice."

10. Joachim Jeremias, *The Eucharistic Words of Jesus*, trans. Arnold Ehrhardt (Oxford: Basil Blackwell, 1955), p. 172.

CHAPTER 12. TRIAL AND ERROR

1. J. Duncan M. Derrett, *The Anastasis: The Resurrection of Jesus as an Historical Event* (Shipston-on-Stour, Warwickshire: Peter Drinkwater, 1982), p. 55, referring to Josephus, *Wars of the Jews* 4.317.

2. Woody Allen, "Hassidic Tales," in *Getting Even* (New York: Vintage Books, 1971), p. 51.

3. Uh, asked them *what*, exactly?

4. This sort of thing is by no means unknown in the textual tradition. See Bart D. Ehrman, *The Orthodox Corruption of Scripture: The Effect of Early Christological Controversies on the Text of the New Testament* (New York: Oxford University Press, 1993).

5. Leibel Reznick, *The Mystery of Bar Kokhba: An Historical and Theological Investigation of the Last King of the Jews* (Northvale, NJ: Jason Aronson, 1996), chap. 18, "The Bar Kokhba Temple," pp. 65–76.

6. Géza Vermes, *Jesus the Jew: A Historian's Reading of the Gospels* (London: Fontana/Collins, 1976), p. 149.

7. Ethelbert Stauffer, *Jesus and His Story*, trans. Richard Winston and Clara Winston (New York: Alfred A. Knopf, 1960), pp. 183–84; Hans-Joachim Schoeps, *Paul: The Theology of the Apostle in the Light of Jewish Religious History*, trans. Harold Knight (Philadelphia: Westminster Press, 1974), p. 161.

8. Graham Chapman, John Cleese, Terry Gilliam, Eric Idle, Terry Jones, and Michael Palin, *Monty Python's Life of Brian (of Nazareth)* (New York: Ace Books, 1979), pp. 111–12.

9. Isaac Bashevis Singer, *Satan in Goray*, trans. Jacob Sloan (New York: Fawcett Crest, 1955), pp. 156, 163.

10. Alfred Loisy, *The Birth of the Christian Religion*, trans. L. P. Jacks (London: George Allen & Unwin, 1948), p. 118.

11. *Miracle on 34th Street*, directed by George Seaton (1947, Twentieth Century Fox Film Corporation).

12. Though I wouldn't be surprised if Eric Holder did it, releasing a prisoner from Gitmo as a Ramadan gesture to Islamo-fascist terrorists.

13. Gershom Scholem, *The Messianic Idea in Judaism and Other Essays on Jewish Spirituality* (New York: Schocken Books, 1971), chap. 4, "Redemption through Sin," trans. Hillel Halkin, pp. 78–141.

14. Eusebius, *The History of the Church*, trans. G. A. Williamson (New York: Penguin Books, 1965), pp. 349–50.

15. Theodore J. Weeden, "The Two Jesuses," in *Forum*, New Series 6, no. 2 (Fall 2003).

16. Burton L. Mack, *A Myth of Innocence: Mark and Christian Origins* (Philadelphia: Fortress Press, 1988), p. 318.

17. Ibid.

18. Steve Mason, *Josephus and the New Testament* (Peabody, MA: Hendrickson Publishers, 1992).

19. Mack, *Myth of Innocence*, p. 167.

CHAPTER 13. CROSS EXAMINED

1. C. D. Yonge, trans., *The Works of Philo* (Peabody, MA: Hendrickson Publishers, 1993), p. 728.

2. René Girard, *Violence and the Sacred*, trans. Patrick Gregory (Baltimore: Johns Hopkins University Press, 1977), pp. 159, 162.

3. And remember, as we saw in the last chapter, the Barabbas scene can be shown to be fictive on other grounds anyway.

4. Jacob Neusner, *Rabbinic Literature & the New Testament: What We Cannot Show, We Do Not Know* (Valley Forge, PA: Trinity Press International, 1994).

5. Graham Chapman, John Cleese, Terry Gilliam, Eric Idle, Terry Jones, and Michael Palin, *Monty Python's Life of Brian (of Nazareth)* (New York: Ace Books, 1979), p. 63.

6. Philostratus, *The Life of Apollonius of Tyana*, vol. 2, trans. F. C. Conybeare, Loeb Classical Library 16 (Cambridge, MA: Harvard University Press, 1912), pp. 403, 404.

7. See Charles H. Talbert, *Luke and the Gnostics: An Examination of the Lucan Purpose* (New York: Abingdon Press, 1966), pp. 30–31; Elaine Pagels, *The Gnostic Gospels* (New York: Random House, 1979), chap. 1, "The Controversy over Christ's Resurrection: Historical Event or Symbol?" pp. 3–27.

8. Hugh J. Schonfield, trans., *The Authentic New Testament*, A Mentor Religious Classic (New York: New American Library, 1958), p. 99, appeals to an old Hebrew text of Matthew for his reading "has no floor to lay his head." The point is the same, though less strikingly put, in the Greek.

9. Plutarch, *Agis and Cleomenes*, *Tiberius and Gaius Gracchus*, *Philopoemen and Flamininus*, trans. Bernadette Perrin, Loeb Classical Library 102 (Cambridge, MA: Harvard University Press, 1921), p. 141.

10. John has only retained the ladies' auxiliary from Mark, though he has omitted the occasion for their visit. John is doing a bit of harmonizing, too, for he includes both the Markan/Lukan version (Mark 16:1–8; Luke 24:1–11), in which the women do *not* see Jesus at the tomb (John 20:1–2), and the Matthean version where they (just Mary Magdalene in John 20:11–18) *do* get to see him and grasp hold of him (Matt. 28:8–10).

11. David Friedrich Strauss, *The Life of Jesus Critically Examined*, trans. George Eliot (Mary Ann Evans), Lives of Jesus Series (1835; repr., Philadelphia: Fortress Press, 1972).

12. I once sheepishly asked a prominent Evangelical apologist, with his PhD in New Testament, if he had ever chanced to read Strauss's *Life of Jesus Critically Examined*. He had not. Things began to become clear to me. He didn't know that all his trusty arguments had been thoroughly refuted many decades before he was born.

APPENDIX 1. WHEN WERE THE GOSPELS WRITTEN?

1. Timothée Colani, "The Little Apocalypse of Mark 13," *Journal of Higher Criticism* 10, no. 1 (Spring 2003): 41–47, excerpted from Timothée Colani, *Jesus-Christ et les croyances messianiques de son temps*, trans. Nancy Wilson (1864), pp. 201–14.

2. Hermann Detering "The Synoptic Apocalypse (Mark 13 par): A Document from the Time of Bar Kochba," *Journal of Higher Criticism* 7, no. 3 (Fall 2000): 161–210.

3. Arlo J. Nau, *Peter in Matthew: Discipleship, Diplomacy, and Dispraise* (Collegeville, MN: Liturgical Press. A Michael Glazier Book, 1992).

4. Adolf Harnack, *The Date of the Acts and of the Synoptic Gospels*, trans. J. R. Wilkinson, New Testament Studies IV, Crown Theological Library (New York: Putnam's, 1911).

5. W. Ward Gasque, *A History of the Criticism of the Acts of the Apostles* (Grand Rapids, MI: Eerdmans, 1975).

6. Walter Bauer, *Orthodoxy and Heresy in Earliest Christianity*, ed. Robert Kraft and Gerhard Kroedel. Translated by a team from the Philadelphia Seminar on Christian Origins (Philadelphia: Fortress Press, 1971), pp. 82–83.

7. Horton Harris, *The Tübingen School* (New York: Oxford University Press, 1975).

8. Eduard Zeller, *The Contents and Origin of the Acts of the Apostles, Critically Investigated. To Which Is Prefixed, Dr. F. Overbeck's Introduction to the Acts, from DeWette's Handbook*, vols. 1 and 2, trans. Joseph Dare, Theological Translation Fund (London: Williams & Norgate, 1876).

9. J. C. O'Neill, *The Theology of Acts in Its Historical Setting* (London: SPCK, 1961).

10. Richard I. Pervo, *Dating Acts: Between the Evangelists and the Apologists* (Santa Rosa, CA: Polebridge Press, 2006).

11. Hans Conzelmann, *The Theology of St. Luke*, trans. Geoffrey Buswell (New York: Harper & Row, 1961).

12. Conzelmann believed the first two chapters were a later addition to Luke, so he did not make this connection, but it seems to me to fit his theory pretty well.

13. Charles H. Talbert, *Luke and the Gnostics: An Examination of the Lucan Purpose* (New York: Abingdon Press), p. 196.

14. Ibid., p. 196.

15. Günther Klein, *Die Zwölf Apostel: Ursprung und Gehalt einer Idee* (Göttingen, Germany: Vandenhoeck & Ruprecht, 1961).

16. J. C. O'Neill, *The Theology of Acts in Its Historical Setting* (London: SPCK, 1961)

17. Jack T. Sanders, *The Jews in Luke-Acts* (Philadelphia: Fortress Press, 1987).

18. Rudolph Otto, *The Kingdom of God and the Son of Man: A Study in the History of Religion*, trans. Floyd V. Filson and Bertram Lee Woolf (Boston: Starr King Press, 1957); Walther Zimmerli and Joachim Jeremias, *The Servant of God*, trans. Harold Knight, *Studies in Biblical Theology* no. 20 (London: SCM Press, 1965).

19. Richard I. Pervo, *Profit with Delight: The Literary Genre of the Acts of the Apostles* (Philadelphia: Fortress Press, 1987); Stephen P. Schierling and Marla J. Schierling, "The Influence of the Ancient Romances on Acts of the Apostles," *Classical Bulletin* 54 (April 1978); Susan Marie Praeder, "Luke-Acts and the Ancient Novel" *SBL Seminar Papers* (Chico, CA: Scholars Press, 1981), pp. 269–92.

20. Rosa Söder, *Die Apokryphen Geschichten und die romanhafte Literatur der Antike. Würtzburger Studien zur Altertumwissenschaft* 3 (Stuttgart: Kohlhammer Verlag, 1932).

21. Robert M. Price, *The Widow Traditions in Luke-Acts: A Feminist-Critical Scrutiny*, SBL Dissertation Series 155 (Atlanta: Scholars' Press, 1997), chap. 6, "Chaste Passion: The Chastity Story of Joanna," pp. 127–52.

22. Söder, *Die Apokryphen Geschichten.*

23. Steven L. Davies, *The Revolt of the Widows: The Social World of the Apocryphal Acts* (Carbondale: Southern Illinois University Press, 1980); Dennis Ronald MacDonald, *The Legend and the Apostle: The Battle for Paul in Story and Canon* (Philadelphia: Westminster Press, 1983).

24. Gerd Lüdemann, "The Acts of the Apostles and the Beginnings of Simonian Gnosis," *New Testament Studies* 33 (1987): 420–26.

25. "What I have done is to show that any serious consideration of the window of possible dates for P^{52} must include dates in the later second and early third centuries. Thus, P^{52} *cannot be used as evidence to silence other debates about the existence (or non-existence) of the Gospel of John in the first half of the second century.* Only a papyrus containing an explicit date or one found in a clear archaeological stratigraphic context could do the work scholars want P^{52} to do. As it stands now, the papyrological evidence should take a second place to other forms of evidence in addressing debates about the dating of the Fourth Gospel." Brent Nongbri, "The Use and Abuse of P^{52}: Papyrological Pitfalls in the Dating of the Fourth Gospel," *Harvard Theological Review* 98, no. 1 (2005): 23–48.

26. C. H. Dodd, *The Interpretation of the Fourth Gospel* (New York: Cambridge University Press, 1953).

27. Rudolf Bultmann, *The Gospel of John: A Commentary*, trans. G. R.

Beasley-Murray, R. W. N. Hoare, and J. K. Riches (Philadelphia: Westminster Press, 1975).

28. Raymond E. Brown, "The Qumran Scrolls and the Johannine Gospel and Epistles," in *New Testament Essays* (Garden City, NY: Doubleday Image Books, 1968), pp. 138–73. See also, e.g., F. F. Bruce, *The New Testament Documents: Are They Reliable?* (Grand Rapids, MI: Eerdmans, 1960), p. 58.

29. Robert T. Fortna, *The Gospel of Signs: A Reconstruction of the Narrative Source Underlying the Fourth Gospel*, Society for New Testament Studies Monograph Series 11 (New York: Cambridge University Press, 1970).

30. C. H. Dodd, *Historical Tradition in the Fourth Gospel* (New York: Oxford University Press, 1963).

31. Thomas Cottam, *The Fourth Gospel Rearranged* (London: Epworth Press, 1952).

32. Raymond E. Brown, *The Gospel according to John (I–XII)*, Anchor Bible 29 (Garden City, NY: Doubleday, 1966).

33. David Trobisch, *The First Edition of the New Testament* (New York: Oxford University Press, 2000); David Trobisch, "Who Published the New Testament?" *Free Inquiry* 28, no. 1 (December 2007/January 2008): 30–34.

34. Robert M. Price, "Is John's Gospel Gnostic?" *Christian*New Age Quarterly* 23, no. 1 (Summer 2013).

APPENDIX 2. DO ANCIENT HISTORIANS MENTION JESUS?

1. Pronounced "penis," poor devil. See Shlomo Pines, *An Arabic Version of the Testimonium Flavianum and Its Implications* (Jerusalem: Israel Academy of Sciences and Humanities, 1971).

2. Edwin M. Yamauchi, *Jesus, Zoroaster, Buddha, Socrates, Muhammad* (Downers Grove, IL: InterVarsity Press, 1972), pp. 43–44.

3. Never mind that some of the same writers take refuge in precisely such proposals when they are the only remaining expedient for denying an error in the Bible: "Oh yeah? Prove this error was in the original autographs! Go ahead! It must have been a scribal alteration." *¡Ay caramba!*

4. Theodore J. Weeden, "The Two Jesuses," in *Forum*, New Series 6, no. 2 (Fall 2003). Steve Mason, *Josephus and the New Testament* (Peabody, MA: Hendrickson Publishers, 1992) revives the view of a less timid scholarly generation, arguing that Luke-Acts made significant use of Josephus, too, not merely paralleling it. See his chap. 6, "Josephus and Luke-Acts," pp. 185–225.

5. Dennis Ronald MacDonald, *The Homeric Epics and the Gospel of Mark* (New Haven, CT: Yale University Press, 2000), pp. 154–55.

6. William Whiston trans., *The Works of Flavius Josephus* (London: Ward, Lock & Co., n.d.), p. 25.

7. Steve Mason, *Josephus and the New Testament* (Peabody, MA: Hendrickson Publishers, 1992), p. 213.

8. Robert Eisenman, *James the Brother of Jesus: The Key to Unlocking the Secrets of Early Christianity and the Dead Sea Scrolls* (New York: Viking Penguin, 1997).

9. Ibid., pp. 286–89.

10. Ibid, p. 881.

11. Ibid., chap. 25, "The Conversion of Queen Helen and the Ethiopian Queen's Eunuch," pp. 883–95.

12. F. F. Bruce, *Jesus and Christian Origins outside the New Testament* (Grand Rapids, MI: Eerdmans, 1974), p. 22.

13. Ibid., pp. 25–27.

14. Ibid., p. 21.

15. Robert E. van Voorst, *Jesus outside the New Testament: An Introduction to the Ancient Evidence* (Grand Rapids, MI: Eerdmans, 2000), p. 39.

16. J. N. D. Anderson, *Christianity: The Witness of History* (London: Tyndale Press, 1969), p. 19.

17. William Hansen, trans., *Phlegon of Tralles' Book of Marvels* (Exeter, UK: Exeter University Press, 1996).

INDEX OF MODERN AUTHORS

Allen, Woody, 271
Anderson, J. N. D., 276
Aslan, Reza, 262, 266

Baigent, Michael, 10, 255,
Barclay, William, 57, 259
Bauer, Walter, 273
Baur, Ferdinand Christian, 21, 221,
BeDuhn, Jason, 265
Bock, Darrell, 10
Brandon, S. G. F., 127, 128, 129, 130, 131, 132, 133, 263, 266, 267
Brodie, Thomas L., 9
Brown, Dan, 9, 241, 276
Brown, Raymond E., 9, 15, 233, 256, 258, 263, 270, 275, 276
Bruce, F. F., 266, 275
Bruce, Lenny, 30
Bultmann, Rudolf, 94, 232, 233, 258, 259, 263, 267, 274

Cadbury, Henry J., 265
Casey, Maurice, 257
Cayce, Edgar, 151, 187
Chapman, Graham, 259, 260, 264, 271, 272
Chilton, Bruce, 258
Cleese, John, 259, 260, 264, 271, 272
Colani, Timothée, 215
Collingwood, R. G., 21, 22, 88, 255, 256, 262
Conzelmann, Hans, 223, 224, 256, 273
Copan, Paul, 28
Cottam, Thomas, 275
Craig, William Lane, 10, 28, 81, 202, 257
Crossan, John Dominic, 202
Culler, Jonathan, 265
Cullmann, Oscar, 262, 263

Davies, Stevan L., 274
Davies, W. D., 261
Dawe, Donald G., 266
Dawkins, Richard, 10
De Jonge, M., 55, 259
Derrett, J. Duncan M., 270
Detering, Hermann, 216, 217, 273
Dibelius, Martin, 16, 256, 257, 267, 268
Dodd, C. H., 232, 23, 274, 275
Doyle, Arthur Conan, 64

Eaton, J. H., 264
Edersheim, Alfred, 83
Ehrman, Bart D., 256, 271
Eisenman, Robert, 247, 248, 263, 276
Eisler, Robert, 45, 258, 263
Emmerich, Anna Katharina, 14
Evans, Craig, 10, 28, 256

Falk, Harvey, 258
Fitzmyer, Joseph A., 9
Flusser, David, 259
Fortna, Robert T., 275
Fowler, Robert M., 112, 265
Funk, Robert W., 263

Gaer, Joseph, 269
Gärtner, Bertil, 90, 263
Gasque, W. Ward, 273
Gibson, Mel, 9, 14, 260
Gilliam, Terry, 259, 260, 264, 271, 272
Girard, René, 272
Gladden, Washington, 269
Goodacre, Mark C., 87, 262
Goodspeed, Edgar J., 57, 259
Gunkel, Hermann, 264

Hamburger, Käte, 259
Harnack, Adolf, 27, 122, 219, 220, 257, 266, 273
Harris, Horton, 273
Harvey, Van A., 258
Hendrickx, Herman, 9
Hoffmann, R. Joseph, 268
Hooker, Morna D., 141, 268

Jaubert, Annie, 164, 270
Jeremias, Joachim, 142, 171, 230, 261, 268, 274
Jones, Terry, 259, 260, 264, 271, 272

Kee, Howard Clark, 184
Keener, Craig, 28

Kermode, Frank, 269
Klein, Günther, 273

Leigh, Richard, 10, 255
Lemche, Niels Peter, 30, 257
Levine, Amy-Jill, 259
Lewis, C. S., 119, 120, 121, 266, 269
Lightfoot, John, 73, 261
Lincoln, Henry, 10, 255
Loisy, Alfred, 169, 170, 179, 270, 271
Longenecker, Richard, 264, 268
Lovecraft, H. P., 109, 265
Lüdemann, Gerd, 274
Luhrmann, T. M., 256

Maccoby, Hyam, 157, 258, 269
MacDonald, Dennis Ronald, 274
MacGregor, Geddes, 269
Mack, Burton L., 83, 90, 130, 131, 133, 138, 184, 185, 234, 262, 263, 266, 267, 268, 271
Mamet, David, 10
Manson, T. W., 269
Marshall, I. Howard, 256
Martin, Ralph P., 270
Martyn, J. Louis, 259
Mason, Steve, 271, 275, 276
Meier, John, 9
Michaels, J. Ramsey, 47, 258
Moreland, J. P., 10
Mowinkel, Sigmund, 264

Nau, Arlo J., 218, 273
Neusner, Jacob, 272
Ninehan, Dennis E., 266
Nongbri, Brent, 274

Oesterley, W. O. E., 270
O'Neill, John C., 273
Otto, Rudolf, 274
Overbeck, Franz, 221, 273
Overman, Andrew J., 262

Pagels, Elaine, 272
Palin, Michael, 259, 260, 264, 271, 272
Phipps, William E., 13, 255
Pervo, Richard I., 221, 273, 274
Pines, Schlomo, 239, 275
Praeder, Susan Marie, 274
Price, Robert M., 274 275

Ratzinger, Joseph, 163, 164
Reznick, Leibel, 271
Rice, Tim, 261
Robbins, Vernon K., 267

Salm, Rene, 256, 260
Sanders, E. P., 70, 261
Sanders, Jack T., 228, 261, 268, 274
Schechter, Solomon, 268
Schillebeeckx, Edward, 9
Schoeps, Hans-Joachim, 271
Scholem, Gershom G., 263, 264, 271
Schonfield, Hugh J., 57, 259, 272
Schweitzer, Albert, 27, 36, 120, 257, 259, 260, 262, 265, 266
Singer, Isaac Bashevis, 179, 271
Smith, Morton, 149, 260, 266, 268, 269
Sobrino, Jon, 9
Stauffer, Ethelbert, 178, 271
Steiner, Rudolf, 86, 187
Stendahl, Krister, 264
Strauss, David Friedrich, 18, 23, 76, 118, 180, 201, 202, 256, 257, 261, 263, 264, 265, 267, 270, 272
Strobel, Lee, 257

Talbert, Charles H., 272
Taylor, Vincent, 267
Theissen, Gerd, 87, 262, 270
Todorov, Tzvetan, 55, 154, 259, 269
Torrey, Charles Cutler, 261
Trobisch, David, 275

Van Voorst, Robert E., 276
Vermes, Géza, 256, 259, 271

Weeden, Theodore J., 271
Wells, George A., 257
Weymouth, Richard Francis, 57, 259
Wrede, William, 255, 257, 260, 262, 263, 267

Yamauchi, Edwin M., 275
Young, Bruce H., 258

Zeller, Edward, 221, 256, 273

SCRIPTURE INDEX

Genesis

1:26, p. 141
2:2–3, p. 140
4:12, p. 155
4:20, p. 131
4:21, p. 131
5:28–29, p. 131
9:4, p. 169
9:20, p. 131
17, p. 248
17:9–14, p. 248

Exodus

3:14, pp. 178, 265
4:10–16, p. 25
12:46, pp. 101, 104, 105
15:1, p. 149
20:4, p. 144

Leviticus

7:26–27, p. 169
17:10–14, p. 169
19:18, p. 145

Numbers

6:4, p. 145
9:12, pp. 101, 104, 105

Deuteronomy

12:16, 23, p. 169
21:23, p. 101
21:22–23, p. 104

Joshua

10:26–27, p. 104

Judges

15:14–15, p. 49

1 Samuel

9:3, p. 162
9:11, p. 162
9:6, p. 162
9:18, p. 162
9:19, p. 162
28:4–5, p. 102

2 Samuel

18:9–10, p. 160

1 Kings

12:16, p. 79
17:8–24, p. 99
17:10, p. 99
17:23, p. 99

2 Kings

25:6–7, p. 102

Tobit

1:16–19, p. 174
2:3–4, 7–8, p. 174

Psalms

2, pp. 94, 119
8:2, pp. 133, 134
8:4, p. 141
22:1, p. 196
22:7–8, p. 196
22:16, pp.101, 195
22:18, p. 195
27:12, p. 102
22:18, pp. 101, 196
27:12, p. 101, 102
34:20, pp. 101, 105
35:11, p. 102
118:26, p. 117

Wisdom of Solomon

2:12–20, p. 196

Isaiah

1:10–20, p. 127
7:14, p. 106
26:19, p. 150
29:13, p. 85
40:3, pp. 36, 37
50:6, pp. 101, 103
53, p. 248
53:9, 12, p. 197
56:7, pp. 60–61
61:1–2, p. 58
62, p. 61

Jeremiah

7:9–11, p. 126

Ezekiel

25:2, p. 141
37:1–14, p. 95

Daniel

7, p. 225
9:26, p. 244
12:2–3, p. 150

Hosea

11:1, p. 106

Zechariah

9:9, pp. 115, 116
11:12, pp. 155, 160
11:13, p. 156
12:10, pp. 101, 103

Malachi

3:1–3, p. 266
3:1, p. 36
4:5, pp. 36, 79

Matthew

1:22–23, p. 196
1:23, p. 106
2, p. 14
2:2, p. 94
2:3, pp. 18, 20
2:5–6, 15, 17–18, 23, p. 196
2:12, p. 16
2:15, p. 106
3:3, p. 196
3:7, p. 34
3:9, p. 135
3:13–15, p. 42
3:15, p. 43
4:13–16, p. 196
5–7, p. 68
6:1–18, p. 217
6: 9–15, p. 217
8:5–10, p. 70
8:20, p. 196
8:21, p. 174
8:28, p. 114
9:9, p. 67
9:18–19, 23–26, p. 96
9:27–31, p. 114
10:2, p. 227
10:3, p. 67
10:5, p. 218
11:2–3, p. 76
11:6, p. 77
11:12, p. 45
12:17–21, p. 196
12:40, p. 111
13:14–15, p. 196
13:35–36, p. 196
13:52, pp. 146, 156
14:28–29, p. 218
14:28–31, p. 64
14:30–31, p. 218
15:15–20, p. 64
15:33, p. 198
15:38, p. 198
16:17–19, p. 88
16:17, p. 89
16:18, p. 65
16:19, p. 218
16:22–23, p. 64
16:21–28, p. 110
17:9–13, p. 110
17:13, p. 267
17:20, p. 88
17:22–23, p. 111
17:24–26, p. 64
18:3, p. 56
18:4, p. 57
18:18, pp. 191, 218
18:21–22, p. 64
19:3, p. 146
20:17–19, p. 111
20:30–34, p. 114
21:1–3, p. 114
21:4, p. 196
21:4–5, p. 116
21:9, p. 116
21:14, p. 133
21:18–19, p. 123
23, p. 84
24, p. 150
25:14ff, p. 225
26:63, p. 176
26:6–13, p. 72
26:8, p. 156
26:14–15, p. 155
26:63–64, p. 258
27:3–10, p. 156
27:19, p. 180
27:26, p. 184
27:32, p. 190
27:43, p. 196
27:49, p. 27
27:51–53, pp. 198, 219
27:52–53, p. 199
27:56, p. 261
27:57b, p. 174
27:62–66, p. 199
28, p. 218
28:1–4, p. 199
28:8–10, p. 272
28:18–20, p. 191

Mark

1:2, p. 196
1:2–3, p. 36
1:10–11, p. 38
1:11, p. 94
1:4–8, p. 34
1:5, p. 34
1:16–20, p. 64
2:1–12, p. 260
2:13–17, p. 260
2:14, p. 67
2:23–28, p. 140
3:1–6, p. 138
3:13–19a, p. 65
3:14, p. 227
3:17, p. 166
3:18, p. 67
3:19, p. 91
5:2, p. 114
5:22–24, 45–33, p. 96
5:39, p. 99
5:43, p. 82
6:2–6, p. 58
6:8–11, p. 217
6:11, p. 227
6:14, pp. 80, 113
6:14–15, p. 87
6:16, p. 80
6:18, p. 46
6:49, p. 60
7, p. 85
7:6, p. 196
7:6–7, p. 85
8:27–30, p. 35
8:28, pp. 80, 87, 113
8:31, p. 265
8:31–33, p. 110
8:34, p. 190
8:38, p. 56
9:1, pp. 216–217, 225
9:5–6, p. 64
9:9–12, p. 110
9:13, p. 267

9:19, p. 50
9:31, p. 265
9:31–32, p. 111
10:2–9, p. 145
10:13–16, p. 134
10:15, p. 56
10:17–22, p. 77
10:22, p. 261
10:23, p. 261
10:32–34, p. 265
10:32–34, p. 111
10:44–45, p. 167
10:46–52, p. 114
11:9–10, p. 116
11:11–14, p. 123
11:11, p. 123
11:12–14, 20–21, p. 124
11:14, p. 50
11:15–19, p. 124
11:16, p. 128
11:17, pp. 61, 126
11:21–23, p. 64
11:22–25, p. 124
11:27–33, p. 142
12:1–3, p. 124
12:17, p. 144
12:13–17, p. 142
12:18–27, p. 148
12:28, 34, p. 174
12:28–34, p. 144
12:32–34, p. 145
13, pp. 215, 253, 273
13:1–2, p. 124
13:10, pp. 216, 225
13:13, p. 77
13:14ff, p. 220
13:30, pp. 150, 216, 225
14:3–9, p. 72
14:4–5, p. 156
14:10–11, p. 155
14:13, p. 162
14:14, p. 162
14:12–16, p. 162
14:16, p. 162
14:27, pp. 112, 196
14:29–31, p. 64
14:61–62, p. 258
14:61, p. 184
14:62, pp. 176, 177, 225
14:64, p. 174
14:65, pp. 103, 184
15:6, p. 181
15:7, p. 128
15:17b, p. 189
15:18–19, p. 103
15:21, p. 190
15:29, pp. 184, 196
15:33, p. 198
15:34, p. 196
15:38, p. 198
15:39, p. 198
16:1–8, p. 272

Luke

1:35, p. 94
1:44, p. 42
2:25, 38, p. 174
2:41–52, pp. 30, 123
2:49, p. 30
3:7, p. 34
3:8, p. 135
3:15–16, p. 40
3:21–22, p. 41
3:22, p. 38
4, p. 58
4:13, p. 224
4:16–30, p. 57
4:38, p. 66
5, p. 66
5:1–11, p. 66
5:8, p. 75
7, p. 75
7:11–17, p. 96
7:15, p. 99
7:18–19, p. 76
7:18–20, p. 41
7:23, p. 77
7:29, p. 34
7:30, p. 34
7:36–50, p. 157
7:39, p. 74
7:40–43, p. 75
7:41–43, p. 74
7:44–46, p. 74
8:1–3, p. 231
8:27, p. 114
8:40–42a, 49–56, p. 96
8:45–46, p. 64
9:20, p. 87
9:22–27, p. 110
9:27, p. 225
9:43–45, p. 111
9:45, p. 111
9:36, p. 110
10:18–19, p. 224
10:38–42, p. 72
11:46, p. 261
12:6, p. 121
12:7, p. 121
12:35–37, p. 168
12:41ff, p. 64
13:6–9, p. 125
13:14, p. 139
13:16, p. 224
15:16–18, p. 125
15:27–32, p. 77
16:2–5, p. 125
16:14, p. 157
16:16, p. 223
16:19–31, p. 100
16:30, p. 101
17:6, p. 124
17:20, p. 174
17:20–21, p. 225
17:22, p. 125
17:26–27, p. 184
18:4–5, p. 125
18:17, p. 56
18:31–34, p. 111
18:35–43, p. 114
19:11, pp. 125, 174, 225
19:37–40, p. 134
19:38, p. 116
19:43, p. 220
19:46, p. 126
20:38b, p. 226
21, p. 150
21:8, p. 225
21:8, 23–24, p. 125
21:20, p. 220
21:26b, p. 224
21:32, p. 225
22:3–6, p. 157
22:15, p. 163
22:26–27, p. 167
22:39, p. 153
22:39, p. 153
22:67–70, p. 258
22:67–69, p. 176
22:69, p. 225
22:70, p. 176
23:1, p. 174

23.6–12, p. 179
23:14–15, p. 180
23:34, p. 22
23:26, p. 190
23:50b–51, p. 174
24:1–11, p. 272
24:13–21, pp. 156–57
24:16, p. 111
24:25, 43–44, p. 228
24:26–27, 44–46, p. 112
24:34, p. 75
24:36–43, pp. 60, 193
24:39–40, p. 194

John

1:1, p. 94
1:7, 32, 34, p. 48
1:8, 20, p. 40
1:19–28, p. 35
1:29, pp. 46, 105, 164
1:34, p. 43
2:10, p. 50
2:16, p. 52
2:23, p. 54
3:3, p. 57
3:3, 5, p. 56
3:11, 22, pp. 48, 55
3:16, pp. 56, 61
3:26, p 48
3:25–30, p. 40
4:39, p. 48
4:44, p. 48
5:16–18, pp. 47–48
5:18, p. 30
5:31–35, p. 48
6, p. 48
6:35, p. 118
6:51, p. 165
6:52, p. 170
6:53, 54, p. 165
6:67, p. 36
7, p. 94
7:1–9, p. 93
7:1, 19, 25, 30, 32, 44, p. 48
7:2, p. 184
7:50–52, p. 174
8:12, p. 118
8:13–18, p. 48
8:40, 45, p. 48
8:42, pp. 118, 265
8:58, p. 118
8:59, p. 48
9:1–2, p. 180
9:16, 24, p. 48
9:22, pp. 56, 179
10:11, p. 118
10:1–18, p. 27
10:24–25, 31–33, 39, p. 48
10:30, p. 118
10:33–36, p. 31
11, pp. 72, 95
11:1–44, p. 73
11:8, p. 48
11:11, p. 100
11:12–14, p. 100
11:25, pp. 95, 118
11:39, p. 100
11:45, p. 101
12, pp. 73, 159
12:1–8, p. 72
12:6, p. 157
12:6, p. 90
12:13, p. 116
12:14–16, p. 115
12:48, p. 86
13:1, p. 163
13:1–17, p. 166
13:2, p. 158
13:6–11, p. 64
13:14–15, 17, p. 166
13:29, pp. 163, 164
14:9, p. 118
15:1–11, p. 27
15:1, p. 118
16:1–2a, 4, p. 179
16:1–4, p. 56
18:10–11, p. 64
18:28, p. 164
18:31, p. 179
19:9, p. 184
19:17, p. 190
19:31–34, p. 194
19:31–36, p. 104
19: 34–35, pp. 194, 234
19:34–37, pp. 26, 27
19: 36–37, p. 194
19:34, p. 194
19:36, p. 276
19:37, p. 103
19:38, pp. 174, 175,
19:39–40, p. 198
20:1–2, p. 272
20:11–18, p. 272
20:19–23, pp. 191, 192, 193
20:24–29, p. 191
21, pp. 66, 75
21:20–23, pp. 215, 216
21:21–22, p. 64
21:23, p. 225
21:24, pp. 26, 55, 234

Acts

1:6–7ff, p. 225
1:10–11, p. 225
1:21–22, pp. 222, 227
2:1–4, p. 193
3:1–8, p. 222
3:13, p. 229
4:27, p. 229
5:15, p. 222
5:36–37, p. 246
7, p. 228
8:1, p. 227
8:9–10, p. 247
8:18–23, p. 222
8:22, p. 231
9:36–40, p. 222
10–11, pp. 222, 247
10:38, p. 224
11:27–28, p. 247
12, pp. 188, 247
12:6, p. 230
12:6–10, p. 222
13:6–11, p. 222
14:8–10, p. 222
14:8–19, p. 230
15, pp. 222, 229
15:20, p. 229
16:25–26, p. 22
16:26, p. 230
17, p. 230
18:14–15, p. 245
19:11–12, p. 222
19:23–41, p. 231
20:9–12, p. 222
20:20, p. 228
20:25, p. 220
20:28, p. 228
21:20–24, p. 222
21:20–25, p. 229
21:24, p. 222

21:33, p. 230
21:38, p. 246
23:6, p. 222
24:24, p. 247
25:13, p. 247
26:29, p. 230
28:1–6, p. 230

Romans

1:3–4, p. 94
8:28, p. 162
8:32, p. 154
10:9–10, p. 56
13:3–4, p. 12

1 Corinthians

1:1:22–23, p. 25
2:6–7, p. 228
2:6–8, p. 12
5:7, p. 46
7:1, p. 269
7:6, p. 146
7:10, 25, p. 25
10:14–22, p. 229
11:23, p. 154
14:37, p. 25
15:5, p. 75
15:8, p. 292
15:42–50, pp. 193, 228

2 Corinthians

5:1–4, p. 226

Galatians

1:15–19, p. 223
2, p. 222
5:12, p. 249

Philippians

1:23, p. 226
2:5–11, p. 270
2:6–11, p. 167

Colossians

1:6, p. 216
2:9, p. 121
2:13–15, p. 12
3:13b, p. 166
4:14, p. 25

1 Thessalonians

4:13–14, p. 226
4:15–17, p. 25

2 Thessalonians

2:1–3, p. 225

2 Timothy

2:2, p. 228
411, p. 25

James

2:10–11, p. 144

1 Peter

1:8, p. 192
2:13–14, p. 12
3:9, p. 193
3:18, p. 228
5:2, p. 144

2 Peter

3, p. 216
3:3, p. 216
3:3–4, p. 215
3:4, p. 225

1 John

2:18–19, p. 234
4:2, p. 60

Revelation

11, p. 215

SUBJECT INDEX

Abraham, 17, 48, 100, 101, 118, 135, 149, 175, 221, 226, 248, 265
Akiba, 177
Alexander Jannaeus, 12
Ananda, 63
Andrew, disciple, 65, 66, 165, 167, 209, 231
angels, 12, 145, 56, 134, 201, 208, 216
Anna, 19, 20, 223
Annas, 176, 182
Antiochus IV Epiphanes, 170
Apollonius of Tyana, 96, 192, 230, 263, 272
apologists/apologetics, 8, 10, 33, 39, 42, 47, 53, 82, 91, 95, 106, 119, 129, 176, 184, 185, 202, 215, 219, 220, 226, 227, 228, 229, 230, 237, 239, 240, 243, 251, 252, 253, 272, 273
Apuleius, Lucius, 97, 98 263, 264
Archelaus, 13, 20, 143
Archons, 12
Asclepiades the physician, 97
Augustus Caesar (Octavian), 11, 12, 14, 17

Barabbas, 128, 129, 181, 188, 272
Bartimaeus, 114
Batman, 218
Beloved Disciple, 168, 173
Bethlehem, 18, 19, 20, 203
Bhagavad Gita, 118
Book of Enoch (1 Enoch), 46
Book of Mormon, 24
Brian of Nazareth, 178, 260, 264, 270, 272
Buddha, 63, 64, 275

Caesarea Philippi, 35, 36, 65, 79, 87, 218
Caiaphas, 128, 158, 159, 173, 175, 176, 177, 178, 185, 199
Carabbas, 188
Cephas, 65
Cerinthus, 258
cheesemakers, 68
Church Lady, 158
Claudius Caesar, 12, 247, 248, 251, 252
Cleomenes, 197
Cleophas, disciple, 207
Cyrus the Persian, 37

David, 79, 94, 103, 116, 117, 119, 133, 141, 160, 177, 178
Dead Sea Scrolls, 105, 163, 233, 244, 263, 276
Dhammapada, 69
Dialogue of the Savior, 118
Dio Cassius, 16
Dionysus, 50, 170
Docetism, 60

Ebionites, 41
Egypt, 12, 19, 20
Elijah, 35, 36, 58, 59, 79, 80, 87, 99, 110, 177, 267
Essenes, 148, 201
Eusebius, 22, 23, 229, 232, 240, 253, 256, 267, 271

Frank, Jacob, 182
Frankenstein, Wolf von, 100
Frankenstein's monster, 42

Gabriel, 205
Galilee/Galileans, 36, 42, 45, 52, 56, 68, 69, 79, 79, 80, 81, 85, 89, 143, 165, 179, 206, 207, 209, 210, 211, 246, 256, 259, 260, 262
Galilee, Sea/Lake of, 207, 211
Gematria, 106
Gethsemane, 112, 128, 129, 153, 166
Gnostics/Gnosticism, 12, 72, 118, 196, 221, 226, 228, 232, 233, 234, 272, 273, 275
Golgotha, 22, 128, 155, 187, 190
Gospel according to the Ebionites, 41
Gospel of Thomas, 23, 59
Gribble, Dale, 8

Helena (queen of Adiabene), 247, 248, 249, 276
Hercules, 12, 96, 167
Herod (brother of Herod Antipas), 46
Herod Agrippa I, 188, 247
Herod Antipas, 11, 12, 41, 44, 46, 68, 77, 79, 80, 81, 87, 109, 179, 180, 185, 245
Herodias, 46

Herodotus, 12
Herod the Great, 11, 12, 14, 15, 16, 17, 18, 19, 20, 109, 181, 207
Hillel, 146
Holmes, Sherlock, 64
Hulk, Incredible, 12
Hunter, Jeffrey, 60

Idle, Eric, 259, 260, 264, 271, 272
Ignatius Loyola, 14
Infancy Gospel of Matthew, 23, 29, 30, 50, 258
Iron Man, 12
Isis, 12

James, son of Damneus, 243, 244
James, son of Zebedee, 65, 66, 83, 165, 166
James the Just, 59, 222, 229, 244, 276
Jerusalem, 13, 18, 19, 20, 37, 51, 54, 68, 79, 89, 93, 93, 103, 109, 111, 112, 114, 115, 117, 123, 132, 134, 148, 177, 180, 183, 184, 203, 206, 207, 208, 209, 212, 216, 221, 222, 225, 227, 228, 229, 241, 247, 248, 249, 258, 263, 266
Jesus ben-Ananias, 182, 183, 184, 185, 241
Jesus, son of Damneus, 243, 244
Jews, 12, 13, 14, 15, 19, 26, 30, 34, 35, 37, 45, 46, 47, 51, 52, 54, 55, 56, 58,59, 69, 70, 79, 80, 81, 83, 84, 85, 86, 90, 101, 104, 117, 126, 127, 128, 129, 130, 131, 132, 137, 138, 139, 141, 143, 144, 146, 147, 148, 149, 155, 158, 163, 164, 169, 170, 173, 174, 175, 179, 180, 181, 182, 183, 184, 185, 187, 188, 191, 194, 218, 221, 222, 228, 229, 233, 237, 238, 239, 242, 243, 244, 245, 246, 248, 251, 252, 256, 258, 259, 261, 262, 263, 264, 266, 268, 269, 270, 271, 274
Johanan ben Zakkai, 89
John of Gischala, 132
John, son of Zebedee, 26, 65, 66, 83, 87, 165, 166, 231, 234
John the Baptist, 27, 33, 34, 35, 36, 37, 40, 41, 42, 43, 44, 45, 46, 65, 66, 75, 76, 77, 80, 113, 117, 135, 142, 208, 223, 233, 244, 245, 258, 263,267
Joseph, father of Jesus, 13, 18, 19, 20, 29, 30, 58, 207
Joseph of Arimathea, 55, 173, 174, 175, 198, 201, 202, 241, 242
Josephus the historian, 13, 15, 17, 18, 29, 44, 45, 46, 128, 131, 132, 174, 180, 182, 183, 184, 185, 198, 237, 238, 239, 240, 241, 242, 243, 244, 245, 246, 247, 249, 250, 251, 256, 258, 262, 270, 271, 275, 276
Judaism, 69, 70, 71, 83, 84, 129, 137, 147, 148, 149, 169, 174, 181, 222, 228, 229, 233, 248, 261, 262, 271
Judas Iscariot, 73, 74, 89, 90, 91, 142, 153, 154, 155, 156, 157, 158, 159, 160, 163, 168, 191, 210, 224, 232, 269
Judas not Iscariot, disciple, 209
Judas of Galilee, 143, 246, 247, 262
Julius Caesar, 11, 109
Justin Martyr, 219, 226, 229, 230

Kabbalah, 106, 264
Koran, 30
Kringle, Kris, 120
Krishna, 17
Kronos, 16, 17

Law of Biographical Analogy, 16, 29
Lazarus, 48, 72, 73, 95, 96, 99, 100, 101, 159, 168, 226, 264
Lebbaeus, disciple, 211
Levi the tax collector, 67

Marcion, 147, 268
Mary Magdalene, 71, 72, 73, 82, 159, 198, 206, 207, 272
Mary, mother of Jesus, 13, 18, 19, 20, 59, 207, 223, 258
Mary of Bethany, 72, 73, 159, 206
Mary, wife of Clopas, 206
Matthew, disciple, 22, 29, 67, 68, 210
Mishnah, 24, 69, 84, 138, 141, 268
Mithras, 16, 71
Moon, Sun Myung, 57
Mort, twin brother of Thomas, 211
Moses, 15, 17, 25, 35, 83, 140, 145, 146, 147, 149, 177, 182, 208, 213, 221, 229, 241
Muhammad, 24, 275

Nazareth, 13, 20, 25, 33, 37, 57, 60, 61, 154, 202, 208, 212, 256, 260, 262, 264, 266, 271, 272
Nero Caesar, 16, 249
Nicodemus, 53, 54, 55, 56, 57, 61, 173, 174, 175, 198, 201, 259
Noah, 130, 131, 184, 208, 213

Osiris, 12, 170

Papias, 22, 23, 25, 232
Parthian Empire, 16
Passover, 13, 46, 48, 51, 53, 54, 104, 105, 109, 115, 117, 161, 162, 163, 164, 169, 170, 175, 181, 182, 194, 252, 265
Pausanias, 50
Peter, disciple, 22, 23, 24, 25, 35, 36, 63, 64, 65, 66, 67, 75, 79, 80, 83, 87, 88, 89, 110, 123, 155, 156, 168, 173, 206, 207, 210, 212, 216, 218, 222, 223, 224, 225, 227, 229, 230, 231, 235, 247, 260, 273
Pharaoh, 15, 16
Pharisees, 30, 31, 34, 35, 37, 54, 68, 69, 71, 73, 75, 81, 82, 83, 84, 85, 86, 134, 138, 141, 146, 148, 157, 163, 222, 258, 261, 268
Philip, brother of Herod Antipas, 46
Philip, disciple, 165, 167
Philip the evangelist/deacon, 232, 247, 248
Phlegon, 237, 253, 276
Pilate, Pontius, 26, 129, 164, 173, 174, 179, 180, 181, 182, 184, 185, 187, 194, 199, 219, 238, 239, 242, 249, 252
Pistis Sophia, 118
Pliny the Elder, 16
Pliny the Younger, 237, 250, 251
Plutarch, 12, 197, 272
Principle of Analogy, 49
Protocols of the Elders of Zion, 182
Pythagoras, 66
Python, Monty, 178, 260, 264, 271, 272

Q Source, 23, 34, 41, 68, 76

Ralph, disciple, 207, 208, 209
rationalistic paraphrase, 30, 38, 60, 109
Rationalists, 200, 201, 202, 203
Rhea, 16
Ricardo, Lucy, 114
Robin Hood, 7
Robin the Boy Wonder, 218

Sadducees, 34, 86, 148, 149, 150, 243, 268
Salome, 46
Samaritans, 79, 142, 218, 227
Samson, 49
Sanhedrin, 53, 54, 55, 80, 86, 112, 128, 129, 130, 148, 153, 155, 156, 173, 174, 175, 177, 179, 181, 219, 225, 243, 244
Saul, son of Kish, 162
Satan, 110, 139, 157, 158, 179, 205, 218, 223, 224, 271
Sepphoris, 13
Shammai, 146
Sicarii, 89, 246, 247
Simeon, 19, 20, 223
Simon bar Giora, 132, 241
Simon bar Kokhba, 177, 216, 271
Simon Magus, 142, 227, 231, 247
Simon Peter. *See* Peter
Simon the leper, 72, 73, 159, 160, 261
Simon the Pharisee, 71, 73, 74, 75, 157
Simon Zelotes (the Zealot), disciple, 89, 165, 166, 210
Smith, Joseph, 24
Söder, Rosa, 724
Soprano, Tony, 146
Suetonius, 16, 237, 251, 252
Superboy, 50
Superman, 7, 114, 159
Synoptic Gospels, 27, 47, 48, 65, 90, 127, 154, 161, 162, 163, 190, 198, 233, 257, 258, 259, 262, 265, 267, 273

Tacitus, 237, 249, 250, 251
Talmud, 84, 89, 149, 182, 255, 261
Testaments of the Twelve Patriarchs, 221
Thaddeus, disciple, 211
Thallus, 237, 252, 253
Theudas, 246, 247
Thomas, disciple, 29, 37, 165, 166, 191, 192, 193, 205, 210, 211, 231, 235
Tiberias, Lake of, 207, 211
Tiberius Caesar, 199, 207, 249, 272
Tinkerbell, 18, 19
Tiridates, 16

Uranus, 16

Vishnu, 38

Wandering Jew, 155, 269
Watson, Dr., 64
Wise Men (Magi), 14, 15, 16, 18, 19, 20, 203

Ygor, Old, 100

Zealots, 89, 90, 131, 132, 166, 262, 263, 266, 267
Zeus, 16, 17,166, 251
Zoroaster, 17, 275